*dizzy* & jimmy

# ∂izzy & jimmy

## My Life with James Dean

### *a love story*

## LIZ SHERIDAN

## ReganBooks
*An Imprint of* HarperCollins*Publishers*

Lyrics from "Fugue for Tinhorns (from *Guys and Dolls*)" by Frank Loesser © 1950 (renewed) Frank Music Corp. All rights reserved. Used by permission. Lyrics from "In the Wee Small Hours of the Morning" by Bob Hilliard and David A. Mann © 1955 (renewed) Bourne Music Corp. All rights reserved. Used by permission. Lyrics of "I Got Rhythm" by George and Ira Gershwin, by permission of Warner/Chappell Music, Inc. All rights reserved. Used by permission.

HarperCollins books may be purchased for educational, business, or sales promotional use. For information please write: Special Markets Department, Harper Collins Publishers Inc., 10 East 53rd Street, New York, NY 10022.

FIRST EDITION

Designed by William Ruoto

Printed on acid-free paper

Library of Congress Cataloging-in-Publication Data

Sheridan, Liz.
    Dizzy & Jimmy : my life with James Dean : a love story / Liz Sheridan.—1st ed.
      p. cm.
    ISBN 0-06-039383-1
    1. Sheridan, Liz—Relations with men. 2. Dean, James, 1931–1955—Relations with women. 3. Actors—United States—Biography. I. Title: Dizzy & Jimmy. II. Title.
PN2287.S3719 A3 2000
791.43'028'092—dc21
    [B]                                   00-042525

00 01 02 03 04 ❖/RRD 10 9 8 7 6 5 4 3 2 1

*1%00*
*BAT*

For Stephanie

And my deepest gratitude and love for my husband, Dale,
for his help and knowledge and for the poetry
in his heart and in his mind.

———————————

Thank you to Matt Storey for his valuable advice and to the
small army of family, friends, and acquaintances for their
patience and input in helping me to piece together my past:

| | |
|---|---|
| Marcus Winslow | Bill Bast |
| Fran Lassen | Adrienne McCalley |
| Sue Hight | Guy Little |
| Art Ostrin | Tamar Cooper |
| James Brock | Charlie Connelly |
| Lavonne Slaybaugh | Charles Corbett |
| Ann Roberts | Marvin Schwartz |

Special thanks to Cal Morgan, editorial director of
ReganBooks. For the services of Mark Rubin Photography,
and to James Whitmore, Tom Cole, and Joyce Chopra for
their wisdom and support.

Liz Sheridan, 1950s

James Dean at Jerry's Bar, 1955

# prologue

A long time ago, when I was a young dancer in New York City, struggling to make it on Broadway, I fell in love with Jimmy Dean and he fell in love with me. Back in those days when nice girls didn't, I did. It was 1951, and he hadn't yet become James Dean, public property . . . the Rebel, the Icon. When we fell in love, he was just my Jimmy. A skinny, near-sighted kid not yet twenty-one, whose glasses always seemed to be sliding down his nose. He was shy and broke and he mumbled. And I adored him.

For more than a year, we lived in a sheltered dream created out of our hopes for the future and our passion for each other. I was an inch taller and two years older, but somehow he always made me feel that I was his treasured little girl.

Our love story is sweet, and funny. I'm going to tell you the way it was, because other writers who have tried to capture our relationship haven't quite done it. I've never been interested in joining the group of writers with claims of being Jimmy's friend, enemy, confidant, or lover. But after

Jimmy was killed only one person was left in the world who knew what really happened between us. Me.

Many of those writers have spent their time on James Dean the dark prince of rebellion—the rude and twisted victim of his own destiny. People who know little or nothing about our relationship have filled page after page in book after book, leaving out everything that was truly important to us. Looking back over his short, turbulent life, I think I now see how crucial our time together was, to him as well as to me. Someone needs to remember the Jimmy who was warm and funny, sweet and polite, and capable of profound love.

I have talked with more than a few interested writers myself over the years, but I have never divulged to anyone the full story of our love. I just stuck to the few details that were common knowledge and kept to myself what took place when we were alone. That much has been mine to keep.

Now, almost a half century later, I think it is an important story to tell. I'm going to do my best to convey the way it was, the way he was, the way we were in the early 1950s. So here is my overture to the past. My duet for one. I remember ...

# *1*

It was the fall of 1951. I awoke on one of those iron gray mornings when the blues tugged at me like a bad memory rolling around in my thoughts, refusing to fade. It had been raining off and on since the night before. I never wake up singing, but on this morning I was positively glum and a little frayed around the edges. I felt like staying in bed all day.

I thought I heard someone at the door. I was still a little groggy with sleep, trying to pull myself awake. *What's that noise?* I finally realized that what I heard wasn't at the door but at the window. Across the room rain was splattering against the glass panes. A torrent of rain. Hard and heavy. Crawling out from under the covers, I padded over to take a look, only to stub my toe on the foot of the bed.

"Ouch. Son of—God *damn* it!"

I grabbed my foot and began hopping around, trying to get my balance. The noise woke up Larri, who was trying to sleep in after a late night.

"SHUT UP, DIZZY!" she yelled.

That woke up Ann, who always slept late. She made a noise—some sort of mumblelogue—rolled over and went back to sleep.

Larri Thomas and Ann Chisholm were my roommates. All of us were dancers, which I suppose is why Miss Carleton placed us together. Larri was blond, stunning, a lot of fun—a true gypsy. She got jobs on Broadway all the time. Ann was very tall, with heavy lips and a strong body. An extreme narcissist. She loved to look into the mirror, pouting and stroking herself slowly. Slowness was her whole style. She chewed slowly, exercised slowly, and spoke slowly. She claimed a slow metabolism, though as far as I could tell she was just an hour and a half behind the rest of us. But she was a hell of a dancer. We all got along well enough to be roommates.

When my toe stopped throbbing, I tiptoed quickly across the room and put my hand up to the window. The pane was cold. As the rain sluiced down just beyond my fingertips, I could feel the dampness go through my entire body. I shivered. Then I threw a coat over my T-shirt and went down the hall to the bathroom, where I stood at the sink, bleary-eyed, staring at myself in the mirror. I pushed back a limp lock of hair, then picked it up and let it fall. No question about it, my hair really needed washing. It was so thick and long that it was always a major deal, and I really didn't feel like bothering, so I tied it in a knot, went back to my room, threw on some clothes, and headed down the huge staircase leading to the main hall of the Club.

The Rehearsal Club—a chaperoned boardinghouse for aspiring actresses, singers, and dancers who dreamed of becoming stars—was located in a double brownstone on Fifty-third Street, between Sixth and Seventh Avenues. My father, a classical pianist who felt I'd be much safer here than out on my own, had made it possible for me to buck the long waiting list to get in by playing a benefit concert for the Theatre Guild. The Club was overseen by the sharp eyes of Miss Kay Carleton, a middle-aged lady of pale demeanor who was firm but understanding, and quite nice under all the reserve. She saw the Club as a little paradise for her girls. To us, it seemed more like a finishing school, with all the advantages of a convent. When I moved in she sat me down, looked into my eyes, and said:

"I want to instill in you the proper behavior for a young lady of virtue." *Are you kidding?* No, she wasn't.

"Gentlemen are not allowed above the first floor," she warned me. *Okay by me. I don't have a gentleman.* I'll never forget clutching my suitcase, focusing on Miss Carleton's rigid back, and following her dutifully upstairs. The higher we got, the lonelier I felt.

Now, as I pushed open the heavy front door of the Club, the rain had stopped, but the sky was still gloomy and I could tell the lull wouldn't last. I hit Fifty-third Street and turned toward Sixth Avenue.

I loved my neighborhood. The Museum of Modern Art was just up the street, with its tranquil sculpture garden where I could sit and drink coffee all afternoon and think about beauty and art and life and all the other things that filled me with wonder.

In the other direction, on the corner was Baden's drugstore with its friendly counter, its steaming coffee and fresh doughnuts. A block up the avenue on Fifty-fourth Street was

Jerry's, our neighborhood bar. It was warm, dark, and cozy, a place where actors could exchange theater news and gossip, trade information on auditions, and find out who was doing what all over town. Between the drugstore and the saloon was a little French restaurant called Faisan d'Or, where the food was first-rate and cheap and you could get a whiff of Paris from the kitchen.

The wind was blowing along Sixth Avenue that day, making ripples across the puddles; people on the sidewalks were pulling their overcoats tighter as they toughed their way around town through the gusts. I doubled my scarf around my neck but still felt my shoulders hunching up in the cold. I was getting chilled through, though I wasn't ready to go find warmth. Not just yet. I'd started to think about my friend Tony and his teeth.

Tony Marcello and Fabio Diaz were my dancing partners. We called ourselves "The Sheridan Trio"—not very catchy, I suppose, but I thought it had a touch of class. (What the hell—it was a lot better than "The Three Troubadours" or "Two Guys and a Gal.") We'd met when we were all auditioning for chorus jobs on *The Noro Morales Show,* a popular television show at the time. They got the job, I didn't, but the three of us struck up a friendship that led us to the idea of a trio, and it clicked. We started rehearsing together every day, and finally we got pretty damn good. We started picking up a small job here and there—then a few more.

This Friday night we were doing a show at a club up in Harlem. Normally we would have been rehearsing that today, but we had to cancel our plans because Tony needed a root canal. Why wouldn't he go to the dentist? Why did he have to wait so long? Now he needed *surgery*! What a mess.

It had started to rain again, and the wind began to blow right through me. I'd had enough. I turned back toward the Club, scooted up the front steps, turned the big brass doorknob, and breathed in a gust of warm air. The smell of soup simmering in the cafeteria floated up from downstairs, mingling with the scents of mahogany, old velvet, and perfume. By now it was getting close to noon. *Maybe Sue's ready for lunch.*

Sue Hight was my best friend. She was a beautiful, tall brunette, with a lovely voice—a wonderful singer and actress. She had gone on from the New England Conservatory of Music to sing on Broadway in several shows, among them *South Pacific* and *Gentlemen Prefer Blondes*, working hard and sleeping late. But I thought I'd take a chance.

I tapped gently on her door.

"Sue? Sue, are you awake?"

"Nooooo."

Her musical voice drifted through the door, making me smile. I opened the door and peeked in. Sue was sitting on the floor, doing her exercises. God, she was religious about her regimen. I decided to sit on the bed and watch her puff and grumble. She had a lovely body with a tiny waist, but she hated her hips—which were perfectly fine, as far as I could see—and she was always fighting her weight. As I walked in, she was just finishing the series of long slow stretches she did every morning. "Hi, Diz," she gasped as she sank to the floor.

"Hi, Sue."

I plopped down on the bed and lit a cigarette.

"Do you want to go to Baden's and have lunch?"

"No, I want to finish torturing myself so I can have a cigarette, too. Besides, I feel like I should eat downstairs, Dizzy. It's free, for God's sake." I'd forgotten about Sue's New England frugality.

"I know, but I really feel like a doughnut and coffee. Please come with me. I'm restless and I'm in a lousy mood. Come on—you can munch on some lettuce. *Pleeassse?* I'll buy."

"Oh, Lord, all right," she said, laughing. "Just be a friend and sit there and talk to me until I finish, okay? Or get down here and fanny-walk with me. If you leave now I'll cheat. Oh, the hell with it—I'm going to cheat anyway. Give me a smoke."

Lighting another cigarette, I sat down next to Sue, passed it over, and began to fanny-walk with her. We were in hysterics. There we were, stretching our legs straight out in front of us and somehow, without using our hands, inching our buns across the floor, one cheek in front of the other, with cigarettes dangling from our lips, and singing the "Fugue for Tinhorns" from *Guys and Dolls*:

> *I got the horse right here*
> *His name is Paul Revere*
> *And here's a guy that says if the weather's clear—*
> *Can do, Can do*
> *Da, da . . . says the horse can do.*

As we got to the other end of the room, I looked at Sue and said, "That should do it. I feel thinner already."

"That's easy for you to say," she panted. "You *are* thin. No fair!"

I shrugged. "Fair or not, I need a couple of doughnuts and coffee."

"See what I mean?" she whined. "I can't sniff a doughnut without gaining a pound."

I shrugged again and started to sing another song from the show: "*Sue me, sue me, what can you do me* . . . . I'll meet you downstairs in fifteen minutes, okay?" And I was gone.

Through the door I heard Sue yell, "*Twenty!*"

How crazy it all was. Sue being a singer and me being a dancer, both of us depending on our lungs and diaphragms for a living, smoking like there would always be a tomorrow. Almost every dancer I've ever known was a hard-core smoker. I don't know why; it didn't make any sense. But no one seemed to be aware of the dangers back then.

Baden's was almost empty when we got there. The weather, I guess. We passed long rows of shelves filled with bottles and boxes and tubes and jars of every size and sat down at the long, J-shaped soda fountain that stretched all the way to the rear of the store. The soda jerk took our order, and we leaned against the counter, talking shop.

"I need a new pair of shoes," I said. "I've gone through my soles again and we've got a job Friday night. I wish they weren't so damn expensive. They've got us dancers where they want us. We're a captive market."

"Don't skimp on shoes," Sue said. "Remember what happened to me? I told you, didn't I?"

"I'm not sure," I said.

"Oh, God, it was awful. Really ridiculous. All the girls had chartreuse, satin-dyed, high-heel, A. S. Beck shoes for four ninety-nine a pair. Can you imagine, buying cheap shoes like that for a Broadway show and expecting them to last? Anyway, of course, my heel gave out. It was Halloween night—isn't it funny that I should remember that?—and my heel came off during the show, while I was onstage. My ankle was broken, and they had to call the company doctor. After I healed and went back into the show, I demanded new shoes for me and all the girls. Well, it worked. A few days later, a huge carton of shoes arrived backstage. Every girl in the company got reshod. Brand-new reinforced I. Miller shoes! I remember it was New Year's Eve, and we all threw our old shoes into the carton near the elevator. Fifteen minutes later, sitting in my dressing room, I heard this shrieking and giggling and running back and forth. I went into the hall and all the chorus boys were trying on our shoes. By the time the curtain went up, the carton was empty. Isn't that a howl?"

"That's hysterical, but I don't have a company manager behind me paying for my shoes."

"I know," she said. "But do the best you can. Listen, I've gotta go. I'm going to be late for my lesson."

I paid the check and we left. Out on the street the day was looking gloomier than ever. Sue went to her singing lesson at Carnegie Hall Studios and I had my shoes to buy, so we said good-bye and headed off in different directions, promising to check in with each other later.

After I found some shoes I liked, I went back to the Club and found a message for me pinned to the bulletin board next to the phone. "Dizzy, call Fabio," it said, so I did. He said that Tony was okay but completely miserable. Still, it was only Tuesday, and the dentist was saying he'd be fine for our performance on Friday night. We arranged a rehearsal for the next day no matter how Tony felt—the show must go on—and I rang off, still feeling restless.

I couldn't settle down. My body had been longing for the rehearsal; I felt like a competitive runner who becomes edgy if she doesn't get in her regular five to ten miles. I had been ready to go out and move and express myself. I was a very physical person, and dancing was my emotional outlet. Now everything felt dammed up.

Looking around for something to do, I started to prowl the Club, searching for a friendly face, someone to talk to. The parlor, as it was so quaintly called, was deserted. The room ran the entire length of the building, and it was enormous. The walls were covered with photographs of early theater casts and productions. Oil paintings hung above the overstuffed couches, which were covered with linen dustcovers that Miss Carleton saw were laundered once a month. The windows overlooking the street were very tall and half hidden by heavy brocade drapes. There were large chairs arranged around coffee tables with vases of fresh cut flowers and Tiffany lamps that glowed with warmth. Everything reeked of order and restraint. I can still hear Miss Carleton laying down the rules: "No slouching, ladies. Feet on the floor, ladies. Posture is everything. Remember, we are all ladies here."

Miss Carleton's office was at the rear of the parlor, behind huge sliding doors. And on the other side of the brownstone was a dorm with twenty beds lined up against each wall. It looked more like a barracks than a lady's boudoir. The dorm was for girls who were only staying a short time. Upstairs, the living quarters consisted of single, double, and triple rooms for those of us who were boarding for longer than a month. All the floors were covered with deep forest-green carpeting.

When I couldn't find anyone downstairs, I decided to wash my hair, so I went back upstairs. The room I shared with Larri and Ann was in the front of the building. I liked that because whenever I felt bored, I could sit on the wide windowsill and watch the street. Each of us had a bed, a dresser, and enough room to add whatever stuff we collected.

I washed my hair, and while I was brushing it dry I mentally ran through all the steps for our engagement Friday night. Then I decided to take a nap. By now the rain pelting the window was really beginning to get to me. I tossed and turned, then after touching the wall with my fingers so I would feel safer, I finally went to sleep.

Around five, I roused myself and wandered back downstairs to the parlor. By now the room was darkening—that dusky darkness at the end of a fall day. The rain was still coming down. Here and there the lamps were lit, creating small pools of yellow light within the Old World charm of that large room.

At first I couldn't see anyone. Then, as my eyes adjusted to the darkness, I noticed a young man slumped in a couch against the far wall. He hadn't bothered to remove his raincoat. He was rumpled from head to foot. Soggy and wet. So soggy, you could practically see the steam rising from him. His feet were on the coffee table. God forbid Miss Carleton should walk in and see such wanton disregard for her precious furniture! The light played across his sandy hair and boyish face. His glasses had slipped far down his nose, and he appeared to be reading a magazine. *Now, here is someone different,* I thought to myself. The flash was instant.

I plopped myself down on the small couch across from him and picked up a magazine from the coffee table. We were the only two people in the huge room . . . total strangers. But the patter of rain on the windows, and the soft lamplight falling on our shoulders, made everything seem very intimate. He looked up, nodded at me, and smiled. I nodded back, and we both returned to reading our magazines.

I didn't want him to see me staring, so I would sneak a peek every time I turned a page. He was smoking, and I liked the way he put his cigarette to his lips, gracefully cocking his head as he inhaled, his hand covering his chin. He had a manner that made him seem manly and self-assured far beyond his years. He started to mumble something. But he wasn't talking to me, and it took a minute before I realized that he was reading out loud:

"Although the birds returned tethered to oranges," he said . . . and then there was a long pause, as though he was waiting. I decided to take a chance. Glancing down at my own magazine, I read some gibberish. Words taken from here and there that made no sense together:

"Egg salad sandwiches were raining everywhere."

Without looking up, he added another line. "The pancakes of the Universe fell through the cracks . . . "

"Who reinvented the future if not Mother Goose? . . . That's what I want to know," I read back.

Back and forth, on and on, we kept up this surreal exchange until we were both howling with laughter.

"Who *are* you?" he finally asked me. "I'm Jimmy."

I sat up, suddenly struggling to catch my breath. My stomach did a little flip-flop.

"I'm Dizzy."

"No, you're not at all."

"My *name* is Dizzy. I mean, people call me Dizzy."

"Dizzy, Dizzy, Dizzy, I love it." He giggled. "Why Dizzy?"

"My sister started it. When we were very little, she couldn't pronounce Elizabeth; it came out Dizabeth and ended up Dizzy. It probably sounds strange to you, but I'm used to it."

"It isn't strange . . . just different and funny," he said. "It's funny nice."

"You mean, instead of funny peculiar?"

"Yes, right, not funny peculiar."

We smiled at each other. I felt a tingle and I liked it.

"Are you an actress?" he asked.

"Well, sort of," I answered. "But mostly I'm a dancer. That's where my heart is. And you?"

"I'm an actor. I did a few plays in college, and a couple of bit parts in movies."

"Movies, how exciting!" I gushed.

"No, no, they were nothing. I just had a few lines." He changed the subject. "Do you like living here?"

"Well, except for some dumb Victorian rules, yes, I like it all right." A long pause; then I blurted out, "What about you? Where do you live?"

"Here and there," he said with a shrug. "Right now I'm at the YMCA up on the West Side."

"And do you like living there?"

"Well, I wouldn't call it living, but it's an okay place to sleep. It'll be even more okay when I get the bedroom set I ordered."

We both laughed again. The awkwardness was passing.

"You're very funny," I said. "Do you have a last name?"

"Dean, Jimmy Dean. What about you? Are you just Dizzy?"

"I guess." I stared at him.

"No, I mean . . . "

"I know. That's just my silly answer to that question."

"People must ask you that a lot, huh?"

"Well, it's a logical thing to ask. My whole name is Elizabeth Ann Sheridan. My mother is the only one who calls me that, though, and only when she's angry with me."

"Dizzy Sheridan." He said it as if he were trying it on. "I like that. I'll call you Dizzy . . . unless I'm mad at you. Then I'll call you Elizabeth."

"Are you planning on getting mad anytime soon?"

"You never know."

"Is there a warning sign?"

"I'll warn you."

"Before the warning sign?"

"Yeah."

"Good." I smiled at him. There was a moment of quiet as we looked at each other. *Interesting.* I went on. "You must be from out of town if you live at the Y."

"Yeah, all the way from California. I'm looking for work. I was told that this is the place for actors to be, but my coins got a bit thin, so I got a job on a game show . . . you know, *Beat the Clock.*" *My coins got a bit thin. How cute!* "A girl who lives here, Ann Roberts . . . well, we test stunts for the show. She said she thought I looked like I needed a hot meal."

"Do you?"

"Do I what?"

"Need a hot meal."

"Oh. Yeah, I guess so."

By this time several of the girls had begun drifting into the parlor. Tantalizing smells were floating up from the kitchen below. Just then Ann came downstairs to see if Jimmy had dried off enough to escort him downstairs.

"Hi, Dizzy," she said. "I see you've met. You ready, Jimmy? God, you're still wet."

"Yeah," said Jimmy. "Well . . . you know, it's raining."

"Diz, do you want to join us?"

"No thanks, I think I'll wait awhile."

I wanted to sit by myself and think about things. I wondered what there was about him that intrigued me so instantly. I wondered if he belonged to anyone, if he was Ann's or somebody else's boyfriend. I loved his face; it seemed to me to be shadowed with secrets. A mischievous face. I loved his smile, shy and tentative but warm—a warmth in his eyes. He looked young—my age, I guessed, maybe a little younger. I loved the way his glasses slipped forward when he said hi, and the way he pushed them back up his nose.

I was lost in thought when the first girls began coming upstairs, pairing off, joining friends, settling into the parlor for the evening. We had playing cards, checkers, and chess. A radio played softly in the background. (I can't remember if we had a TV yet.) The murmur of gossip, girlish laughter, and the steady patter of the rain filled the room.

Just when I was losing hope that he would ever come back, he reappeared, bobbing up the stairway, and wandered over.

He jammed his hands deeply into his pockets. He was rocking back and forth, looking down at the ground, mumbling something. I couldn't make it out.

"What?" I asked.

"Um, er, uh—do you, er, maybe have an extra umbrella?"

"Oh, sure, of course . . . I mean, wait right here and I'll go get it."

I only had one umbrella, but what the hell? I wasn't going anywhere. I raced upstairs to get it for him, stumbling on the landing, tripping on the stairs, then bumping into the wall on the way back down. *How cool could I be!?* I was lucky to arrive back in one piece, but there I stood, handing the umbrella to him.

"I'll bring it back tomorrow," he said. "Tomorrow afternoon. First thing. Promise."

"Fine." That's all I could get out. Suddenly I didn't care if it went on raining forever. I was going to see him again.

Neither one of us wanted to say good night, I could feel it, but all at once we both became very shy and tentative. His hands fumbled with the umbrella, and I couldn't think of anything to say.

Finally, after an awkward silence, as he was backing into the front door, he blurted, "Okay, I'll see you tomorrow, Dizzy. Maybe we can go someplace and talk?"

"All right," I said, hanging on to the doorknob. Just then one of the girls shouted from inside, "Dizzy, telephone!"

"I better get that—it might be important. I'll see you tomorrow."

I headed back to the hallway, behind the stairs, where the phones were. I turned for one last look, but he was gone.

# 2

The next morning I woke up earlier than usual. I'd had a busy night, toying with possibilities and *what-ifs*. Throwing on my tights, I grabbed my little record player, went downstairs for a fast bite of breakfast, then hurried off to rehearsal. I could feel the anticipation in my body. I couldn't wait to stretch out, raise some sweat, and dig into rehearsals.

The studio on Eighth Avenue in Midtown was small and dusty, but it met our needs. Large windows overlooking the street, a ballet bar, a piano, some chairs, and enough room to work.

Tony looked awful. His mouth was swollen, and his jaw was still killing him. But ever the trouper, he said, "Forget about it," and so we all did.

Fabio was slight and exotic-looking. With his almond-shaped eyes and light mocha skin, he looked like a Mexican bandit—a *nice* sort of Mexican bandit. I looked more like a Gypsy than the all-American girl; Tony was Italian, a butcher's son, beefier than Fabio and more athletic. If there were lifts in a routine, Tony did the hoisting. In his powerful hands, I felt like a bird taking off for the heavens.

Our job uptown wasn't exactly the Palace, but we didn't care. It was a paying job and a chance to showcase our new routine, which was choreographed by Sue's boyfriend, a wonderful dancer named James Brock. It was a French apache routine: two guys, one girl, an imaginary lamppost, flared nostrils, stamping feet, and a lot of attitude. Sounds hokey, but we were good. We loved to dance, and it came across the footlights. We also did a lot of our own choreography, but Brock was usually around to lend us moral support and new ideas.

I was having trouble concentrating that morning. All through the rehearsal, Jimmy's funny way of looking at me kept sneaking back into my thoughts. He looked at me almost in wonder, as if he were just discovering something hidden in a dream.

Our rehearsal went well, but we all thought we needed one or two more before we'd really be ready, so we planned to get together the following day.

I was very eager to get back to the Club to see him again, and I didn't want to take any chances on missing him if he brought my umbrella back early. Just thinking about him made me excited. So by late afternoon I was running back up the steps to the Club.

No sign of him yet. I could feel myself wilt. Maybe he hadn't felt the same connection I had. I had to dump my feelings onto someone—but not just anyone. So I went upstairs to see Sue. I knocked on her door, but this time I didn't wait for her to answer, I just went barreling through. She was sitting on her bed, reading, waiting for dinnertime.

"Sue, I've gotta talk to you," I said, and plunged on. "I just met this boy . . . it's too early to talk about . . . but it's driving me crazy."

I was pacing feverishly. Sue stared at me calmly, amused, waiting, book open on her lap.

"He was s-o-o *cute*—we had this sort of immediate thing, you know—I mean, we touched each other, I think—well, not *really* touching!—I think he felt the same way I did— God, I hope so!—His name is Jimmy, Jimmy Dean—I gave him my umbrella—now he's got to come back, right?—Oh, Lord, Sue, I'm sorry I bothered you—I'll see you in the cafeteria." And with that I was out the door, where I left Sue still sitting on her bed—undoubtedly wondering, *What the hell was that?*

I went to my room, undressed, left my clothes where they fell, put on my robe, and went to take a shower. *I'm going to have to calm down.* I tried to concentrate on Jimmy's hands. His fingers were strong and faintly stained with tobacco. I didn't remember seeing any rings or even a watch.

Sue was already in the cafeteria when I got there. She smiled and patted the chair next to hers.

"I saved you a place . . . can't wait to hear more."

"He's *so* cute," I gushed.

"You said that," she said.

"I love the way he uses his hands. Sort of like a puppeteer working his strings." More gushing.

"I haven't the slightest idea what you're talking about." Sue stared at me. I ignored her and went through the line, picking up a salad, a roll, and some chocolate milk.

"You must think I'm insane," I said, sitting down.

"Yes, of course I do. But so what? That's why I love you. Tell me more."

"That's just the point. There's nothing more to tell—and even if there were, I don't know if it's a something or a nothing, and if it is a nothing, then I don't want to feel foolish."

"What?! God, Dizzy, I get so mad at you when you use your own language," Sue replied.

I changed the subject. "Are you and Brock coming to see us on Friday night?"

"Wouldn't miss it. Somebody said they had a great dance band up there. I have a morning singing lesson on Saturday, though, so we can't stay too late."

Then she said she felt like a nap and went back up to her room.

After dinner the usual bunch of girls was sitting around the parlor. Just when I was beginning to give up on Jimmy, the front doorbell rang. I was on my way upstairs, but I whirled and bolted down to answer the door. There stood Jimmy with a sly grin on his face and my umbrella in his hand.

"Hi," he said. "I'm back."

"Hi."

My heart flipped over and I just stood there. He reached into his raincoat pocket and, pulling out a crumpled pack of cigarettes, offered me one. I took it; I remember touching his hand as he held the match. It was so cold and raw I wanted to hold it in both of mine until it was warm.

"I'm sorry I didn't bring this back earlier," he said. "But I got hung up working . . . anyway, I hope you didn't need it . . . ."

His voice trailed off. I was trembling. I could hardly hear him.

"It didn't rain today, so you're lucky." I tried to screw my face into what I hoped was a fierce look of displeasure. I succeeded more than I meant to. He held out the umbrella and started backing away, not quite sure what to make of my reaction until I burst out laughing.

"I was just kidding," I said.

"Well, you got me pretty good there."

The parlor seemed crowded and I didn't want to share Jimmy with anyone.

"Let's go sit on the stairs, it'll be a little more private."

We went over to the staircase and I sat down on the first landing. Jimmy leaned against the banister and we started talking. His shyness was irresistible. He would look at me and then his eyes would dart away; I waited for them to come back to me, and when they did there was something so intense in them that I felt stripped of everything. As if he could see right through me. As if he knew what I was feeling.

"Was your rehearsal today?"

I nodded.

"I'd love to come watch you. Do you think that would be okay? I'd sit in a corner and be quiet as hell."

"That's an oxymoron."

"Who's a moron?"

*Great! We're having fun again.*

"I'll have to ask my partners if it's okay."

"I just want to see you again." *God, was he blushing?*

"In that case, what are you doing Friday night? We're working in a place up in Harlem. Maybe you'd like to come."

"Great . . . Great . . . Harlem! Really? What kind of a place is it?"

"It's this big dance hall, with a bar, and they have a great big swing band. It's a very popular place and the music is supposed to be really great."

"I've never been to Harlem. Can I go with you?"

"Sure—I'll let you know."

We started to talk about other things. We talked for a long time, sitting on the big staircase. He told me he'd grown up on a little farm in Indiana.

"Oh—did you have horses?"

"No. The farm was small. Pigs, chickens, a few cows, you know . . . like that. Why, do you like horses?"

"I *love* horses. All animals, really, but horses are my very favorite. When I was a little girl, I was always threatening to run away and become a cowboy—uh, cowgirl, I guess. Then, when I got a little older, I wanted to be a cowgirl *and* a matador . . . or is it matadoress?"

"Oh, Christ," he said, "that's one of my big passions—bullfighting!"

"Really?! Did you see *Blood and Sand*?"

He nodded, and I kept going.

"Wasn't it exciting? Tyrone Power as the matador in the suit of lights . . . and another thing I love—the sound of the Spanish words—*matador, capote, muleta, banderilleros*—they sound like music, don't they? And there was another movie about this bullfighter from Brooklyn, Sidney Franklin .... Robert Stack played him, I think. What was the name of that movie? Oh, you know—"

He interrupted me. "I can't believe this. I know him."

"Who? Robert Stack?"

"No, Sidney Franklin. Actually, he's kind of a friend of mine."

"You're kidding! Really? How?"

At this point, the traffic on the stairs was getting heavy. He was mumbling something about Sidney Franklin, but I couldn't get it.

"What? . . . I can't hear you."

People were stepping over us and between us, and no matter how often we shifted we were definitely in the way.

"Could we go somewhere?" Jimmy said. "Maybe have a drink?"

"Sure. Jerry's Bar is only a half a block away," I said quickly. "It's dark. Full of actors. You'll love it."

"Great, let's go."

We walked up the street, talking all the way. Jimmy told me he'd become friends with Mr. Franklin when he was in California, and that he had talked him out of a bloodstained bullfighter's cape—a prized possession he'd brought with him to New York.

"Oh, could I see it sometime?" I asked him. "*Puhl-e-e-e-z-e?*"

"*S-u-u-r-e,*" he said, gently mocking me. He drew out the line, making it match mine, relishing each consonant and vowel. In the months ahead it was to become our favorite expression. We used it constantly, making it our own little security blanket, cooing it to each other the way you would to a child:

"Do you love me?"

"S-u-u-r-e."

"Are you hungry?"

"S-u-u-r-e."

"Will you rub my back?"

"S-u-u-r-e."

Jerry's was pretty full. Most of the regulars were there at the bar; some were at the tables; most of the booths were taken, but one was vacant. The very last booth in the back. I grabbed Jimmy's hand and practically dragged him toward it.

I liked Jerry's. It was a world-class neighborhood bar on the corner of Fifty-fourth Street and Sixth Avenue. There were two entrances, one on Sixth, the other around the corner. A long, dark, stained wooden bar stretched down the right side of the big room. In the back on the right was a bank of telephone booths. The back wall was covered with bulletin board messages. Tables filled the center of the room, and the most popular place to sit was the row of booths with leather seats lining the wall opposite the bar.

Like me, most of the girls from the Club used Jerry's as a home away from home, an office where they could pick up their messages on the bulletin board or drop playbills announcing anything exciting that one of us was doing. We felt safe and comfortable there, and the food wasn't bad.

One of the regulars was an older woman, maybe fifty or sixty, always gloomy, who drank at the bar every day. She always wore a hat, a beret-type thing that hid her hair, except for a few gray wisps that trailed down her forehead and ears. She concealed her body underneath baggy sweaters, even in the summer. She ordered her meals at the bar, and when they came she would wolf down a few bites, then pour the rest into an enormous purse she always carried—mashed potatoes, gravy and all. If anyone dared laugh, she would spin around and glower. I wish I could remember her name. She deserved that.

As we headed for the back we passed Ann Chisholm, who was sitting in a booth with Tamar Cooper, an actress from the Club. Tamar was very Russian-looking, with high cheekbones and hair cut in bangs. Ann recognized Jimmy and called out "Hi!" We stopped a moment to say hello. I introduced Jimmy to Tamar, who seemed interested in what we two were all about. But when she invited us to join them, Jimmy said, "No, thanks, we have some things to talk over," and pulled me away.

We settled into the last booth. "Would you like a drink?" Jimmy asked me.

"Maybe a beer."

"Have you ever tried Champale?" he said. "It's like beer, only with bubbles. I recommend it."

"S-*u-u-r-e*."

He leaned forward and studied my face.

"Damn—you're the most interesting girl I've ever met."

"Yeah? That's a pretty good line. You don't even know who I am."

"Are you hungry?"

"Not really."

"Me either."

"Want to share a burger?"

"Okay."

Then we both started talking at the same time.

"Who are you?"

"Go ahead."

"No, you go."

"Like I said, I'm a dancer."

"Like I told you, I'm an actor."

"You first."

"No, you." He was giggling. My stomach was in knots. Then he paused for a moment, and in a formal way he began to recite the story of his life.

"All right, I'll start. Then you, okay? My name is James Byron Dean. I was born in Indiana. My mom died when I was nine, and my father moved to California and sent me to live with my aunt Ortense and uncle Marcus on their farm in Winslow. My father was in teeth. Still is." He laughed at his own joke. "Actually, he's a dental technician. He still lives in California. We're not exactly close. He has his life and I have mine. I came to New York to be an actor, but sometime before I die, I want to fight a bull. Definitely. Maybe a lot of bulls. Shall I keep going?"

I nodded.

"The farm was okay. My aunt and uncle raised me. They're really nice folks, but I couldn't wait to get out on my own. I really didn't know what I wanted to be. I had so many voices in my head pulling me in different directions, but I knew I wanted to be somebody really important. Maybe a star athlete or a lawyer or a musician. I played sports in high school—track, baseball, basketball. I was pretty good, too; I could have been a professional, maybe ... but then I did some acting."

As the words came tumbling out they became more and more passionate.

"I knew right away, deep down in my soul, that I wanted to be an actor—well, actually, I realized I *was* an actor, and that by being an actor I could be anyone, a scientist, a lawyer, or a musician. I could be Mozart or Bach. I could be a general, a king, or even the president. When I act I'm in a different world. I don't know how to explain it—"

"You don't have to explain it," I broke in. "I know what you mean. That's exactly the way I feel when I dance. I've felt that way since I was a little girl. It's just like you said—in my soul I always knew I was a dancer. *Am* a dancer. Did you see *An American in Paris*?" He nodded. "Do you remember that great big smile Gene Kelly had on his face when he was dancing with the little kids of Paris? Like he felt something inside that no one else could feel?"

I started singing, and all at once we fell into a duet, just the way we had over our magazines the day before—just the way the kids and Gene Kelly had in the movie:

"I got ... ," I sang.

"Rhythm," Jimmy answered.

"I got ... ," I sang.

"Music," Jimmy answered.

"I got ... ," I sang.

"My gal," Jimmy answered.

"*Who could ask for anything more?*" we both chimed in, trying to harmonize. It was god-awful, and without thinking, as if it were the most natural thing in the world, we reached for each other's hands across the table and laughed.

"It's a good thing you didn't want to be a singer," I ribbed. "Anyway, when I'm dancing, it's like I'm telling a story with my body, and I'm telling the story in a way that nobody else can. Am I making any sense? I have a hard time expressing my feelings with words. Talking with my body is easier."

"Yes, I know," he said. "I know exactly what you mean. You're daring to be true to yourself, removing all the barriers between you and your audience, and when it's going really well you feel in complete harmony—almost as if you're in control of destiny."

A shout from the bar. "Hey, Diz, who's the boyfriend?" My roommate Larri.

"Wouldn't you like to know?"

The waiter came up with the burger and the drinks. I leaned around to ask him for some mustard, and when I turned back to take a sip of my Champale, there, in my glass, were two white shapes. I didn't know what to think.

"Can I have my teeth back?"

I looked up. Jimmy was banging on the table, whooping and cackling. He had a big gap where his two front teeth should have been. Someone had knocked his teeth out—later he told me it happened during basketball practice when he was still a kid in Indiana—and his two removable caps had made their way into my drink when I wasn't looking. I got the feeling he didn't miss them one bit. As I'd soon find out, he loved dropping them everywhere—in your glass, on your plate, down your back. Then he'd grin that toothless-idiot grin and ask for his teeth back.

We talked more about bullfighting.

"It's amazing, you being interested in all that. Most women find it disgusting."

"Not me! It's really quite beautiful. Like a dance—a dance of death. Almost stately, in slow motion; you don't know how it will end, and you can't take your eyes away. It's cruel, no doubt about that, but it's beautiful too. I hate it that the bull has to be killed, though. What's the point? I don't really understand the whole concept . . . the reason for—"

"Would you rather they shake hands and go home?"

"Wouldn't *that* be neat?" I smiled. "After all, a prizefighter doesn't have to kill his opponent just to prove he's better."

"To me, it's all about fear," Jimmy said. "Overcoming your fear. To look death in the face and walk away. To challenge death and conquer your fear. If you can overcome your fear, you can do anything, right? I don't know—maybe you have to be Spanish to really understand."

"Well, I'd have thought that just getting in the ring and turning your back on a killer bull would be pretty much conquering your fear—but, as you say, I'm not Spanish."

Jimmy drew a bull with horns on his paper napkin; I took his pen and drew a tree on mine. The same wintry tree I had been drawing since I was a little girl and could first hold a crayon.

"You sketch very well. I love your bull."

"It's yours," he said, handing it to me.

"Would you like a dead tree?" I said, handing him my napkin.

"Yes, thank you." He folded it neatly and put it in his pocket.

We talked and talked until we heard the bartender signal for last call. I looked around the room—we were the only ones left, except for a few hard-core drinkers at the bar.

"Would you like a nightcap? Should we split another beer?"

"No, thanks. We should go, don't you think? We've been here all night."

"Yeah, I guess. I'll walk you home."

We headed back to the Club. Jimmy put his hands in his pockets and I put my arm through his and we walked side by side. Holding him, I felt a tension in his body. I liked the feeling. We sat on the brownstone steps, sharing a last cigarette. Neither of us wanted to part, as chilly as it was.

"I'm glad I met you, Dizzy. I don't hardly know anyone here. I could use a friend."

"You don't like New York?" I asked.

"Don't get me wrong. I love New York. It just seems all I've done since I've been here is go to the movies. I study the actors. Would you like to go sometime? To the movies, I mean. You know . . . with me. Maybe tomorrow?"

He was adorable.

"Yeah, I guess so. Might be fun. Maybe I'll turn out to be that friend you could use." I was smiling.

"I didn't mean it like that!"

"I'm teasing."

"Oh, yeah, I know. So what time?"

"I have a rehearsal tomorrow and a few things to do. Why don't we meet at Baden's drugstore at seven?"

I hoped he would try to kiss me good night, but he just squeezed my hand and looked at me with that goofy smile. "Okay. Tomorrow at Baden's. I had so much fun tonight."

"Me too."

"Good night."

"Good night." I stood with my hand on the door and watched as he walked away.

The next morning I awakened and lay there thinking about Jimmy, how easily we had taken to each other, how much fun we had. I remembered the touch of his hand, his slanting smile and easy laughter and the warmth I felt enfolding me while I was with him. And, strangely enough, I couldn't help but wonder if he had any real talent—if this shy, mumbling, crumpled little guy could act at all.

That afternoon I met Tony and Fabio at the studio, and we spent a good two hours rehearsing. Tony's face looked a little better, though not much. I told them that Jimmy had been wanting to watch us rehearse. Said Tony, "Why not?" He could come watch tomorrow, and then we'd all go up to Harlem together.

A good workout was just what I needed to get my mind off the big date. I had to start concentrating on other things and do what I thought I did best—dance. I put the bolero on my little record player, and I entered that other place—a place

I knew so well, a place of power and grace, of harmony and beauty. I felt beautiful when I danced. I felt that anything was possible. My apprehensions melted away. My mind was fluid. My nerves were at rest. And my body seemed to be smiling.

Afterward I dashed back to the Club to grab a bite, bathe, and dress, all the while rehearsing witty things to say to Mr. Dean. I braided my hair in a pigtail down my back and spent a long time putting on what little makeup I wore. By five o'clock I was ready; the next two hours were the longest I had ever experienced.

When I got to Baden's, Jimmy was already there waiting for me at the counter, having a cup of coffee.

"Hi—so you want a cup of coffee or something?" he asked.

I felt a little nervous, and I could tell he was too. "No, not really. Why don't we just go?"

We started walking in the general direction of Times Square, still uncertain where we were going. Jimmy was holding on to my long pigtail as we strolled along.

"What do you want to see, Dizzy?"

"I don't care, what do you want to see?"

"It doesn't matter to me. I've already seen every movie in Times Square. I've seen *Streetcar* I don't know how many times. I love Brando."

"Oh, me too! He was so crude and menacing, wasn't he?"

"Yeah, he played the part perfectly. You never knew what he was going to do from one moment to the next. That's what great acting is all about—surprise."

As we neared the corner of Sixth Avenue and Fifty-first I

saw a figure dressed in a poncho and black leather from head to toe, squatting in a doorway. It was Moondog, the blind poet and musician. A woolen cap hid his face almost entirely, except for the mustache and beard covering his mouth. Most of the time he wore a Viking helmet with horns, but I guess tonight it was too cold.

Moondog had been a city fixture for decades; he was also my friend, and I always stopped to talk to him. Quiet and thoughtful, he made primitive instruments and wrote poems and songs that he sold to tourists and passersby. He had told me he was a vegetarian, and so on some days I would bring him a banana or an apple. We would sit in a doorway while he patiently listened to my hopes and worries or we would just chat, about anything and everything, sitting side by side, sharing a piece of fruit on the edge of a bustling city street. Sometimes I would shut my eyes so I could experience something of the darkness in which he lived, just for a few minutes.

At first I thought Moondog might be sleeping, but I wanted to stop and introduce him to Jimmy. I wanted Jimmy to know him, to like him.

As we approached him, Moondog raised his head and smiled. I never knew how he did it, but he always knew I was coming.

"Hi, Dizzy," he said quietly. "Who's your companion?"

I loved that. It must have been essence of Dizzy that let the blind man know.

"Hi. I want you to meet a friend of mine," I said. "Moondog, this is Jimmy."

Moondog held out his hand. Jimmy took it in both of his, which I found very touching, and said, "It's a pleasure to meet you, sir."

"Likewise. How are you, Dizzy? I haven't talked to you in a couple of days. Crazy weather."

"I'll say. Everything is good with me," I answered.

Jimmy was admiring a little drum that Moondog had beside him. It was a crude, tribal-looking, stretched-skin, tom-tom sort of thing.

"May I try out your drum, sir?" Jimmy asked.

Moondog chuckled. "Of course." He held out the drum along with a felt-wrapped mallet. "Are you a musician, Jimmy?"

"Yes, I am. I play the recorder," Jimmy replied, accepting the little drum. He put it under his arm, cocked his head for several moments, as if he were thinking of what he was going to do, then started beating out a simple rhythm and began chanting and dancing, as if he were an Indian around a campfire.

"A*ye-a-yee-o-aye-a-yee-o.*"

It wasn't hokey or mocking, it was rhythmically valid and entirely sincere. Of course I joined in immediately, improvising little steps and spins. I liked the way Jimmy moved. Not that he was doing anything spectacular; it was just the opposite, and his steps were simple and fluid. Then, to our amazement and delight, Moondog started intoning a counterchant to Jimmy's and mine, and before we knew it the three of us had a little thing going. A few passersby stopped to enjoy our impromptu performance.

After a while Jimmy ended with a shave-and-a-haircut beat on the little drum. Moondog laughed; we all laughed.

Moondog pushed forward a cigar box and opened the lid, offering us a few pieces of dried fruit that were inside.

"No, thanks. We're off to the movies," I said.

"Well, you two have fun," Moondog said. "And thanks for cheering me up tonight. Come by again anytime." As if he were inviting us back into his living room. Which, in a way, I suppose he was.

We said we would, and we were off, dancing down the street to the next corner.

"That was such fun. I didn't know you played the recorder."

"Well, actually, I'm just learning. I'm not quite ready for Carnegie Hall yet," he said, chuckling. "I'm totally fascinated with music, though. I can practice for hours."

"Speaking of Carnegie Hall, my father gives a concert there two or three times a year. He's a pianist."

"Really, a concert pianist? That's fantastic! Can I meet him sometime?"

"Sure, I guess so. But I have to warn you, he can be extremely difficult."

"Great artists are *supposed* to be difficult!" Jimmy shot back.

*Well, okay, if you say so.* That shut me up for a while. I didn't see it that way.

"I'll tell you about my father sometime, when I know you a little better. What movie do you want to see—or should I say, what movie haven't you seen? How about something scary?"

"Perfect!" he said.

What it was, I couldn't tell you. I was too swept up in Jimmy to remember the name of the movie we weren't seeing. What I do remember is that the theater was less than half full and the flickering darkness was welcoming.

We sat on the side, way over by the wall and started whispering.

"I keep wanting to touch you," he said.

"Go ahead," I told him.

"I'm so happy I found you."

"I'm happy I found you, too."

We didn't wait long. He put his arm around my shoulder, and with his other hand he gently caressed my cheek. He pulled me close to him and turned my face to his. We looked into each other's eyes, and then we kissed for the first time. So sweetly. So easy and natural. Tentative at first, then our lips explored and grew bolder. We kissed each other's faces, as if we were two puppies cleaning each other. Between kisses we panted:

"I can't . . . you know . . ."

"Yes . . . I know . . . Don't talk . . . kiss."

We tumbled into a world all our own.

Finally we came up for air and looked at each other. I was trembling from sheer ecstasy; I remember feeling as if stars were exploding inside of me. Exploding stars of pure joy. The movie ended and the lights came up and people slowly shuffled their way back to reality.

"Could I have one more kiss?" I asked.

"Suure."

I don't know how long that kiss lasted, but when we came up for air this time, we were all alone in the deserted theater.

"Do you want to stay and actually watch the movie this time?" Jimmy asked.

"No, wet's go for a lalk, I need to get thuum fweeling bwack in my wips." That cracked him up.

Back on the street, I took his hand. "That was the best movie I've never seen. Thank you."

"Oh, you're very welcome," he said formally.

"I mean, thanks for not getting fresh. I don't know what I would have done. Probably nothing."

"I wanted to touch you everywhere, but I didn't want you to think I was only after one thing, you know?" he said. "'Cause I'm not. Your face is a . . . I love your face. We just met, but I feel like . . . I don't know . . . I've never felt this way about anyone before."

"Really?"

"Yeah, really, and I didn't want to do anything to screw it up. I know you're a good girl, Dizzy."

"And you don't mind?"

"No." He smiled. "I'm glad. Maybe things will just happen when they happen."

As for me, I was torn. I was a good girl; still, all I really wanted to do at that moment was get naked with this boy and be bad. But good girls didn't have sex on the first date. Not in those days. Everybody knew that. And I didn't want him to think I was some dumb pushover. I didn't want to do anything to derail this racing romance. I remember feeling, even so early on as that moment, that this was destined to be someone special.

We walked and talked for hours, up to Fifty-ninth Street, then east along Central Park South, then down Fifth Avenue, past the Plaza, Bergdorf's, and Tiffany's, back over to Times Square and Broadway. We ducked into more than one doorway to hug and kiss and we stopped under every theater marquee we passed, telling each other that someday our names would be up there in lights.

"Sheridan and Dean," I said.

"Dean and Sheridan," he corrected. "You know, like Lunt and Fontanne."

"Oh, it's gonna be that way, is it? You Tarzan, me Jane?"

"You want to be Tarzan?" he asked.

"Sure, can I?"

"No, I'm Tarzan. You're Jane."

"Okay."

He put his arm around my waist and drew me closer.

As we walked around Times Square, we improvised silly dialogue from the plays we passed:

"Oh, Colonel, do tell me how you lost your arm!"

"I lost it fighting the Fuzzy-Wuzzies in the Sudan, don't you know."

"I do now. Can I make you a nice spot of tea?"

"A spot of tea would be nice."

Finally, we made our way back to the brownstone steps of the Rehearsal Club. Even after all those hours we could hardly bear to end the evening.

"It's scary, isn't it—all this happening to us, so terribly fast?"

"No—*wonderfully* fast," he said.

"Oh, I almost forgot—I talked to my partners and they said it would be okay for you to come watch us rehearse tomorrow. That is, if you still want to . . ." Then, before he could answer, I put my arms around him, pulled him close, and kissed him one more time.

"Good night, Dizzy."

"Good night, Jimmy."

I ran upstairs, undressed, and jumped right into bed. I didn't want to wash the evening off. I couldn't remember ever being so happy. I closed my eyes and replayed the whole evening in my mind, and just as I was wondering how I would ever be able to sleep, I fell asleep.

When I got to the studio, Jimmy was there waiting for me. He had already introduced himself to the boys, and they all seemed to be getting along well. Jimmy sat in a chair in the corner, and he was as quiet as he had promised to be.

We began to rehearse. It was glorious being able to express my emotions in motion. A simple step, a full extension of the right leg, arms reaching out, then a fast spin into Tony and a lift over his head. At one point I lost my concentration on the release; peeking over to see Jimmy's face, I almost knocked Tony over. My elbow landed in his stomach.

"Jesus, Dizzy, concentrate!" Tony yelled. Poor guy! He didn't need any more trouble.

"Sorry, Tony." I pulled myself together, and we went through our routines quickly. The trio was slick and tight; we were finally ready for our gig.

I started putting my record player away.

"So what do you do, Jimmy—act?" Tony asked.

"Yeah, I'm an actor. You guys were great. Thanks for letting me sit in. I've never seen such movement. What style is that?"

"I don't know. It's just dancin', man. A little of this, a little of that, you know. It's like telling a story, only no words."

"Well, you were all marvelous—I mean it."

"Yeah, thanks. But I'm dying here," Tony groaned. "I gotta get to the fuckin' dentist." His teeth were still giving him trouble. "Later. Jerry's Bar at seven, right?"

"Oh, *pobrecito*! I'll go with you, man," Fabio said, and they disappeared.

"Thanks again," Jimmy said. "God, that was . . . you were *marvelous*." That word again. It sounded phony, but I could tell by the expression on his face that he was sincere.

"I've seen all the Hollywood musicals," he said, shaking his head. "And I've never seen anyone move like you do. You were so free and natural . . . like an animal. You were just . . ."

"Marvelous?" I teased.

I wanted to throw myself in his arms, but I was all sweaty—and he was still sitting down.

"I gotta run," Jimmy said. "I got an audition."

"Me too. I've got a million things to do. Like wash my hair, for one. I always wear it down when I perform."

"I hope so."

Walking downstairs together, we suddenly both seemed shy.

"Meet us tonight at Jerry's," I said, "and we'll all go uptown together. Okay?"

He smiled at me and said, "You're marvelous," and we both cracked up. He turned on his heel and off he went down the street, still laughing.

It was pretty cold that night. We were all wearing winter coats and gloves—except Jimmy, who arrived in his raincoat. As we hit the street, he turned up his collar, thrust his hands deep into his pockets, and leaned into the chilly night.

"Jimmy, aren't you cold?" I asked him.

"Nah, I'm a hardy farm boy," he said between shivers. "You know what we call weather like this in Indiana? Summer."

We headed for the subway station at Eighth Avenue and Fifty-ninth, locking arms four abreast as we hustled along. Tony was in obvious pain, head down, lugging the suitcase with our costumes. Jimmy started to make chug-chugging train sounds, and I started to sing Duke Ellington's theme:

> *Why don't you—go take the A Train*
> *You'll find it's the quickest way to get to Harlem.*

Fabio chimed in with sound effects and lyrics—"Choo, choo—hurry, hurry—hurry—take the A train!" Only poor Tony didn't want to play our game. The whole left side of his face was swollen and he could only growl sideways at us like W. C. Fields: "Forget about it!"

The club was a big place, probably a theater in an earlier time; there was a proscenium stage at one end where the band was playing. There was a big dance floor in the middle of the room surrounded by tables and chairs. A long bar ran along one side, and at the time we arrived, the joint was really jumping. The crowd was about 90 percent black. Everyone was laughing, drinking, dancing, necking—having a wonderful time.

Sue and Brock had gotten there early because they loved to dance together, which is just what they were doing when we came in. I waved to them from the sidelines, and Sue pointed toward a ringside table she had saved for all of us. Jimmy and I went over and sat down.

Looking over my shoulder, I saw some of the girls from the Rehearsal Club crowded around an adjoining table. In those days, single girls with any sense of adventure thought nothing of going up to Harlem to dance or listen to jazz. I ran over to say hello to Ann Chisholm and some other girls from the Club. Tamar was there too, with some friends of hers I didn't know.

"Thanks for coming, you guys. Have fun."

"Oh, we will. Break a leg, Dizzy."

When I got back to our table, Jimmy was talking to Sue and Brock. Sue winked at me as I sat down. It felt good to be warm again—with my friends and with Jimmy.

The band really sounded great, and when they struck up a swing tune—"Jumping at the Woodside," I think—I asked Jimmy if he wanted to jitterbug. He smiled a crooked little smile.

"I'll wait for a slow one."

So I pulled Tony out of his chair and we danced. Tony's face was so funny, I could hardly keep from laughing out loud. He looked like an angry dog with a ball in his cheek, but as soon as we started jitterbugging around the floor Tony seemed to forget his pain. The sweetest half-smile spread across his face as he fell into what he loved to do most— dancing.

When the song ended, the band segued into a ballad, and the two of us returned to the table where Jimmy was standing up—applauding. I took his hand and I led him out to the floor, and we slow-danced for the very first time. The vocalist began to sing.

*When we walk hand-in-hand,*
*The world becomes a wonderland—it's magic . . .*

I don't know when we stopped dancing and just began swaying back and forth, pressing against each other, barely moving. Now our bodies knew what our lips had already discovered. We were made for each other. Jimmy whispered in my ear. "I know it's crazy, but I'm falling in love with you."

Then the song was ending and I couldn't speak. My thoughts had drifted into a place they had never been before, except perhaps in daydreams. For the first time in my life I was beginning to believe someone might truly love me. And we had met just four days before.

"Did you hear me?" Jimmy asked.

"No—um, yes—I mean, *yes*, I heard you and *no*, it isn't crazy, because I'm falling in love with you too."

He was smiling. Glowing. We looked at each other, and then he kissed me very gently for a long time. No one had ever kissed me quite the way he did—our lips lightly touching, the kiss lingering.

After a long while, someone yelled at us: "Enough already." We opened our eyes and found we were all alone on the dance floor. We smiled at each other. Jimmy kept his arm around my waist as we made our way back to the table. The emcee announced an intermission, telling the crowd that the evening's entertainment was about to start: "STARRING THE TALLEST MAN IN THE WORLD—THE PUERTO RICAN GIANT—AND THE FABULOUS DANCING OF— THE SHERIDAN TRIO!" I still had a show to do.

Backstage (if you could call it that), the dressing room (if you could call it that) was a small, dingy cubicle with a table, two folding chairs, and a cracked mirror. It didn't even have a door. A burlap curtain almost covered the entrance. So much for privacy.

Tony, Fabio, and I quickly undressed and got into our costumes; then we went into the wings offstage, where the tallest man in the world was standing with his sleazy agent. I found myself staring up at the saddest face I'd ever seen. The Giant was dressed all in black in a hand-tailored suit that still fit him badly, a rumpled shirt, and a tie. His shoes looked like a pair of rowboats, and topping off this funereal ensemble was a big black homburg.

"Hi, I'm Dizzy Sheridan—and you're the tallest person I've ever seen." I held my hand up to him. The Giant took it in his. My hand looked like a golf ball in a catcher's mitt. It felt as if I were looking up at a tree . . . or a statue in the park.

"How do you do," he said in a very deep voice. "*Mas despacio, por favor.* Please speak slower."

Before I could say anything, his agent interrupted us and started to give him a pep talk.

"Okay, now, you ready? Do your stuff. And remember to smile."

Out on the stage, the emcee introduced the Giant with a stupid old tall joke, and the agent nudged his client out toward the spotlight. The Giant trudged to center stage—and just stood there. Some people left their tables and came to crowd around the stage as Mr. Sleaze stood in the wings, shouting:

"Energy. Turn around. Smile. I said *smile!*"

The Giant turned around slowly a few times. Then he just stood there, looking straight ahead, with a frozen smile, his arms dangling like dead logs. The crowd was kind; they cheered and whistled and applauded. Inevitably, some dimwit shouted, "How's the weather up there?" In reply, the Giant made a formal bow, one hand on his stomach, just like a little boy. That was his act. He was tall . . . that's all. Then he made his way laboriously offstage, still smiling his blank smile.

The emcee began wowing the crowd with even more crude tall jokes. It made me feel sick. So I approached the Giant again, and speaking as slowly as I could I told the Giant how much I had enjoyed his . . . *bravery*. Bravery wasn't the word I meant to say, but it was the only word I could think of. I knew it wasn't right and I didn't want to offend him. I tried to stammer my way through an apology: "I mean—I think you were, you know—I mean, I thought you had a lot of dignity out there—"

The Giant stopped me. "It's okay. I know what you are trying to say. I'm used to it. And besides, it beats the circus."

Then I heard the emcee saying, "The FABULOUS SHERIDAN TRIO," and all at once we were on.

I wanted our routines that night to be especially good, because Jimmy would be watching. We opened with a "Slaughter on Tenth Avenue" kind of thing with a Latin twist, if you can imagine that. We were wearing our apache costumes, and Fabio and Tony were tossing me all over the stage. At one point, I got so carried away trying to be good for Jimmy that I crashed into a ringside table and fell into a man's lap, breaking his chair. We hit the floor together. "Sorry," I said, and without missing a beat I spun into my next step. Fabio, always the consummate show-man, ran over, picked up a chair leg, and pretended to threaten me with it. The man whose lap I landed on took it well. After the number ended, I ran over and apologized to him again. He smiled and said he was used to having pretty girls fall all over him. Before we were through we'd done two encores.

After the show I got back into my street clothes, brushed and braided my hair into a single long pigtail, and returned to the table just in time to say good night to Brock and Sue.

"Will you be around the Club tomorrow?" she asked me. I knew she wanted to tell me what she thought about Jimmy.

"I will in the morning. I'll stop in and say hello, but I think I might go see Mom this weekend. I'm not sure when."

"I have a singing lesson, but I'll see you before you go. I have to tell you, Diz, you always knock me out, but tonight you were special. Tonight you were on fire, Diz girl." Brock gave me a squeeze, and then he and Sue left. Tony and Fabio told me they were going to an after-hours club in Queens where they could dance until the sun came up. They said they'd pick up their pay on Monday at rehearsal, and headed out for the subway.

"Jimmy, I have to go pick up our pay. I'll be right back." I was walking away when he called after me:

"Dizzy, do you think I could meet the Giant?"

I turned back and took his hand. We went backstage together, where the Giant was standing, obviously waiting for his pay too. Jimmy and I approached him together.

"Senor, I'd like you to meet a friend of mine. This is Jimmy Dean."

"How long have you been in show business, sir?" Jimmy asked the Giant.

Placing his hand over Jimmy's head, the man responded: "Ever since I was this high." Then a huge, deep laugh rumbled through him. He had a wonderful sense of humor; I'm sure it came in handy.

"I've been in show business for a long time. *Muchos anos—* many years. I started in a little circus when I was young. We traveled around Puerto Rico, playing little towns. Then we went to Venezuela, and all around South America, and now I'm here."

"You seem happy . . . ," Jimmy said, pressing him quietly.

"*Sí*, I think so. I try. I know I will be much happy when I can go home. Save money for a little farm. Raise vegetables, have a donkey. The simple life. *Entiende?*"

"Yes," Jimmy said. "I *entiende*."

After I collected our pay, the Giant's agent came over to his client; poking his finger up at him, he said, "You were pretty good tonight. They loved you. Trust me, you're going straight to the top. You'll be big. Big, I tell ya."

"I'm already big," the Giant told him. And the sweating agent just looked at him blankly. I'll never forget the sight of that kindly man, driving away a few moments later in his undersized car. Jimmy later told me he felt a powerful kinship with the Giant we met that night, but he could never explain why.

We went back inside to our table and closed the club, talking and dancing and touching and laughing. All around us, the waiters began clearing the tables and stacking chairs. "Last dance, everybody," the bandleader called across the room. We moved onto the dance floor and Jimmy took me in his arms.

"I've never seen anyone dance like you. I love the way you move. Have I told you that I love the way you move?"

"Yes, but tell me again."

"I just did. You remind me of a beautiful white panther."

A *white panther*. He pulled me closer and I purred in his ear. "I want to be alone with you so much," he said. "Really alone. Do you know what I mean? I think I could borrow some money for a hotel room—I mean, if you don't think it's, you know, too tacky? I mean, would you? Could we go somewhere and . . . you know . . . make love?"

"God, I sure hope so." I laughed. "You must know that I want to be with you too. I say, tacky, *schmacky*."

The music stopped. We picked up our coats and walked to the subway. The train was almost deserted. An old man was nodding off at the far end of the car. I was beginning to feel those special feelings somewhere between exhilaration and exhaustion that I always experience after a good performance. I was a little sore from the fall, so I put my head on Jimmy's shoulder and started to think about the weekend ahead. Mom was still expecting me in Larchmont, which gave me an idea. But I didn't want to scream over the roar of the subway. I must have been laughing, because Jimmy was nudging me.

"What is it? What?"

"Not now!" I yelled as the A train sped, banging and clattering its way back downtown. "I'll tell you later."

# 3

The subway left us on the platform at Fifty-ninth Street. Jimmy had a healthy grip on the pigtail that hung down below my cap, and he wouldn't let go.

"Ouch," I yelled as he gave a yank; we were running up the stairs into the fresh air. "That *hurts*, goddammit. Let *go!*"

"Not until you tell me that great idea you're dying to tell me."

"Weelll . . . there's a tiny hotel in Larchmont. The Bevan Inn. It's down by the water next to the Horseshoe Harbor Yacht Club, where my stepmother used to take me sailing."

"Sounds great."

"Mom is expecting me for dinner Sunday, and I thought we could take the train up Saturday, spend the night at the Bevan, and go to Mom's the next day."

"Great."

"Why don't you call and make the reservations? We need a man's voice."

"Great."

"You sure say *great* a lot."

"Well, since I met you, everything is *g-r-e-a-t*." He smiled. I started running down the street, shouting, "That's just *great!*" When we got back to the Club I told him to give me a kiss and go home and get warm; he kissed me on the stairs and I floated up to my room—relieved that we weren't going to wind up in some Midtown fleabag hotel.

The next day, I packed a few things in a small suitcase. We met at noon in Jerry's. I was wearing my hair upswept in a bun, a black dress, a strand of pearls with earrings to match, and my best pair of heels. I thought I looked rather sophisticated. Jimmy's eyes lit up when I walked in.

"Oh, baby, you look so beautiful. My beautiful girl."

"Thank you," I curtsied. "But look at you." He was wearing a jacket; he'd even borrowed a tie. He looked adorable. "I got the number of the Bevan last night, from information. Should I call now?"

"Yeah, that would be a good idea—we're all dressed up with no place to go." Jimmy stepped into one of the phone booths. Dropping into a rich baritone, he intoned: "Do you have a vacancy tonight? Perhaps with a view? Accommodations for two—the wife and I." *Oh, God, what if they don't have a room? It's Saturday.* I crossed my fingers while he listened intently. As soon as he hung up, I squeezed into the booth next to him and covered his face with kisses. Then I dialed my mother.

"Mom, can I bring a friend with me on Sunday? Someone important? A boy?"

"A boy?"

"Yes, a boy. You've got to meet him."

"You know your friends are always welcome, Elizabeth. I'll cook something special."

I didn't tell her, of course, that we would be there in Larchmont, at the Bevan, a day ahead of time. That was private.

Jimmy had thirty or forty dollars, and I had about sixty tucked in my purse. So we were really loaded. A hundred bucks! We were going in style. The train left for Larchmont at two o'clock, and since we still had lots of time, we decided to have lunch here at Jerry's. We went back to our booth and ordered two Champales and a hamburger apiece.

Leon, our waiter, noticed our finery. "Where you guys going? To a funeral?" he asked as he served up our burgers. Leon was a real character—thin face, slicked-back hair, pencil mustache, and a big heart.

"Actually," said Jimmy with a very straight face, "quite the contrary. We're on our way to audition for a pornographic movie."

"Okay, be mysterious," Leon said as he walked away.

We lingered quietly over our lunch; I guess neither of us wanted to mention what was really on our minds. After about an hour of distracted conversation, it was time to be on our way. Jimmy casually threw a few bills on the table, picked up my little overnight bag, and we were off.

"Thanks, Leon," we shouted over our shoulders.

"Anytime. Have a good weekend."

We grabbed a subway down to Forty-second Street and took the shuttle over to Grand Central Station.

Larchmont was a forty-five-minute train ride from Grand Central. We found seats at the back of the car. The train was only about half full, so we had lots of room to stretch out. Putting our feet up on the seats facing us, we leaned back and relaxed into the comfortable, lulling motion as we rolled along.

"Wouldn't it be fun to go across the country on a train, like John Barrymore and Carole Lombard on the Twentieth Century Limited?" I asked.

Jimmy smiled, but it was such a sad smile. "I don't like trains. I don't feel comfortable."

"Why not?"

"Well, a long time ago I went for a train ride. My mother had just died." He spoke slowly, quietly. "My father put me on a train from California to Indiana with my mom's coffin."

"How old were you?"

"This is going to sound pathetic. I was only nine years old."

"That was a terrible thing to do to a child."

"Yeah, actually, I guess it was. I had never felt so alone."

"Oh, honey, I'm so—"

He didn't let me finish. "But I didn't cry. That's one reason I don't like trains."

"Are there other . . . reasons, I mean."

"Yeah, I'll tell you about it sometime."

"Not today?"

"No, especially not today."

"Okay." It was all I could think to say.

Jimmy took my hand and looked out the window. We stayed that way for a long while. I wanted to break the tension, but I wasn't sure how. Jimmy was obviously back on another train.

"Comfy?" I finally asked him.

"Yeah. You?"

"Yeah." Then I thought I'd see if the old trick would work again. "I hear Mrs. Murphy stopped making her famous chowder."

Jimmy picked it up right away. "Yeah, I heard about that—she found a pair of overalls in her pot."

"She was so upset, she called Mrs. O'Leary and inquired about her cow."

"Unfortunately, I'm sorry to say, I heard her cow kicked the bucket."

"Oh, too bad. I heard he jumped over the moon."

We were laughing again, two parts of one person. Alone, together.

Once we came out of the Park Avenue tunnel and made it past the industrial wastelands in the Bronx, the scenery became more beautiful every mile, as if we'd already entered the countryside. The little train stations in Westchester County were old and rustic but always looked freshly painted. The signs on the depots flew by that day in a lovely blur.

As the conductor called the stations—Mount Vernon, New Rochelle—and Larchmont grew closer, I confess I felt a little apprehensive. I was twenty-two, Jimmy was not yet twenty, but emotionally I was as young and green as any teenager. I kept telling myself that if I could act sophisticated—and Jimmy could keep his two front teeth in his mouth—we could pull this off.

We got off and walked through town, down toward Prospect Street and the water. The Bevan was a country inn right out of a black-and-white movie from the 1940s. Just inside the front door stood a small registry desk, and off to the side was a little bar and restaurant.

My heart was thumping as we walked up to the register. But I knew when I saw the desk clerk that we'd gotten lucky. She was a young girl, immersed in a heated discussion with her boyfriend, who was hanging around the doorway behind her. At first she didn't even notice us.

Jimmy cleared his throat.

"Excuse me. I believe you have a reservation for Dean. James Dean. I called earlier."

Our girl scarcely bothered to look up. "Umm, yes, ah ... here we are, a nice double room with a view. And how long will you be with us, Mr. Dean?"

"Just tonight. My wife and I are going to Boston tomorrow for a few days on business."

She handed him a pen. Putting on his glasses, he wrote "Mr. and Mrs. James Dean" while I tried to look bored and worldly. Then she gave the key to her boyfriend—the bellboy.

We followed the boyfriend up the stairs and into our room; he set my overnight bag on the floor and gave Jimmy the key.

"Newlyweds, huh?"

"How did you know—what gave us away?" I smiled at him.

"When you've been on this job as long as I have, you develop instincts. I can always tell." He was maybe nineteen.

"Well, you sure nailed us," Jimmy said, slipping him a tip. He left, shutting the door behind him. I heard the latch click. And we were alone.

A small window looked out over the front lawn and the quiet street to a pretty pier in the shimmering water of Long Island Sound. The bobbing boats looked snug and safe. Every now and then you could hear the blast of an air horn from a yachtsman who had anchored his boat and was calling for the launch to bring him ashore.

For a long time we stood there in the gathering darkness, looking out the window, holding hands. No one spoke for the longest time.

"I feel kind of strange." I broke the silence.

"I know," he said.

"Are you glad you're here?" I knew he was. I turned and put my arms around him.

"I love you," he said. "I love you."

Those were the words I wanted and needed to hear. Each of us might have fooled around with others before, but we had never felt anything so blessed. We weren't thinking ahead at all. We just wanted to be here alone, to give ourselves to each other. We wanted to make love. It was as simple as that.

"Am I the first one?" he asked.

"You mean, am I a virgin?"

"Yes."

"Well, sort of," I said.

"What do you mean 'sort of'?"

"Well, I'm sorry to say, I lost it one day." I smiled.

"That rhymes. What do you mean, 'lost it'?"

I nestled my head against him. "I lost it when I was sixteen years old, riding a horse. A horse beat you to it, Jimmy."

"Well that's a relief . . . I think," and he laughed. "I bet you were cute as hell when you were sixteen."

"Yuck! I was stupid-looking. I was built like a ten-year-old boy—straight up and down. A skinny kid, and *very* obnoxious."

"Well, it's nice to know some things never change."

"Are you trying to charm the pants off me?"

"Yes," he said with a smile.

"Jimmy, I don't want to disappoint you. I'm not experienced."

"Neither am I. We'll learn together. It'll be okay."

There was nothing left to say. We held each other. We kissed. My whole body was trembling. Would we make it without dying first?

"I love you too, Jimmy."

Then, I don't know what came over me. Losing every pretense of sophistication, I gave him a hug and blurted out: "*Let's do it!*"

If I'd felt self-conscious before, all of a sudden my modesty flew out the window. I pulled my dress up over my head and just stood there. I felt good about my body: slim and tall in my bra and panties, long legs, small breasts—a dancer's body. I wanted to see Jimmy's body. He turned away to remove his jacket, and when he turned back, I reached over to pull up his sweater. Stretching his arms above his head as I tugged, he said, "You're my little girl, Diz. I want to hold you. I want to learn how to love you the way you want to be loved."

He slipped off his tie and out of his shirt and pants and dropped them on the floor. We were both trembling. "I'm so happy right now I could die" was all I could think to say. I pulled his T-shirt up around his head, kissing his face all over. "Hey," he said, laughing. "You want to play rough? Okay . . ." He grabbed my waist, pulling me to the floor.

"Ouch!" I cried out. I'd forgotten about my sore bones from the fall up in Harlem.

"Let me see," Jimmy said. He rolled me gently onto my stomach and caressed the back of my thighs.

"Aww, my little girl. Bad news on your legs. Two big bruises."

He leaned down, his lips caressing the back of my thighs, and I felt a rush of pleasure welling up within me. I turned over and we kissed passionately. No more talking now. He kept kissing me as he tugged at my bra, trying to figure the damn thing out, and then he was on top of me.

"Oh, no. Please, not yet."

"Oh, God, I'm—"

"Me too—"

We both exploded at pretty much the same time—he in his shorts and me in my panties and pearls. And then we were giggling, louder and louder, until we were roaring with laughter and relief. When we finally calmed down, I said, "Well, that was . . . something." We cracked up again.

"Yes, that was really—I don't know what, but definitely . . . *something*." We were hysterical by now. Then a torrent of I *love you*s. We couldn't get enough of each other. After a while, I went into the bathroom, made a bubble bath, and lay there soaking until Jimmy slipped into the tub with me.

"Do you like my bubbles?"

"I love your bubbles."

We lay there, scrunched up and facing each other in the old-fashioned tub, playing with each other's toes. I still had on my pearl necklace.

"I'm sorry about what happened," he said.

"Me, too. But not really. I'm too happy to be sorry about anything. It doesn't matter. We have all night. We can try again, can't we?"

"In a little while we can," he answered.

"Can we try the bed this time?"

"*Suuure.*"

We stopped talking. Closing my eyes, I started to sing. "I was waltzin', with my darlin', to the Tennessee Waltz . . . da da da dum . . . da da da. . . ." And, as if a conductor had given the nod, Jimmy joined in at full voice: "I remember the night, and the Tennessee Waltz . . ." Our faces were glowing, our bodies steaming in the water, our voices bouncing off the bathroom walls. I don't know if there were guests in the next room, but if so they must have loved us.

After a lot of silliness we got out. I washed our soiled underwear and hung them on the tub faucets. "Which one do you want, hot or cold?" I asked him.

"Surprise me."

We swore we would love each other forever—again— then dried our bodies carefully, patting each other with our towels. Jimmy's body was very pretty—everything in good proportion. He could have used a little more muscle to cover his bones, but what was there was smooth and fit. When he moved across the room, it was as if he were stalking me.

Then he did a little dance while I lit a cigarette and crawled in bed to watch. He was the Pied Piper leading the children of Hamlin away to safety. He was very seductive. I would have followed him anywhere. He didn't have his recorder that night, thank God. But somehow the way he pretended to play the flute for the children was even more effective. I applauded and he bowed and crawled into bed next to me.

For a while we lay there talking and smoking. I remember everything so clearly. At long last I took off the pearls and let my hair down. Jimmy was stroking it, still calling me his little girl. His hands were soft, warm, and loving. I kissed his fingertips and placed them on my breasts, and he started to caress me slowly and with such gentleness that my whole body began to move with intense quivering waves. Then we were both moving in rhythm, touching each other everywhere, making love slowly, taking our time—a long, long time. When Jimmy entered me, I rose up and then cried out. He was moving deep within me, touching places I had never known before, secret even from myself. I thought I would break apart with thrills I'd never known. I had never felt such joy, such completeness.

When we were finished, we held each other and whispered in the dark.

"What do you want to be when we grow up?" I asked him.

"Marlon Brando. What about you?"

"Isadora Duncan. But can I still be your little girl too?"

"You'll always be my little girl. Do you want to make love again?" he whispered.

"Only if you do. I couldn't possibly feel any more complete than I do at this moment."

"Me too. We did it, didn't we, Diz, we really did it."

"Yes, we did, and it was so—so perfect."

Finally, like tired children exhausted from too much play, we fell asleep.

In the first pale light of morning, we got out of bed and stood at the window, looking at the most beautiful sunrise. Everything was more brilliant than even the night before: the colors more astonishing, the sun, the sky, the water more perfect. And we were lovers. We tumbled back into bed and fell asleep again in each other's arms.

When our 10 A.M. wake-up call came, Jimmy picked it up and groggily ordered room service—Danish and coffee, all very continental. The night before we had totally forgotten to eat; now we smeared jam on each other's faces and licked it off, playfully. We goofed around until everything was consumed, and we were left with an hour before checkout time.

"What do you want to do, Mr. Dean?"

"I don't know. What do *you* want to do, Mrs. Dean?"

We giggled and did what we both wanted to do, one more time.

# 4

I remember strolling along that day, feeling the afternoon wind on my face, so clean and crisp. I looked at Jimmy and felt such happiness. He met my gaze, looked intently in my eyes, and smiled.

"Don't be afraid, little girl. I will protect you."

"Protect me from what?"

"From all things boring."

"You already have." I wrapped my arms around him, and we hugged so long and so tightly, I almost ran out of air.

We walked along, chatting dreamily. "Diz?" he said. "How does 'together forever' sound to you?"

"Like music."

I pulled away and waltzed up the street, through the yellow and brown wind-blown leaves. I whirled around and around while Jimmy clapped his hands, running after me to catch up. Down the street we skipped and twirled, lighthearted and in love. We passed a florist shop and Jimmy grabbed my pigtail gently, pulling me to him.

"Let's go in. I'd like to bring your mom something."

We must have spent a good half hour there, minutely inspecting every flower, marveling at the exquisite colors and the amazingly intricate structures—bold, fragile, delicate, and flamboyant. Some were outrageously sensual, with their insinuating shapes and fragrances. How can one describe the architecture of a rosebud? The perfect symmetry of the petals makes a sheath for its hidden heart preparing to open and reveal secret interiors, like a woman at love. I felt I knew a little about such things now.

We fell into an easy improv. I started:

"Oh, look, darling, these hyacinths would look ever so perfect in the music room."

"Ah, yes, and the birds-of-paradise would be *maahhvelous* in the library in that big crystal vase Muffy gave us for our anniversary. Remember?"

"Yes, and let's not forget something *really* special for the Chippendale table we brought home from Paris." We went on and on. The florist stood watching us silently, one hand on his hip, unamused.

Jimmy finally decided on a single long-stemmed yellow rose.

"How much for just this one?"

"That'll be fifty cents."

"Isn't that a lot of money for only one flower?" I asked.

"It's almost winter, you know," the florist snapped icily. "And by the way, miss, those were not hyacinths." We ran out of there giggling like naughty children.

"Does your mom know where we were last night?" Jimmy asked.

"Of course not—no one does. I thought last night should be just for us."

"I'm glad, but do you think she would understand? I mean, is your mom one of the good guys?"

"Well, she might not understand; she's a mom, after all. But she's a really good person, I think you'll like her. She's had an interesting life. She was a concert singer."

"What do you mean?"

"Well, my parents eloped to Paris and ended up staying two years. They appeared together in concerts, billing themselves as 'The Sheridans.' They were great—they gave recitals all over Europe. "

"Does she still sing?"

"Well, not professionally anymore, but she sings at her church services, and she goes up to Sing Sing—you know, the prison up the Hudson River? They have services there, like maybe once a month for the Christian Science prisoners, and she sings for them. Isn't that funny?"

"Oh, no, man, that's great!"

"She sang in churches when she was young, and she was in vaudeville as one of the 'Blend Sisters.'"

"With her sister?" Jimmy asked.

"No, she doesn't have a sister—they just called themselves that. The other lady's name was Casey. But Casey had a lot of problems, I guess, and she committed suicide. So I guess that was the end of the Blend Sisters."

"And Casey too," he said.

Jimmy leaned over and kissed me, and we were quiet for a while.

"Jimmy, do you remember your mom very well?"

"I remember the sad things better than the happy ones. I

think of my mom now as kind of ethereal, like a spirit. That's the way I prefer to remember her. I know she'd approve of me being an actor." He was silent for a while. *I wonder if I shouldn't be asking him to talk about his mother.* Then he said, "When she was first put in the ground, I wondered if she was cold. If she was aware of the change of seasons—you know, like the snow falling on her grave? Sounds kinda weird, I know, but I was just a little kid." I nodded. "I'm sure I feel her presence. I know this sounds crazy, Diz, but I talk to her. I consult her whenever I have a difficult decision to make and don't know what to do. *What do you think, Mom? What should I do?* I mean, I know I'm a part of her, but in some way now she's a part of me too. Aaah—I don't know how to explain it; it's just a bunch of strong feelings, all mingled together.

"Dizzy, I've never told anyone this before, but I feel she's *with* me somehow—that she's always been with me, like I said. She's a part of me—maybe the feminine part. I think about her all the time; I wonder if her spirit, her soul, is intertwined with mine. I'm sure it is. Do you think I'm nuts, Diz?"

"No, not at all. I think that's very sweet and as it should be. I believe that if the bond between you and her is strong enough, anything is possible. Why not? I think there are a lot of spiritual things we aren't supposed to understand, just *feel*, and—"

He paused; then he went on: "It was always difficult for me to live around my father. We didn't communicate. I wondered if he even liked me. It's hard to miss something I never remember having. It's complicated—I do love him, I think. I could never seem to please him, no matter what I did."

"I can relate to that."

"When my mother died, I felt like I'd been thrown off a cliff—like I was all alone in empty space, not falling, just hanging there. When my dad sent me to live with my aunt and uncle, it was kind of like a release. They are really nice folks. They've always been good to me, and I liked growing up on the farm. I want them to meet you someday. You'd really like them, and I know they'd love you."

His eyes started to tear. His emotions were so close to the surface. I put my arm through his, and we walked silently for a while as Jimmy drifted through his own reverie.

For my own part, all this conversation started me thinking about my mother. What an exciting life she'd led, and yet how naive she still seemed to be, as if she had been cloistered her entire life. She came from strong English stock—her family from Staffordshire, a city famous for its pottery. Her parents moved to St. Louis, where Mom grew up and studied singing. She was gifted and blessed with a beautiful contralto voice, and when she met my father, a pianist of extraordinary talent, they fell in love, eloped to Paris, and stayed a few years, billing themselves as "The Sheridans," touring Europe and garnering wonderful reviews along the way.

I've often tried to imagine what those years in Paris in the 1920s must have been like for them. They were part of the elite musical circle of the times, my father being a member, along with the prominent composer Darius Milhaud, in the famous musical ensemble Groupe de Six. How romantic their life must have been—in love, in Paris, sharing a flat in the Longchamps Hotel Apartments overlooking one of the beautiful racetracks near the city.

After they returned home, Mom made her New York debut, in a recital at the Princess Theatre. I still have her notices all these years later: "She sang with rare sensuous beauty," "had an unusual mastery of technique," "sang with unusual intelligence and taste." She also performed in the concert halls of Harvard, Yale, and especially Princeton, where my father taught. Even with all those accolades, and such a wonderful artistic life, she remained a sweet, modest woman, living very much in my father's shadow.

When Daddy left her for the next of the many other women he would marry, she was devastated. When I got older, I wondered why she didn't get on with her life the way he did—why she didn't continue with her career and find a man to love her. But I don't think it even occurred to her. She never got over the breakup; she withdrew from life, became a Christian Scientist, and quietly waited for my father to come to his senses and return to her. It was a futile hope. I always felt that life had not dealt my mother a kind hand, and what was most unfortunate was that she seemed no longer interested enough in the game to play her cards the way she might have.

She stopped singing professionally but continued to work with an accompanist and, yes, make the occasional trip to Sing Sing to sing to the prisoners. It was a rough day for her, taking the train up the river and back at her own expense, but she loved doing it. I remember her telling me how much the inmates appreciated her coming. I know she must have felt that the little joy she spread made a difference in their lives.

I think of Mom often, even today, and when I do I remember her in a cotton housedress, an apron, and a smock covered with tiny flowers. She's in her kitchen, where she seemed to be the most comfortable, humming Irish melodies and preparing to please. I see her with a few strands of hair hanging over one eye, her round dimpled arms, plump and freckled, working back and forth over the stove as she served up one of her extraordinary dinners. Her hair was the most beautiful color: a light, light white around her temples, spreading outward into different shades of gray. She was a woman of some height, good posture, and exquisite poise. She gave my sister and I whatever she could, whenever we needed it. And yet I've always felt that she disapproved of almost everything I did. Understandably so, perhaps, for the life I chose began when I ran away from home at sixteen, and carried through days and years spent racing stock cars, taking cross-country trips, moving abroad, having affairs for reasons right and wrong, suffering gunshot wounds ... I guess she had good reason to disapprove. But all of that is another story.

Jimmy and I finally arrived, having walked all the way from the Bevan. It took us maybe an hour with our frequent stops, so we were chilled to the bone but red-cheeked and exhilarated.

Mom lived alone, in a small one-bedroom apartment two blocks away from the center of the village of Larchmont, and a half a block from the railway station. My sister, Fran, was staying with her for a while; her husband was away in Okinawa with the air force at that time, and Fran was biding her time at home with a baby on the way. Mom and Fran were waiting for us at the door; they must have heard us laughing as we came down the hall.

"Hi, Mom."

"Hi, Elizabeth. And this must be Jimmy?" She smiled.

"Yes. Jimmy, this is my mom and this is my sister, Fran."

Jimmy presented his flower to Mom. "This is for you, Mrs. Sheridan. I'm sorry it's not a dozen. Thanks for inviting me, I'm real glad to be here. I haven't had a home-cooked meal in a long time."

Mom beamed. "Oh, it's beautiful—it's the thought that counts, you know. Come on inside, you must be cold."

I kissed my sister and gave her tummy a little pat.

"How ya doin', Fran?" I asked. She looked a little tired.

"Okay," she said. "It's just getting a little hard to sleep through the night. I take so many naps now, I feel like a slug." I laughed along with her, but I don't think Fran was having an easy time of it. Her husband was far away, and I wondered about the separation; I don't think it was a particularly happy marriage.

Fran is three and a half years older than I am; she's short, like my father, and has the loveliest face. A generous mouth, blue-gray eyes, sleepy eyelids—very pretty indeed. She was popular with the boys, mad about all sports, and a very talented pianist. She still plays at her church to this day.

Mom's dinner was wonderful: pot roast with all the trimmings. "This is so good, I can't stop!" Jimmy said. "I haven't eaten like this since I was home on the farm."

Jimmy seemed comfortable. He was funny and dear, helping Mom in the kitchen, and showing great patience and interest with Fran; he asked about her life as an air force wife and made us all thankful that what could have been an awkward evening turned out to be so enjoyable.

After dinner Mom smiled and started clearing dishes; Jimmy immediately jumped up to help. She tried to dissuade him, but he persisted—"Please, I need the exercise"—and we could hear them through the door as they chatted in the kitchen.

"Diz tells me you have a beautiful voice, Mrs. Sheridan. I mean, that you sing—"

"Oh, yes, a little. I go into the city and work with my friend"—her accompanist—"now and then. But other than my church, I've pretty much given it up."

"What about Sing Sing?" asked Jimmy.

"Oh, my Lord—she told you about that?" Mom laughed. "Yes, I love to sing in Sing Sing." She laid into the line as if it were her favorite play on words.

"You should learn that song 'Sing, Sing, Sing.' Then you could sing 'Sing, Sing, Sing' in Sing Sing!"

Mom roared with laughter. I could tell she was having fun. I think Jimmy felt compassion for my mom because, in his mind, she was neglecting her career. He felt tied to her artistically, somehow, as he felt they were both artists. Jimmy was driven by his desire to show the world his talent, and nothing was going to stop him. What he needed from her, I don't know, but I was so happy that they hit it off right from the start.

I came to know that Jimmy could always charm women, when he really wanted to. I'm sure he was well aware of his effect on women, and with his arsenal of grins, stammers, and pauses, his respectful manner—and the way he would modulate his voice and use his eyes—you just wanted to put your arms around him and mother him.

Fran smiled at me. "I like him, Dizzy. He's cute. A little strange, but cute."

"That's the part I like the best," I said. "The strange part."

We were moving furniture around, pulling chairs away from the table, clearing a big space in the living room so we could camp out on the floor. Mom said she was tired and excused herself, retiring to her bedroom. Jimmy, Fran, and I arranged pillows and blankets on the floor. Fran took the couch, where she was staying anyway. Jimmy and I made ourselves comfortable on the floor. We all settled down to what felt like an old-fashioned pajama party.

"Is Hollywood a romantic place?" my sister asked Jimmy.

"No," he said, "but then I don't know much about Hollywood the movie town. I was in college out there, and when I did work in movies, I just had bit parts here and there. I did a tiny part in a Dean Martin–Jerry Lewis movie. Those two guys are really crazy—at breakfast on the set one morning, they ran around pouring pancake syrup over everyone's head, cast and crew and everyone. It held up production for hours. I thought it was hilarious. The director was mad as hell, but they didn't seem to care. Someone told me they're always doing stuff like that."

"How did you end up in New York?" asked Fran.

"Well, I was taking acting lessons from James Whitmore—"

"Oh yeah—I *love* him."

"Yeah, he's great. Anyway, I got to know him, and I sort of asked his advice about a lot of things. He told me that if I was really serious about acting I should come to New York and do theater—study hard and learn my craft. So here I am!"

We all told stories, laughing and goofing long past midnight, until we finally fell asleep, well fed and happy.

Mom was up early. I could hear her moving around in the kitchen quietly and then I smelled the coffee. I opened my eyes as shafts of light pierced through the blinds, warming my face, and felt a sense of quiet pleasure. I glanced at Jimmy, lying close, curled up on the floor next to me. He looked about twelve years old with just his head peeking out from the blanket. Fran was snoring lightly on the couch above us, her back turned away.

We all enjoyed a nice and easy breakfast, but soon we needed to hurry to the station. At the door Jimmy turned to Mom and smiled.

"I had a good time, Mrs. Sheridan. Thanks for the hospitality. And I just want you to know that I love your daughter."

My heart leapt. *He sounds so formal. But he's so adorable.*

"I can see that by the way you look at each other," she said. "Love is a wonderful gift. Treasure it. Next time you come, you kids can borrow my car so you can see some of the pretty scenery around here."

"I'd like that a lot," he said. Being in a family atmosphere seemed to draw out a part of him he otherwise kept hidden. I suppose he must have felt safe.

We were sleepy and full of food when we got back on the train, late on that Monday morning. The train was nearly empty; all the commuters had come and gone. The stale smell of tobacco and bodies clung to the maroon velvet cushioning, but we were leaning back into it, our feet resting on the opposite seat. Jimmy had taken his jacket off. His hair was falling over his eyes; his shirt was wrinkled, and he looked like a stray puppy. We reached for each other at the very same time.

"I miss our little room on the water," Jimmy said, playing with my hair.

"It was magical, wasn't it? The best night of my life."

"Mine too," Jimmy said. "But we can't do that again for a while. I wish to hell I wasn't so broke. I just want to be able to hold up my end. Sorry, kiddo—I'm such a damn dud."

"A damn dud?! That's so funny. From now on, I'm going to call you my 'damn dud,' maybe 'Dudley' for short."

"That's longer, not shorter." He smiled. "I'm serious, I need a job. I need some money. I need to be with you."

"What you need is an agent. Then everything will start to get better. And I know you'll find one. You haven't been in New York all that long. Have a little patience." I tried to sound confident.

"As long as I have you, it helps."

"You got me, Dudley," I said, and he laughed—but sadly.

"We need to be together all the time. You make me feel so full of life, you know? You've given me something I didn't even know I needed. I feel more complete, somehow."

"I need to be with you too, you know. Do you think we could save up some money and maybe get a little place together?" I asked.

"Wouldn't that be perfect?"

"Are you sure?"

"Yes." He leaned over and kissed me softly, with great gentleness, and then, with a little tug on my pigtail, said, "Yes, I'm *suuure.*"

We had known each other for almost a week.

## 5

Jimmy and I talked constantly on the phone, but it was a few days before I saw him again. We met at Jerry's. He was in a foul mood.

"What's wrong?" I asked him.

"I got fired. Christ, do you believe it? I actually got fired from *Beat the Clock!*"

"Why?"

"The producer told me I did the stunts too easily. Do you believe that? I got fired because I was doing too good a job."

"Oh, Jimmy, I'm so sorry. What a dumb reason to lose a job." I scrambled for something to say. "Maybe it's a good thing."

"How can it be a good thing?" He glared at me. "I don't have a job!"

"I didn't mean *good* . . . I guess I meant maybe it's for the best . . . . I don't know what I meant." I felt terrible. "Don't worry, something will come up. It always does. We'll be all right."

"Tell me something good," he demanded.

"Well, you got me. Is that good?"

"Oh, yeah, that's really good."

Leon, our favorite waiter, came to the booth. "Hiya, kids. Why so glum?"

"I just lost my job because I was doing it too well," Jimmy said.

Leon was overly sympathetic. "Those sonsabitches don't know what the hell they're doing!"

"I couldn't have put it better myself," Jimmy replied. "Could you bring us a Champale and two glasses, please?"

"You got it."

When he returned he put two glasses and two bottles on the table, winked, then turned and left without a word.

Jimmy didn't want to go home, so we stayed until well after midnight, and I managed to cheer him up a bit.

"Let's go find Moondog," I said. "Do you want to?"

"Okay, but I doubt if he's still on the street. He's probably home by now. It's pretty late."

We walked by his usual spot, but he wasn't there, so we headed over to Fifth, stopping now and then, looking in windows, wondering if we would ever have the things we saw there. All the department stores along the avenue had wonderful holiday displays. Tiffany's was fun for a minute or two, but our absolute favorite was F. A. O. Schwarz, the toy store. It was a wonderland for kids of all ages, and in the coming months we would spend countless hours inside, goofing. Tonight, as we peered in the windows, we saw a menagerie of stuffed animals, life-size Wonderland Alices and Raggedy Anns; a long shiny train was sinuously moving through the huge display, up and down, over trestles and around bends, disappearing on one side of the vast room and emerging from a tunnel on the other side through the feet of an enormous stuffed King Kong. It was pure magic.

Fifth Avenue was illuminated that night by thousands of twinkling lights stretching all the way down to Washington Square; steam rose from the manhole covers. It was our kind of night. Jimmy was gradually relaxing and starting to enjoy himself. I couldn't resist the urge to dance in the middle of the street; it helped that there was hardly any traffic—only a few cars now and then—to worry about. I ran to the middle of the street, stood over the rising steam, and started moving very slowly to an exotic, bluesy kind of melody I heard in my head. I motioned enticingly for Jimmy to join me. He usually preferred to watch me dance, but tonight he was into it: curling himself inward and crouching, he began moving like a cat, doing that mysterious bent-kneed walk of his I loved so much.

We danced and twirled and swirled all the way down to Forty-third Street, then decided to head over to Grand Central Station. We entered the side door on Vanderbilt.

Big-city railroad stations are usually busy, bustling places, but there was something haunting about this beautiful, imposing space when it was empty. I danced down the sweeping staircase with its gorgeous copper railings, and whirled out to the center of the floor where the information booth stood. Jimmy slid down the banister and landed on the marble floor running. He pretended he was playing basketball, bouncing an imaginary ball over the great expansive floor.

Then I heard his voice from behind me: "Toro, toro, toro." Jimmy wanted to play matador, and I was ready. I wheeled and stomped and made snorting sounds and ran for the imaginary cape over and over until I heard someone say:

"My, oh my, that's something. Whew, you two are crazy."

We both stopped and glared, a little offended and maybe a little embarrassed. But the speaker recovered quickly: "Uh, but in a good way!"

There was a man over in a corner leaning on an enormous broom. It looked about six feet wide, and so did he.

"How long have you been working here?" Jimmy asked.

"About twenty years." He smiled back.

We laughed, completely out of breath. "No, I mean, how long have you been watching us?"

"Oh yeah—well, since you made your big entrance down the stairs. What are you, some kind of weird dance team or something?"

"Yes," Jimmy said. "Yes. We are definitely some kind of weird dance team." Then he added, mischievously, "We can't afford to rent a dance studio, so we come here at night to practice."

"That's a good one." He laughed. "Yeah, that's a good one. I don't believe you—I would have spotted you. But that's a good one." And he started pushing his broom, chuckling and shaking his head.

About a week after Jimmy lost his job, I answered an ad in the paper and got a part-time job at Lord & Taylor's in the umbrella department—and, of course, on my first and only day it rained. I have never been good at mathematics. Before I could even get started people were lined up, waiting for me to make change while I struggled with coins and often as not dropped half of them on the floor. The truth is, I know that two and two make four, but I don't really know why, exactly. I lasted for two hours. The personnel manager suggested I try to find a job where basic arithmetic was not involved. To this day, my checkbook is always a mess.

At rehearsal the next day, Tony and Fabio told me about an opening for a female dancer on *The Noro Morales Show*, the show where we'd first met. I hadn't passed my first audition there, but now one of their girls was leaving to get married, and Tony and Fabio were auditioning dancers to take her place.

"It's a good job, Diz," Tony said. "Only one day a week—rehearse in the afternoon, shoot the show in the evening, then go home. Twenty-five bucks. Interested?"

"Oh, yeah!"

"I'll make a call."

We all three huddled around the phone. Tony hung up, snapped his fingers, and said, "It's all set: two o'clock tomorrow. Nothing to it."

"Real easy routines, Diz. We'll have fun. Three boys, three girls—cha-cha-cha." Fabio gave a little rhythm swing with his hips.

Noro and Machito, the Cuban Congeuro, were the two great Latin bands of the time for my money. Forget about Cugat; he was for the society squares. Noro's band was hot and fiery, with a heavy rhythmic underpinning of clave, cowbell, conga, and timbales. And when the band would segue into a melancholy bolero it could tear your heart out.

I arrived a bit early at the studio and changed into my leotard and tights. A small man came running over. "You Deezy?" I nodded. "I'm Chucho. Ya ready?" I nodded again. "Let's do eet!" He put a record on a hi-fi with big speakers. "Follow me. Just do what I do—you theenk you can do dat?"

"Gee, Chucho, I'll try."

"Spunky, huh? I like dat. Here we go!"

We danced alone and together. Spins, turns—basic stuff ending with a spin and dip.

"*Bueno*, you can dance! You don' got much up top—a leetle Kleenex can feex dat. But you got good long legs and you sure can move! Can you start dis Thursday?"

I nodded. No nonsense about Chucho. The whole thing lasted maybe ten minutes.

I showed up Thursday and got fitted for a costume. Chucho introduced me in his inimitable style: "Hey, everybody, dis ees Deezy. Deezy, everybody. Okay, let's go!"

It went easily, a half-hour show. A great band, ruffled sleeves, fake palm trees, a little kootchie-kootchie. Fabio was right, it was fun—for one night. After the show Chucho came up to me and said, "You did real good tonight, Deezy, but I got bad news. De udder dancer? She don't wanna get married. She wanna come back. She's an old friend of Noro's. Been wid us a long time. What can I do? I made a call to an *amigo*. They are looking for a dancer on Meelton Berle." He handed me a card with a name and address. "See dis guy. I tell him you was great. *Muy especial!*"

"Thanks, Chucho, it's been fun. Brief—but fun." I laughed. "I'll see you around."

There was nothing left to say.

♦♦

Jimmy and I spent as much time together as possible, playing in the park or the night streets or at Jerry's Bar; when we couldn't see each other, we talked on the phone four or five times a day. Usually it went something like this:

"Hi, little girl, whatcha doin'?"

"I'm sitting here on the floor talking to the love of my life."

"Sounds like a very lucky guy."

"Oh, he is."

"Oh, yeah? Well, can he play the recorder? Listen to this, Diz—this is a song Moondog gave me." He started playing a simple little riff, over and over and over; half an hour later his voice came back on the line.

"You still there?"

"Yes, that was beautiful," I lied.

"That was a mere bagatelle."

"What the hell is a bagatelle, anyway?"

"It's French."

"I know that, smart-ass."

"Well, if you're going to talk to me like that, I won't tell you."

"Good, cause I gotta go pee."

"*Mais oui.*"

"Don't you mean *mais wee wee*?"

"*Absolutamente*—that's Spanish."

"Well, up yours—that's American. See you later at Jerry's."

Jimmy tried hard to learn some of my favorite folk songs my mom used to sing for us, like "The Fair-Haired Boy" or "Who's

That Pretty Girl Milking Her Cow" or even "Danny Boy"; he wanted to be able to play well enough to sing along with Mom. He was especially keen about "Danny Boy" and asked me to teach him to sing *and* play it. We went to the park and sat on a bench, and I started to sing very softly, "Oh, Danny boy, la, la, la . . . " Jimmy played it very slowly, with great melancholy—so much so that I was starting to feel a little blue. Before too long a few people stopped to listen.

"She's a dancer," Jimmy told them. "Come on, Diz, dance for the crowd."

Crowd? What crowd? "I will if you make it sound a little happier. *Pleease?*" He did. And I danced.

I began moving around, in and out of the "crowd." One person moved away and then the next, until there was only one old guy left standing there, sort of tapping his toes to the music. I swirled around and really got into it, while the old guy stood there entranced. That inspired me even more. When we finished, he applauded. He started to leave, stopped, came back, dug in his pocket, and placed a quarter on the bench beside Jimmy. We thanked him, he tipped his hat, and our day was made.

"Our first paying gig together. How about that?"

"Yeah, how about that?" I smiled.

On our next trip to Larchmont, Jimmy brought his recorder. Mom had really outdone herself with the dinner: roast turkey, mashed potatoes, three kinds of vegetables, and another sensational pie. When we finished eating and everything was put away, we gathered together around the piano. After all our many torturous hours of practice in the park Jimmy was dying to show my mother what he'd learned.

"Is it okay if we start with 'Danny Boy'?" Jimmy asked.

"That's one of my favorite melodies," said Mom. "I sing it in church, only in the hymnal it's called something else."

And she started to sing it through, because she couldn't remember the title of the hymn:

> *Oh, dreamer leave thy dreams for joyful waking,*
> *Oh, Captive rise and sing for thou art free...*

Mom got her hymnal from the piano bench and we all crowded around, reading one another's shoulders. Fran was playing the piano, Jimmy his recorder, and Mom and I were harmonizing. We gave it a damn good try; we were definitely making music—music with feeling—and everybody was on key. (Well, more or less.)

"Will you sing one for me, Mrs. Sheridan? You know, a solo?" Jimmy asked.

"Oh, my heavens, I don't—"

"Come on, Mom," I urged.

"How about 'Ave Maria'?" Fran said. "I know that one pretty well."

"Oh, well, I'll try."

She rose from her chair, pulled herself up very erect, took a deep breath, lifted her head as if she were looking at a far-off star, and sang. She opened her mouth and out it came—that pure, rich sound, natural and warm. When she had finished and the last plaintive note was hovering in the air, we all applauded. The old magic was still there—a little rusty and frayed, but still there. I know I was moist-eyed, but tears were streaming down Jimmy's face.

"That was so beautiful," Jimmy said.

My mom smiled. "I'm glad you enjoyed it, Jimmy, but I'm sorry I made you cry." She laughed.

"No, no, it's all right, Mrs. Sheridan, I'm not ashamed to cry. I love to be moved. It doesn't happen often enough."

He put his arms around Mom and hugged her. "You should go back on the stage," he told her. "People should be hearing you. You should be sharing your voice."

"Well, it's not that easy," she said. "It takes a lot of commitment. I don't mind singing for my church or at the prison, but I can't get back to it professionally. I'm too old, too heavy. I'd have to lose weight. Oh, heavens, I think it's just too late." I know how powerless she felt, but in her lifetime of demurrals I have always taken a lesson—not to let my life slip away, the way my mother's did. Jimmy was drawn to my mother; he said he considered her a kindred spirit—another artist, honest and ingenuous and very aware. His reaction sometimes surprised me, because to be honest she didn't seem to be aware of who I was at all. I think I felt a little envious of him at those moments when Jimmy and my mother seemed to connect. And yet I was so pleased that they liked each other.

The next morning we went for a drive. I took the wheel so Jimmy could play the recorder, although Jimmy's playing was beginning to wear a little thin on Fran by now—too much practicing, too many wrong notes. "How do you take it?" she asked me. "It would drive me nuts."

After a while I realized that we were hopelessly lost. Somehow we had wandered onto a small, narrow road; looking for signs of the Parkway, the only sign we could find read WESTCHESTER SANCTUARY FOR BIRDS.

"Let's take a look. This is really pretty around here. *Sanctuary*—I like that word, don't you?" Jimmy asked.

There was a lock on the gate, but it was low enough for us to give it a try; we all clambered over, but Fran caught the hem of her dress on a nail, and we all heard it rip.

It was as if we'd entered a beautiful patch of countryside, unmanicured and wild—trees, flowers, grass, and the songs of birds everywhere. Perhaps the whole world was like this once, I remember thinking, with the pure sounds of brooks and birds, insects and the wind.

We kept forging ahead, looking for someplace to rest a while. At one point we came to a little brook that Jimmy thought we should cross, and he took charge of the expedition. Suddenly he crouched.

"Shhh—the enemy is behind us. Not a sound. We can cover our tracks across this brook. Quiet!"

I covered my mouth and nodded; Fran, on the other hand, must have been wondering what the hell was going on. She didn't want to play; she wanted to sit down. But I took her hand and winked as we gingerly crossed the brook, jumping nimbly from one stepping-stone to the next. We looked like a high-wire act. I would have much preferred to be an acrobat than a combat soldier, but this was Jimmy's fantasy. We were in Iwo Jima or Okinawa or Bataan, and he was leading our platoon into battle. At that point Jimmy motioned that we were safe—for now—and we should rest. We were almost ready to turn around and go back to the car when we spotted a little cottage on the banks of a muddy pond. It was a stage setting, mysterious and moody. We peeked in the window. It looked deserted, but there was some furniture to play with.

"I want to go inside," Jimmy said.

"We'd be trespassing," Fran said. She was getting more than a little cranky.

"But obviously nobody lives here," I said.

The door wasn't locked; it seemed unlikely that anyone would care if we went inside and rested for a while, and that was enough of an invitation for us. The place was dark and musty, but there was a fireplace, so Jimmy gathered some wood and we made a little fire. There was an arrangement of furniture in front of the fireplace—a couch and two chairs, one for each of us.

"I could make this place look homey in no time," I said. "I could really fix it up."

"If it was yours, which it isn't."

"Wouldn't it be fun to try?" She wasn't about to kill my enthusiasm. "I wonder how we could find out who owns the place."

"Probably the Audubon Society or something like it," Jimmy said. "Maybe it doesn't matter. Maybe it's here for people like us, a haven to stop and rest."

"I think you're right and even if you're not, that sounds right to me." And I plunged ahead to straighten the room. It was still chilly, so we built up the fire a little. I found a sad-looking broom in a corner, sprinkled some water on the floor, and swept the dirt out the front door. There was running water in a tiny little bathroom. The water wouldn't have been left on if the cottage had been deserted. We decided it must have been a caretaker's occasional quarters, but that day it was ours. How great it would be to have a little place like this to come home to—just Jimmy and me.

Fran took her shoes off and lay on the couch while I swept around her. Jimmy was outside checking things. He had given up soldiering and was now playing nature boy. When he came back, he was positively glowing.

"This is such a great place," he said as he settled into a chair and lit a cigarette. "I've never seen so many snails in my life. I feel so sorry for them. They can't hurry; they can't even get out of the way. Isn't that sad?"

"Pretty sad. I wonder if they can think," I said. "And if they have brains, where do they keep them?"

"In their shells," he said.

"You mean like luggage?" I laughed.

Finally Fran chimed in: "Have you ever eaten a snail? I did once. He wasn't wearing his shell. Guess he didn't have his wits about him." Even she was coming out of her shell.

The weather in Manhattan that winter was nasty, with mean little winds blowing through the city. We were well into December. The holidays were approaching rapidly, heralded by jingled bells. The front door of the Rehearsal Club sported a pretty wreath with little red berries, and the walls inside were decked with holly and of course there was a beautiful tree.

Jimmy and I plotted constantly about moving in together, but we were up against it for money. I wondered where Jimmy had gotten the money he did have. I'd guessed he had borrowed here and there. As for me, I'd managed to save a small amount but certainly not enough, and I couldn't keep going back to Mom all the time. She was on a pension, and money from my father came when he felt like giving it. I just couldn't ask.

Sue's rehearsals for *South Pacific* were ending, and she was ready for her part as one of the nurses. I hadn't seen her for a while, as she had been busy learning her way through the show, but she was my best friend and I wanted to talk with her about my plans with Jimmy. One day I bolted through her door the way I usually did, and found her sitting at her little desk going over lines.

"Sue, I'm sorry if you're busy, but I have to talk to you."

"Of course you do, Diz girl." She was so patient with me.

"I can't stand this any longer. Jimmy and I want to live together so badly. We don't have the money, but we're saving for it. What do you think?"

"About what? Living together?"

"Yes, that and, well—I guess just that." All of a sudden I wasn't sure I wanted to hear what she had to say after all.

"Do you think that's wise, Diz?" She looked at me from her perch.

"What, living together?" She just stared at me. "Maybe not, but it *feels* right. Maybe being wise isn't always the best thing to do."

Sue just smiled. "Does it really matter what I think? I know how you are, Diz, when you get an idea in your head and you won't let go. I think you've already made up your mind. You don't need my advice."

"Oh, yes I do, Sue. You're my best friend. But you're right. Maybe I don't need your advice as much as I need your blessing."

"Well then, let's just say I don't think it's wise at all, but that's my puritanical upbringing. I want the very best for you, so of course you have my blessing. But your father went to some trouble to get you into the Club, and I don't think he's going to appreciate this."

She was right; that was going to be a problem. "Yeah, I know. I haven't decided whether to tell him or not. I guess he'll find out sooner or later—but right now later is better."

"God, Dizzy, you're headstrong. And—"

She didn't have a chance to finish. "We've both been waiting all our lives for someone to love, and somehow, by some miracle or fate, we found each other. It seems simple to me. We just want to be together. Does it have to make sense?"

Sue knew I didn't want to argue; I wanted her to be happy for me, but if she couldn't, at least she knew better than to try and talk me out of it. I left and went back to my room, feeling irritable. *Dammit, hasn't she ever been in love?*

I didn't waste any time calling Chucho's friend from the Milton Berle show—or *The Texaco Star Theater*, as it was called. Chucho had put in a good word for me, so when I went to audition, they asked me for a few basic movements—*could* I *hula?*—and when I said yes the job was mine. All excited, I called Jimmy to meet me at Jerry's that evening. He was in a foul mood when I got there.

"Lousy day?" I asked him. I didn't need to ask, his expression said it all. "I have some good news, for me at least. But maybe—"

"I want to hear some good news, even if it can't be mine. Go on, tell me. I dare you." He scowled.

Just then Leon came to our booth to get our order.

I went on. "I just got a job dancing on the Milton Berle show. I don't know for how long, but isn't that neat?"

"Great," said Jimmy. He was really low, but I could tell he was glad for me.

"So, you're gonna work for Uncle Miltie?" Leon broke in. "I have a cousin who knows him. Watch yourself—he can be a real stinker."

I told him I didn't care, and ordered a spaghetti to split. Leon came back with a huge plate of pasta, two plates, and two forks, then left us alone. What a nice guy he was. After he left, Jimmy raised his glass.

"Congratulations, little girl," he toasted. "Now maybe if I can get a job, we'll have enough to get our own place. Let's drink to that."

The Berle show that week had only one production number I had to learn: a barefoot Hawaiian hula number with one other girl and Uncle Miltie in drag—grass skirts, leis, the whole bit.

That night, as we were doing it live for the camera, everything was going well until an overhead light suddenly fell, crashed, and exploded a few feet in front of us. Needless to say we were all startled, but Berle ad-libbed a joke and people thought it was part of the number. Television was live in the early 1950s, so the show kept going and we kept hulaing right through the broken glass. It wasn't until I got back to the dressing room and sat down in front of the mirror to remove my makeup that I realized my feet had started to sting. When I looked down, I saw there was blood all over the bottom of both feet. The other girl came out with a few scratches, but I was the one standing nearest the point where the glass shattered and scattered. I had a pretty large gash on the ball of my left foot and one on the heel of my right. A nurse came and bandaged my feet, and gave me a report to sign; someone else came in and handed me a check, and that was the end of it. Needless to say, I walked kind of funny for the rest of that week.

Jimmy came to the Club the next day to take care of me. As the days rolled by he showed his concern in so many ways: he read to me, helped me maneuver from here to there, and did everything he could to cheer me up. He insisted on taking me up the street to the Museum of Modern Art, where we could sit in the beautiful sculpture garden. It felt good to move around, and I loved his attention. Out of sympathy, Jimmy took to walking the same way I was; the two of us, like twin Quasimodos, created quite a scene. Even for the jaded denizens of New York I suppose we were a bit of a spectacle. Whenever one of the passersby overreacted, Jimmy would shout, "Don't you know it's impolite to stare?"

We entered the museum and Jimmy escorted me to the garden. He sat me down and went to get us something to drink. He came back and handed me a Coke, which I spilled all over the table.

"What am I gonna do with you?" he said. "What am I gonna do with you? You're getting so clumsy!"

"Clumsy, maybe, but I am cute, don't you think?" I wasn't going to let him get away with that. "Besides, I can't help it, it's genetic."

"Yes, you are kinda cute. But are you cute *enough*?"

"Too cute for you. Can we have another Coke—*pleeease*?"

Jimmy began reading to me from an art magazine he had picked up along the way. "*The public and the academicians disliked the Impressionists intensely,*" he intoned. "*How sad not to be appreciated in one's own time—*"

"Yes, how awful!" I broke in. "To be understood and loved only after you're dead."

"I know, but not me. I'm going to let people know who I am—*while* I am."

"You sound like Popeye." I laughed.

"You mean, I am what I am?"

"Yes, you am what you am and I love what you am," I said.

We hobbled through the galleries of the great museum. Jimmy related to van Gogh; I preferred Matisse. He liked the free, broad strokes and the earth tones, and I was passionate about Matisse's colors and patterns. His *Red Room* is my favorite. We talked like two art connoisseurs who thought they knew what they were talking about. We both loved all of the Impressionists and some of the old masters too and, of course, Picasso and Dali, who we thought were unclassifiable. Jimmy played the intellectual very well. He was hungry for knowledge about everything, and he pursued it relentlessly. He almost always had a book with him. He took it as his credo that an actor should know as much as possible about every human emotion; he knew he had much to learn, and he was learning.

One morning, a few days before Christmas, I was lying on the floor exercising (and thinking about Jimmy) when a familiar voice disturbed my reverie.

"Dizzy, telephone. Your father."

Well, that brought me back to reality. "Thanks, Sue."

I limped down to the phone and picked up the receiver. "Hello, Elizabeth. I didn't wake you, did I?"

Whenever I heard his voice, my spine stiffened. "Hi. No, I was just doing some stretches. Is anything wrong, Daddy?"

"No, no, nothing's wrong, I just want to see you. Could you drop by late this afternoon, if you don't have anything better to do?"

"Sure, Daddy, I'll see you later. About five, okay?"

"Perfect." To the best of my knowledge, no one had ever said no to my father. It certainly never occurred to me to try it.

He had a large studio apartment on West Seventy-third Street, just off Broadway at the Sherman Square Studios. The main room was huge. A nine-foot Steinway Concert Grand was in the corner by the windows overlooking Seventy-third Street. The studio was comfortably appointed, with two leather couches, several chairs, tables, ashtrays, and, of course, a well-stocked bar in the far corner of the room, away from his pupils' curiosity. He privately taught a few students whom he felt were almost worthy of his attention, and I assumed he still entertained from time to time. He was a ladies' man, and women adored him. Most of his students over the years were female; one remarkable exception was Benny Goodman's great jazz pianist Teddy Wilson.

My father was always impeccably dressed in a suit with a vest and tie—except when he was relaxing at home, when he would remove his jacket and roll his shirtsleeves up, though the tie always remained in place. He smoked Camels, a lot of them, and he drank only Manhattans—sometimes a lot of them. That was always a good time for me to be someplace else. Whenever I was summoned by my father my heart did a little flip-flop and I would present myself with a certain degree of trepidation. He could be loving and concerned, but that was rare. Usually he was critical and stern, and I never knew what would trigger his anger. You would think his pianist hands would be long and beautiful, with graceful, tapered fingers, but on the contrary, they were short and pudgy and extremely powerful. I remember as a child watching his hands moving over the keyboard; they reminded me of fat little birds flying across the keys.

After returning to New York from a successful two-year sojourn in Europe with Mom, my father had been selected as soloist with the New York Philharmonic. He was the only soloist chosen by the audition committee without a dissenting vote. He gave concerts in New York and all over the world, and was noted as one of the leading interpreters of Chopin, Schumann, and Brahms. He was one of the founders of what is now the Mannes College of Music, which is still going strong, and taught at Princeton for years. His repertoire was wide and deep, encompassing the works of Bach all the way through to the Modernists, but my favorites were the Chopin ballades and nocturnes.

My father also played a yearly solo concert at Carnegie Hall, which my family and I attended faithfully. I remember one of those evenings in particular. My sister and I were little at the time. Fran and I were dressed in tiny velvet outfits with lace collars and patent leather Mary Jane shoes. I remember feeling as though we were on display. We sat in our box and watched Daddy walk onstage with all the pomp of a great artist, condescending to allow his audience to love him. When the last encore had been played and the applause was still thundering he slowly rose, and with one hand on the piano he stood erect and gazed out over his audience. He turned slowly from left to right: first to the boxes, then to the orchestra seats, and finally to the mezzanine and balcony, as if he were looking directly at each individual person. Then he bowed with a look of exhaustion on his face, as if he were drained. In truth, he probably was: his performances were intensely dramatic, his concentration legendary; as a child I found it difficult to differentiate between the artist onstage and the father at home.

Naturally, Fran and I would have to go backstage and wait until the long line of devoted and adoring fans would file by, gushing and breathy with compliments. After observing all this, we would approach from the shadows. I would try to bring fresh compliments to him; I remember being terrified not just that I wouldn't say the right thing, but that it also wouldn't be original enough for him.

My father had been a child prodigy; he was an accomplished pianist before he was ten years old, and he never really had a normal childhood. He once told me that when he was a little boy, he wanted more than anything to play baseball, but instead was forced to practice for many hours every day at the

piano. He probably would have been a happier person if he had
been allowed to follow his dream of an athletic life. His team
was the New York Giants; as a father, he would take Fran and
me to the Bronx if the Giants were playing. He knew the names
and stats of all the players. He wasn't a screamer, but I never saw
him more animated than at a New York Giants game. My sister,
a sports fan, loved it; I was a thorn in my father's side, and I
hated it. He was determined to make me interested in baseball;
I was just as determined to be a pain in the ass, fidgeting whenever I wanted a hot dog or popcorn or needed to go to the bathroom. My only solace as I sat there was to sit and concentrate
on the gorgeous Mel Ott, a star player for the Giants, on whom
I had a whopping crush. Mel Ott gave me a hero to root for, so
any day he was playing would be an involving experience. By
the end of the game, though, Daddy and I had invariably created a bitter standoff. It was always a quiet ride home.

Daddy was a snob. He hated being half Jewish; he felt it was
a stain on his character. I have always felt it was his Jewish
blood that provided him with a good sense of humor. As I've
said, he was moody and stern, with a terrible temper, but he
could be very witty when it suited him. He loved a good battle
of wits—the kind of battle he invariably won, especially with
me. He was critical of everyone, particularly his children. He
said he adored us, but I think it was from afar. We were thor-
oughly intimidated by him, so the farther afar the better. I
wanted to love him, but he made it almost impossible.

When he and Mom divorced, they sent Fran and me
away to boarding schools—first the Riverdale Country School
for Girls, which was up the Hudson River, and then Daycroft

in Stamford, Connecticut. He gave benefit concerts at each school, and I had scholarships to both. Every time he sat down to play, whether at Carnegie Hall, a high school stage, or at home, he made beautiful, profound music. Despite our difficult relationship, I felt from childhood the power of his music and how it could captivate the soul. When he played he seemed to go inside of the music, and the music in turn would emanate through him. Today, when I think of my father and what he really meant to me, it is that memory that comes back—the memory of his stirring music.

That night, I was announced from the lobby of his apartment building. As I got out of the elevator he was standing in the open door waiting for me. I kissed him on the cheek and said, "Hi, Daddy."

"Hello, Elizabeth. Come in. Can I get you something to drink?"

"Yes, please. Do you have any Champale?"

"I'm afraid not."

"I like it," I said defensively.

"Well, I had something else in mind, like tea or coffee or soda. How about a very weak Manhattan? I'll join you. It is cocktail time." I was relieved to find him in good humor.

I accepted, and congratulated him on his Giants' big World Series win.

"Yes, they were glorious. There was this incredible play in the final— But baseball's not your game, is it?" he said rhetorically. (With just a taste of sarcasm.) "What's wrong with your foot?"

I told him about my job in Harlem with the trio and about *The Noro Morales Show*. Then I told him about the Milton Berle incident, making it as light and funny as I could, and he laughed.

"You should have called me—I might have watched."

"Oh, it was nothing. I would like you to come and see my trio sometime, though. I'm very proud of it."

"I might, if you ever work in Manhattan."

"Well," I said, "we haven't had any calls from Carnegie Hall lately."

"You look well, Elizabeth. You're positively glowing."

Since he was being so congenial, I thought it was a good time to tell him about Jimmy.

"I'm glowing on the inside too, Daddy, because I've met the most wonderful boy."

"Oh, a boy. What does he do?"

"He's an actor, Daddy."

"An actor. What is he appearing in?"

"Nothing at the moment. He's auditioning."

"Oh, my God, an out-of-work actor!"

"Well, he just got into town from California, and he's looking for an agent. But I think he's going to be very successful; he has high hopes, and I do too. Anyway, I told him all about you and he was very impressed. He can't wait to meet you." I smiled.

"Well, he'll have to, because I'm going out of town. I have a concert tour and I'll be gone for a while—that's what I wanted to tell you. But I also wanted to give you and Fran a little something for Christmas."

He went to his desk and picked up two envelopes. "Please give Fran her envelope and tell her not to open it until Christmas Eve. That goes for you, too."

"Yes, Daddy. Thank you very much."

"How is Fran, and your mother? I'll call and wish them well before I go."

"They're fine," I said. "We're spending Christmas Eve together. I didn't bring your present with me; I thought I might be seeing you on Christmas Day."

"That's all right, we'll get together when I get back. Tell you what. I'll call and we'll have dinner, just the three of us, all right? Just you and me and your out-of-work actor."

That was all right by me. I finished my drink and left soon after. Once I was on the street I opened my envelope and there was a crisp new hundred-dollar bill. Great! Perfect! Money! I happened to be walking east on Seventy-first Street, on my way to the park to meet Jimmy. I happened to be passing the Hargrave Hotel & Apartments—a nondescript-looking building like all the rest on the block—when I noticed a sign in the front window: FURNISHED STUDIO APARTMENTS TO LET. Without stopping to think, I found myself walking through the dark narrow entranceway leading to the front desk. I inquired about monthly rentals, and an old man wearing suspenders told me I'd have to come back after Christmas—but that studio apartments were eighty dollars a month, plus fifty dollars in key money, whatever that was. The place was a little seedy and the rent would be a monthly hurdle, but just the possibility that this might become Jimmy's and my first home together made the Hargrave look like the Plaza. I couldn't wait to tell Jimmy about it when I met him in the park.

I spotted him leaning against a tree, reading a book. I tried to sneak up on him, but he saw me first.

"Hey, mister, whatcha readin'?"

"Nothin', I was just turning pages till you got here."

"I thought so, 'cause your lips weren't moving."

"Very funny! You're late. How'd things go with your father?"

"Not bad," I said, showing him the hundred-dollar bill. "He's going out of town, but he invited you and me for dinner when he gets back. Then on my way over here I passed an apartment hotel. They had a sign in the window, so I went in and talked to the super and he told me to come back after the holidays when the manager returns. We can check it out then. Whaddya think? I have a few bucks stashed in my underwear drawer. I'll put this hundred in with it, and that'll be our apartment fund."

"As usual, I'm practically broke, but I think my folks will send me something for Christmas. Until I get a job, though, I don't know how I'm going to hold up my end."

"Well, until you get that job, maybe I can hold up your end."

"Could you hold it up right now?" He smiled and pulled me toward him. I grabbed his buns and we ended up rolling around on the cold, hard winter grass, hugging and kissing and laughing.

"You know what I want for Christmas?" he said. "Just you. Only you—and maybe a new pair of jeans—and of course some socks, and a watch from Tiffany's, and—oh, oh, and I almost forgot—"

I clamped my hand over his mouth. "Well, you've already got me, kid," I said, "and it's going to be Christmas every day." Kiss again, wet and sloppy.

"If we're going to be partners, we're going to be partners. If I got it, you got it; if you got it, I got it. Get it?"

"I got it!"

"Good."

For a few minutes we forgot about money and jobs and the cold, and just got lost in each other.

Jimmy was invited to my mom's for dinner Christmas Eve, and I tried everything I could to get him to come, but he was at a very low point, extremely depressed and moody. He walked me to the train and said, "Have a good time, and don't worry about me. I'll be fine. There's something I have to do."

I knew by the look in his eyes that further efforts at persuasion would be futile. I assumed he didn't want to go because he had no gifts for my Mom or Fran, or me for that matter. I hugged him and headed, reluctantly, for my train.

Mom's was as festive as we could make it. We all got a little misty-eyed; Mom may well have been thinking of Daddy, and I know Fran must have been missing her husband. Of course I spent the whole evening thinking of Jimmy's touch, wanting to be with him. We clinked our glasses and reminisced about earlier Christmases when we had all been together with Daddy in our old apartment off Fifth Avenue by the park. It was always open house during the holidays. I was only five or six at the time, but I still remember the famous people who sometimes dropped by. John Barrymore and his wife, Michael Strange, were great friends with my parents; Mom told me that Michael had loaned her a beautiful gown, and helped her with her hair and makeup when Mom made her New York debut at the Princess Theatre.

Only recently, all these years later, have I learned—from my sister, who never thought to tell me before!—that George Gershwin and Isadora Duncan also came by at one time or another. New York seemed like a small town then, especially the artistic community; looking back on it now, it seems as though everyone must have known everyone else. Many of my parents' friends from the theater, ballet, and symphony orchestras came by through the years to sing carols at Christmastime, sipping champagne and being oh so grand. A few of the musicians would bring their instruments; how amusing it is now to think of those world-class musicians peering over Daddy's shoulder to read the music for the simplest Christmas songs.

That night Mom and Fran and I sang a few carols, but our hearts weren't in it. We opened the little gifts we had gotten each other; we Sheridan girls always opened our presents on Christmas Eve—not out of any formal tradition but just because we couldn't stand to wait till Christmas morning. Mom really came through, as usual; this year it was a check for fifty dollars, which she knew I needed because my torn-up feet had kept me from working.

Fran and I were always teasing each other, so I waited until the last gift had been opened before I finally said, "Oh, Fran, I almost forgot. This is for you, from Daddy."

Her eyes got huge; she knew what it was, and she whooped with joy. A hundred dollars was a lot in those days. I told Mom that Daddy had asked about her and would call before he left town. I stayed the night, ate a lovely breakfast on Christmas morning, and took the train back to the city.

Jimmy and I met at Jerry's a night or two after Christmas. One of the reasons I loved Jerry's was that they knew how to take care of their regulars. The bar was colorfully decorated, and drinks were on the house more frequently than usual.

We slid into our regular booth, and Jimmy kissed me sweetly. "How was your Christmas?"

"It was kinda sad. Mom was very disappointed you didn't come. What did you do?"

"December twenty-fifth is the worst day of the year for me. I don't know why, but I just wanted to be alone." I *thought there was something you had to do*, I thought, but I let it slide. There was a certain look that Jimmy would get in his eyes when he didn't want to communicate; I got to know that look well in the coming year, and I knew that was when I should just shut up and hold him. There were times when we would be together for hours without speaking. It was as if silence was an old friend.

January was more or less a blur. We saw each other whenever we could. I know that was the month we discovered the Hayden Planetarium on the Upper West Side. We were intrigued by the stars, and the precision of their movements. We talked about the planets and other galaxies and the mysteries of the universe.

And we agreed that there were definitely other life-forms out there. Even in our "scientific" talks we teased each other.

"They would almost *have* to be superior beings," he said with a sly look.

"Well, takes one to know one," I shot back.

"What the hell does that mean?"

"I don't know," I mumbled.

"See what I mean?"

"I'm gonna let you win this one, Dudley."

What fun it was to be young and goofy and in love. We would hang over the rail at Rockefeller Center, watching the people ice-skating and make up stories about them. Another favorite place was the Metropolitan Museum of Art on the Upper East Side: an amazing place with more beauty than you could possibly see in one day. I'd grown up nearby, and the museum had been a favorite of mine since childhood. There were whole wings devoted to ancient Egypt, full of tunnels and tombs and mummies. It was all very intriguing when I was an impressionable little girl, and it was a perfect place for Jimmy and me to play hide-and-seek.

When we tired of that, we would stroll along the corridors filled with huge paintings by the old masters. To be in the presence of da Vincis and Goyas and Rembrandts was truly awesome.

"Isn't this just—" I started to say.

"Sssssshhh."

"What?"

"Quiet . . . we must be quiet," he whispered.

"Why are you whispering?" I whispered.

"Because we're in the presence of greatness. We have to be respectful." He nodded to the walls.

"Why, they're dead."

"These works will live forever. That's why."

"Okay."

We spent the next hour or so in total silence until we exited the museum, then screamed and hollered as loud as we could, running up the street and into the park. There were lots of places to be together: exploring the museum, walking the streets, nursing a beer at Jerry's, or, of course, the movies. But there was no place we could truly be alone together. We ached to make love again, but for some strange reason, it wasn't a priority. We wanted more than a night of bliss; we wanted night after night after night. We tried to save money, but it kept dwindling away day by day. I had given Sue my hundred-dollar bill from Christmas, to hold for me.

"Promise not to give it to me, no matter what I say. Okay?"

"Ever?" Her eyebrows went up.

"Oh, you're just so funny. No. Just not until we're ready to move."

"Isn't Jimmy helping at all?"

I was afraid she'd ask me that. "Yes, of course."

"Oh, Dizzy, I—" Sue started.

"Don't. I don't want to hear it!"

"All right, sweetie, just consider me the Chase Manhattan Bank."

The truth is, I didn't know if Jimmy had managed to save anything or not. It was a touchy subject; I just couldn't ask. I know he hadn't had a job for a while, just a few unsuccessful auditions. Rejection is a bitch, it's tough on the ego, and some days he would seem very bruised. But Jimmy never had a doubt about his talent; I learned that fast. I knew instinctively when to back off and not to pry.

My feet healed quickly, and I was able to start rehearsing again—a fact that made Tony and Fabio happy, because we had another engagement at a nightclub somewhere in New Jersey. A friend of Tony's had a friend who was part owner of this club, and he talked his partner into giving us a Saturday night. Tony was a good hustler.

In the early 1950s there were literally hundreds of little nightclubs in the greater New York area with live entertainment on the weekends. Every club would feature music and an emcee who told jokes and introduced the acts—singers or magicians or perhaps an exotic dancer. It was thrilling to be in front of an audience again, to satisfy the need for the excitement of performing. I just wished we could have landed a steady weekend job, but it was tough to book a trio.

I was determined to make more money. I checked out the bulletin board at the Club daily. One day I found an interesting notice: RETOUCHERS: EARN AS YOU LEARN. AMERICAN PHOTOGRAPH CO. That sounded vaguely artistic to me. I decided to check it out.

The American Photograph Co. was on Forty-second Street, near Bryant Park and the fabulous Public Library with its big stone lions out front. *Sounds promising,* I thought; *within walking distance of the Club and another one of our favorite haunts. Hmmm . . . how convenient.*

I stood in front of the old building, worn but still beautiful, like so much of the older Manhattan architecture. Solid, sturdy, timeless. I walked into the dreary lobby, which was sadly neglected, but the sliding metal gate made the do-it-yourself elevator a treat. I closed the gate and pressed the button to the third floor. The elevator creaked and moaned its way upward with a sigh; when it came to a grateful stop, all I could think was W*hew*, I *made it.*

I walked to the end of the hall, opened a door, and entered another world. I had to blink. It was dark and almost silent, a startling contrast to the noisy street I had just left behind. I was standing in an enormous room filled with desks in neat rows. At each desk sat a worker hunched over a drawing board with a square hole cut out of the middle, a frosted glass over that, and a lightbulb behind it. On each glass was a photo negative; the muted glare from the bulbs reflected on the workers' faces, illuminating each as softly as a Rembrandt portrait.

As I stood there trying to focus, a short, round man with bulging eyes behind very thick glasses walked up to me and spoke in a raspy German accent.

"You here about de job?"

I jumped. "Yes," I said.

"You got experience?"

"No, not really. But I do some sketching. And this appeals to my creative side."

He smiled and said, "Vell, ve see . . . follow me." And he led me to what I supposed was his office. I couldn't help noticing how much he resembled a frog. He wore a white shirt with the sleeves rolled up, a drab-colored tie, a suit vest, and trousers that matched. I remember it all because my father dressed the same way. His shoes squeaked beneath him when he walked. I will affectionately call him Mr. Frog.

Mr. Frog turned out to be a patient teacher, and I caught on fast. We worked on four-by-five negatives with special retouching pencils. We smoothed faces, filling in age lines, sweeping away acne, and generally making people look as perfect as possible without erasing character. As you can imagine, the work was a strain on the eyes and tiring on the fingers, not to mention my aching back.

After about two hours of training, I was hired. I would be paid so much per negative; the more we did, the more we made. The second we finished a negative, we hit a little bell on our desks, and the floor manager would come around to pick up our work, which was then taken to Mr. Frog. If he didn't approve it, it was returned to us to do over. There was no talking while we worked, so for hours upon hours the only sounds I could hear were the dings of the little bells and the barely audible scratchings of the pencils, like tiny animals whispering or insects singing in the twilight. A little whimsical musing seemed to make the time go faster, and as I worked I would invent biographies of whatever subject I was working on.

When my shift ended and I turned my lightbulb off and left this world of darkness, I walked back to the Club, squinting all the way up Sixth Avenue. I worked three days a week and I got pretty good at it, averaging about seven or eight dollars a day. I tried to talk Jimmy into joining me, but he wasn't interested. On the off days, I rehearsed with the boys.

One day, as I came out of the building, Jimmy was there waiting for me, leaning against a car.

"Jimmy, is that you? What a surprise."

"Hi. Who did you think it was?"

"Well, it takes a minute. I work in a cave. What are you doing here?"

"I was in the neighborhood. Want to go to the library with me?" He took my hand and we walked.

The New York Public Library was a wonderful place to us, its wooden tables in the main reading room filled with people engrossed in their studies—some reading, some writing, some just resting. I took from the experience a sense of privilege, the joy of knowing that this building full of great works was available to everyone for the asking. On this particular day, Jimmy wanted to read about bullfighting. We were there for hours, leafing through old magazines, looking at photos and reading from a small stack of books. We were taken with the mythological rituals: the corrida, the circle of life and death, more eternal than a wedding band; the picadors and the horses; the trumpets' melancholy blare, piercing the blazing afternoon heat. The pageantry was a glorious spectacle against the reality of death.

"What's the point of it all?" I asked Jimmy after a while.

"I told you—conquering your fear. That's the point."

"Jimmy, could you actually kill a bull?"

"I would have to, if I wanted to live. These bulls are bred and trained for only one purpose: to kill a man. It would be him or me. All that dance-of-death, cruel-but-beautiful bullshit, that's for poets. Fear and death is what it's all about. Can you imagine how it must feel to be so close to death? I want to know that feeling. That's what intrigues me."

"Well, that's something I don't think I can watch," I said.

"I thought you wanted to be a matadoress?"

"I do, as long as nobody has to die."

He laughed.

Now that I had steady work—and the trio was getting the occasional booking, to my utter delight—Jimmy was starting to catch up; one day not long after, he told me he had about a hundred dollars, which I assumed had come from his folks. That was all the incentive we needed: we decided to check out the Hargrave Hotel.

I could tell Jimmy was surprised that I picked a location in my father's neighborhood, but he said nothing. When we reached the building he looked at me and grabbed my pigtail. "Don't worry, my little girl, the gods are looking down. I feel the tides changing for us." I looked at him in amazement.

We were still holding hands when we walked up to the front desk. A round little lady with frizzy red hair was sitting on a tall stool behind the counter. I guessed she was somewhere in her sixties. She was overly made-up, but you could tell she might have been quite a beauty when she was young. Her manner was aggressive but cheerful. We asked if we could see the studio apartment.

"For yourselves?" she asked.

"Yes, for my husband and myself; we just got married. We're newlyweds." I nonchalantly scratched my nose with my left hand; I'd had the foresight to turn around an onyx ring I always wore so it would look like a band. She gave me a knowing look.

"Right this way." She took a ring of keys from a drawer behind the desk. "Watch your heads."

We followed her, passing a large flight of marble stairs, when suddenly she ducked under the stairwell to get to a small elevator on the other side. Jimmy giggled and nudged me. He was loving this, and so was I. We all rode up to the second floor.

"I'm Mrs. Epstein. What business are you two in?"

Jimmy jumped in, with his most theatrical voice. "I am an actor and my lovely wife is a dancer. Perhaps you've seen her on the television show—"

"Television!" she interrupted. "That's what killed vaudeville, you know!"

"I thought it was radio," Jimmy teased.

"That too!" Evidently Mrs. Epstein liked her entertainment live.

I proceeded to tell her about my accident on the Milton Berle show. I told her about the hula number, the falling light, the whole thing. As long as I kept talking, I thought, we would be all right. Jimmy was being very quiet, holding my hand and smiling his most appealing smile.

"Oh, you poor thing," she cooed. "My late husband and I were in vaudeville for almost ten years before it *died*. We played the Keith Circuit, six shows a day. We went everywhere. We were known as the Dancing Darlings. Maybe you heard of us?"

We shook our heads.

"Ahh, you're too young."

Jimmy said, "I guess we missed vaudeville, but I had a feeling you were in show business." She smiled at that.

"How exciting," I chimed in. "My mother played the Keith Circuit too. She's a singer. She was one of the Blend Sisters. Did you ever run into them?"

"If they were on the Keith Circuit, I must have. But it doesn't ring a bell. There were so many sister acts, and my memory isn't what it used to be. If my husband were here, he'd remember. That man, what a mind he had. Here we are, kids."

She opened the door for us. Jimmy looked at me, winked, and went in first. We were show folk, all three of us, and show folk always stick together.

# 6

The minute I walked in, I knew this would be our new home.

It couldn't have been better. Two large windows overlooking Seventy-first Street made the room bright and cheery. A nice-size room with a large bed and a small night table with our own telephone, a comfortable chair, a desk with a little lamp and chair, a dresser, a floor lamp with a tasseled shade, a closet with a full-length mirror on the door, and a tiny bathroom with a shower emptying into an old-fashioned bathtub with funny little lion's-claw legs. But I think it was the bathroom floor that sealed it for me: black-and-white checkerboard tile. I couldn't resist.

"This is one of our coziest studios," Mrs. Epstein said. "You two should be very comfy here."

I turned to Jimmy and said, "Do you think you'll be comfy here, hon?"

"Well, sweetie," he said, "if you'll be comfy, I'll be comfy . . . and then we'll be comfy together."

Mrs. Epstein gave us an incredulous look. "If you two will come back downstairs with me, we'll make arrangements, okay?"

I smiled at Jimmy and then at Mrs. Epstein; Mrs. Epstein smiled at me and then at Jimmy; Jimmy smiled at me and then threw the ball back to Mrs. Epstein. Then we all headed through the doorway together. "I'm sorry." "No, excuse me." "No, after you." Talk about vaudeville: we could have traveled with that routine!

In spite of all the fun we were having together, Mrs. Epstein still wanted her rent up front and her fifty dollars for key money. When we returned the keys, she said, we'd get our money back. It was also a deposit for the telephone. I had a suspicion she didn't believe we were man and wife, but I know she liked us, and that went a long way.

Jimmy said, "Do you mind if we talk it over for a minute?"

Mrs. Epstein nodded, and we walked back under the stairwell. Jimmy whispered, "I've got almost a hundred. How about you?"

"I have forty in my underwear drawer and Sue has my hundred from Christmas, so we have more than enough. Oh, God, we're really gonna do it, aren't we? We're really gonna do it!"

"Yup," he said.

We walked back to the desk.

Jimmy said, "We'll take it, but we have to go to our bank. Will you hold it for us?"

"Sure, if you give me a small deposit. Say, twenty dollars and I'll hold it for a week. Okay?"

"Okay." Jimmy handed her twenty dollars.

She smiled. "I hope you two will be happy here."

Jimmy moved out of the YMCA not far from there. He brought a suitcase, his portfolio, a few books, his bloodstained cape, and a pair of bull's horns—and, of course, his recorder. I left the Rehearsal Club with a suitcase, my dance bag, my radio, my portable phonograph, and an alarm clock. I never for one minute allowed myself to think of what effect this move would have on my parents or what the consequences would be.

Our first evening in our new home was so exciting. We both unpacked what little we had. Every time we passed each other, we hugged and kissed. I decided we had to rearrange the furniture, so I sat cross-legged on the bed and gave directions.

"Over by the window." Jimmy, sandwich in his mouth, was lifting our "comfortable chair." "No, no, no—wait a minute. Against the wall between the two windows. Oh, hell, that looks awful."

"Christ, will you please make a decision," Jimmy mumbled through his sandwich. He looked so cute, barefoot, in jeans with no shirt. I started to laugh, and he put down the chair in the middle of the room and sat down to finish his sandwich.

"That's it!" I clapped.

"What's it?" he said.

"Right there! Where you are! I read in a magazine somewhere that if you make 'groupings' with your furniture, the room will seem larger."

"That probably means if you have furniture to make 'groupings' with."

I ignored that. "If we leave the chair there and bring the lamp over to it and the magazine rack, then we'll have a cozy little group. Don't you think?"

"Well, I have to say, I feel really cozy here in my comfortable chair, right here in this cozy grouping in the middle of the room." We left it right there, and that was fine with me.

We hung Jimmy's cape and horns on the wall over the bed, and his books looked very important on our little desk along with my radio. "Don't you think the lamp on the desk should go right here by the bed?" I asked.

"These are really tough questions," he teased.

"I just think if it was by the bed, then we could read there comfortably."

"Reading is good . . . but this is better." And Jimmy gently pushed me back onto the bed. "I love you so," he said.

We lay there, his hands on both sides of my face, his lips kissing my cheeks, my eyes, the tip of my nose, my neck. He whispered in my ear: "It's been too long. I want it back—the Bevan by the sea. I want *you*." I knew just how he felt. We undressed and left our clothes where they fell; he took my hand and we stood in front of the full-length mirror naked, looking at ourselves. We stood side by side, we faced each other, we faced the mirror; he stood behind me, his hands caressing my body. We turned round and round. We were so beautiful.

Jimmy pulled my hair out so it spread over my shoulders and covered my breasts. He kneeled in front of me and pulled my hair over his forehead to make bangs, and we broke up. He was always playing with my hair.

"I want to make love and fall asleep in your arms, then wake up in our new home as happy as I am now," I said.

We went to bed with the radio playing soft music. We

kept the lights on so that we could see each other. I know we both wanted to recapture the intensity and passion of our first time together. He stroked my body, and I his. We became so emotional this time that we didn't wait; Jimmy entered my body just in time and we exploded together. I started to cry from the sheer joy of the moment. Jimmy kissed my face, licked my tears with a laugh.

"Jimmy, that was so wonderful."

"Yeah," he said. "I'm glad we waited. It was better than wonderful. There's something I want to read to you." He leapt out of bed to get a book from the desk. We lit our cigarettes and cuddled in bed while he read to me from Saint-Exupéry's *The Little Prince*. It was his favorite story: a prince from another planet that was so tiny, there was only room for a chair, a rose, and three volcanoes . . . two active and one extinct. (Why? I never understood that part.) The little prince is in love with the rose, but she is too vain and self-involved to notice. He is so unhappy and too young to know how to love her, so he travels to other planets for enlightenment. Finally, on his journey to Earth, he learns, from a very wise fox, the secret of what is important in life. "'It is only with the heart that one can see rightly,'" Jimmy read. "'The wise fox told him, *What is essential is invisible to the eye.*'" He looked up. "I'm going to tell you a secret. This is it—this simple truth that I strive for when I perform."

Our first few days in our new home were wonderful. We learned so many things about each other we hadn't known before. Jimmy liked sleeping on the right side of the bed . . . so I liked the left. He curled; I sprawled. He was tidier than I thought he would be. He only had two pairs of shorts, so I volunteered to wash his underwear when I washed mine in the tub, after my bath. That became a ritual. So there was always a pair of panties and shorts hanging on the shower curtain rod.

Living was expensive. There was food to buy, occasional cleaning bills to pay, phone bills and carfare money, and of course the rent. We had maid service: once a week, Mrs. Epstein would show up with fresh linen, two bath towels, two hand towels, two rolls of toilet paper, and two little bars of Ivory soap. We walked as much as we could, but we liked going out to Jerry's or the movies or eating around the neighborhood. We bought a hot plate, and that took care of coffee or soups and boiled eggs. We ate a lot of sandwiches and cereals in, and a lot of pastas out.

We walked to the park, which was only a block and a half away, almost every day. Jimmy loved practicing his bullfighting technique, and I served as his bull.

We brought the horns and cape; I held the horns to my forehead, pawed the ground, and charged at him. "Olé!" he shouted, swinging the cape around. "Olé," I snorted back, flying right by him. He twirled the cape and then dragged it on the ground, casting an arrogant glance over his shoulder as he walked away from me. He always made me the bull, so after a while I decided to be the baddest and meanest bull ever. No more fooling around. I *became* that bull, and I started charging him for real. I would burst from the *toril*—the Gate of Frights— feeling the full power of my two thousand pounds. My muscles rippling, screamingly alive with pure power. I would toss and stomp, my eyes mad one instant, thoughtful the next.

"You won't be happy until you're gored," I screamed.

"Are you going to talk or fight?"

That did it: I started charging at him again and again, without letup, until I was exhausted.

"Let's stop," I gasped.

"Just once more," Jimmy said. "I want to try a farol pass." And he dropped to his knees, shaking the cape.

So I charged him one last time—and at the very last moment I went in low and hooked to the right and got him near his groin. He was wearing jeans, but nevertheless, he let out a cry. "Hey! You gored me!"

"That's the point, isn't it? Don't be such a baby. I could have been more accurate, you know."

"Then we'd both be out of luck." He grabbed me and we rolled around on the ground.

I think he never let me be the bullfighter because he thought I might handle the cape more gracefully than he did. When I asked him, he claimed it was because I was so much faster, but I can't believe it. It's possible I might have been more graceful, but there was no way I could have done it with as much cocky strut.

Jimmy had trouble sleeping. He was very much the night owl, so naturally I became one too—and soon enough I got to ignoring the alarm on my retouching days. I would show up late for work and all the desks would be filled. Mr. Frog wondered if I was serious about my work. *Was he kidding?* When he finally warned me that he'd have to let me go if I was late again, I thought, *He wouldn't dare. I'm one of his best retouchers.* The next time I showed up late, he was as good as his word: he let me go.

Jimmy and I spent a lot of time lying in bed reading. I have always had a problem with retaining what I have just read. One night I told Jimmy about it, and he asked me if I wanted help with the problem.

"No, not really."

"Well, I'm going to anyway. Why bother reading if you can't remember what you've read?" He handed me a book of philosophy. "Now, take this and read just these two pages."

"Out loud?"

"No, to yourself. Then close the book and tell me what you read," he said.

"That's silly," I replied. "I have a wonderful memory."

"When you're interested, sure. But this isn't about memory—it's about unscattering your mind."

"Well, that's why they call me Dizzy," I snapped.

"I thought that was because your sister couldn't pronounce your name."

"I lied."

"Really?" he asked.

"No." With a sigh I took the book and started to read. We were sitting on the bed facing each other.

"Can I have a cigarette?" I reached for the pack he had in his hand.

"No." He put them behind his back. "Not till you're through."

"Damn it, who do you think you are?"

"I am the man you love," he said, smiling at me.

"Not at the moment." I went back to reading. He just sat and stared at me.

"I can't do this if you're going to sit there and watch me," I whined.

"That's the whole point," he said. "Concentrate. Shut out everything. Go inside."

Damn, he was maddening! I hated being told what to do. I threw myself into the book, brow knitted in mock intensity, and when I was through I closed the covers and looked up at him.

"Okay," he said. "Now tell me exactly what you read. In detail."

"I have absolutely no idea. Let's make love. I'll concentrate—I promise."

We did a lot of sketching—his bulls and my trees. One day we decided to switch: I would draw a bull and he would draw a tree.

"I can't do this. Every time I try, it comes out looking like a spider," I pouted.

"Try something easier," said Jimmy. And he began to set up little drawing classes for me. Sometimes if he had an appointment or an audition, he'd leave me at home with my homework: sketching an egg, or a book or the lamp or my hand. Easy things—or so I thought. For someone who had trouble drawing anything other than bulls, he was a good teacher.

"All you have to do is look at what you're drawing and see it in your mind. Really see it. It's simple. Just focus. Everything just comes from the inside."

I really tried and it did get easier; soon we had sketches that were good enough to decorate the walls. Just me and him, surrounded by our things. I loved it.

♦♦

Sue and Brock were our first guests. I dusted, cleaned the bathroom, bought some flowers, and Jimmy got some beer and pretzels. We'd planned an evening out, but first we wanted them to see the place.

When they arrived, though, I could hear Sue carrying on down the hall: "My Gawd! It's like a bombed-out building. I wonder if there's a password." Laugh, laugh, laugh. "Dizzy, dear, where the hell are you?"

I opened the door. "Hi, guys."

Brock gave me a hug. "We knew you'd surface if we made enough noise. How ya doin'?"

Jimmy stepped into the hall and made a sweeping gesture of welcome, ushering them into our room.

"Oh, Dizzy, this is really sweet." Sue beamed.

"Really cozy," said Brock.

They were trying too hard. I could see the disappointment on their faces.

Jimmy moved toward the bathroom to get the beers we had chilling in the sink. We had our two chairs for them, and we took the end of the bed.

"My God, what is that?" Sue said. She was looking at the bloodstained cape hanging over the bed—Jimmy's pride and joy.

"That's the bullfighting cape I told you about," I said. "The one that belonged to Sidney Franklin. Remember? Isn't it great?"

"Oh, my God. Is that real blood?" She seemed horrified, which pleased Jimmy no end.

"Sometimes we sleep under it," he said.

"He means not just under it," I added, "but *under* it—around our bodies, like a blanket. Isn't that exciting?"

"Oh, my God!"

We changed the subject—or, rather, Sue did. "I'm going to be staying at my aunt's apartment in Greenwich Village for about a week. She's going on vacation and I just love apartment-sitting for her. I think I might throw a party. What do you think?"

"Great idea. I love the Village," I said, looking at Jimmy.

"Maybe we can love—er, I mean *live* there someday," he said.

"No, you were right the first time." I leaned over to kiss him.

"Well, you two are just so cute!" Sue screamed. "Ain't love grand?" That it was.

The four of us had a wonderful time. After a movie and a nightcap at Jerry's, Sue offered to get us tickets for a Wednesday matinee of *South Pacific* later that week, and we all said good night. By the time Jimmy and I arrived home it had begun to snow. It was so nice to have a place where we could fall in bed together and talk till all hours.

At about five in the morning, we were going over the sad state of our finances. We were both out of work; I was still rehearsing with Tony and Fabio, but no jobs were cropping up.

"I've got to find an agent," Jimmy said. "These cattle calls are getting to me, Diz. Waiting around for two hours to say one line. Fuck it!"

"You'll find one. I know you will."

"When? I'm so depressed. I'm sorry—I've got to get out of here and get some air."

"Where are you going at this hour?"

"I don't know. You wanna come?"

"Can I?"

"Yeah, sure. Let's go someplace we've never been, okay?"

"You're sure you wouldn't rather be alone?"

"No, no. Please come. We'll explore."

I leapt out of bed. "Let's go."

It wasn't too cold—for a snowy late-winter night. Doubled up on clothes, we hopped on a subway, and on the way downtown I had a thought. "Let's go to the beach!"

"Perfect!" Jimmy said. Nothing like an early-morning trip to the absurd.

After a subway change we ended up at Coney Island, just as the sun was trying to break through the fogbound clouds. We strolled along the boardwalk. All the rides were covered with tarps and tied down. The fun booths were all boarded up. The snow had stopped, but everything was covered with a fine powdery cloak.

The beach was deserted, except for a few dozen gulls making crazy paths across the sky. Jimmy had never been to Coney, and he was suddenly elated. "I saw a photograph of this beach in a magazine once. There were so many people—like a million, with big umbrellas and stuff. You could hardly see the sand. But this! This is like standing on the moon!"

The beach was undisturbed by footprints. *Wow, what an amazing dance floor.*

In a heavy Swedish accent I said, "I sure vould like a polka!" and held out my hand.

"Ya! Sure! You betcha!" He took my hand, and we ran down the wooden steps leading to the beach. I started singing "Roll Out the Barrel" and Jimmy joined me, and we started across the huge, white expanse dancing, taking giant polka steps—which isn't easy on the sand—and singing at the top of our lungs. Accompanied by the shrieks of gulls, we sliced through the stark Coney Island morning, singing chorus after chorus as we polkaed over the beach.

After a long while we sank exhausted to the ground. We lay on our backs spread-eagled and holding hands, watching the horizon where the sunlight was beginning to shine through. We lay there for a long time, staring at the ever-changing beauty of the sky. No one spoke. When our breath finally returned, we walked back up the steps to the boardwalk.

"Oh, Dizzy, look what we made!"

Jimmy pointed to the tracks of our dance on the beach. We had left hundreds of circles, intersecting like a giant abstract painting on a canvas of snow that was already melting into the sand.

As we were leaving, we spotted a solitary old woman with a dog down at the end of the boardwalk. She was sitting on a bench, all bundled up, with a black Lab in harness at her feet. Though she was blind, she seemed to be looking out to sea just as we had been. I closed my eyes, as I always do when I see a blind person—as I did with Moondog. I find I listen deeper with my eyes closed.

"Jimmy, close your eyes," I commanded, and together, with closed eyes, we listened to the morning. Then, after a time, we opened our eyes and headed for the subway—back to our city life. We made love and at last we fell asleep, like the weary travelers we were.

When Jimmy and I were together, in that close early time, I forgot everything that made me feel sad, lost, empty, broken, lonely, or forlorn. In their place I found trust and understanding and patience, and he did as well. Jimmy knew he could trust me, and he was learning how to open up and share his feelings.

The Hargrave was our safe house, the one place where we could let all our barriers down. Downstairs, Mrs. Epstein held court. She would sit behind the front desk knitting away, always carefully policing the comings and goings. She was our own private Madame Defarge. We became very fond of her. She was always available for wardrobe tips, medicinal cures, and advice for the lovelorn. Her first name was Sophia, but if she insisted that you call her Sophie, then you knew you were family.

I went to the Rehearsal Club daily to see if I had any messages. One afternoon there was one from my father. I called him immediately.

"I'm home. Can we have dinner? Are you still seeing what's-his-name?"

"Jimmy. Yes. We'd love to." We made a date for a few nights later at one of his favorite restaurants.

That night in the bathroom, as I was taking a bath and Jimmy was brushing his teeth over the sink: "Will I have to dress for dinner when we see your father? I mean, where are we going to go?" he said, toothbrush tucked in his cheek.

"It's a charming little French restaurant. You'll love it."

"Can I have a steak?"

"No." When he threw me a dirty look, I smiled. "Of course you can. You can have two."

I knew he was depressed. He had no job, no money, no decent clothes. He was nervous about the impression he would make. I had told Jimmy a little bit about my father, so I couldn't blame him. I was nervous too.

I was standing in the tub, drying myself after my bath. My skin felt warm and rosy, tingling from the rough rubdown I'd given myself. I wanted to console him, but I knew words wouldn't help. Instead, when he turned and left the bathroom, I noticed he left his glasses on the little shelf above the sink. I quickly put them on top of my head. Surrounded by my upswept hair, they were almost invisible. After a moment I heard Jimmy's voice from the other room.

"Where the hell are my glasses?"

I smiled. "I don't know."

"Well, they couldn't just disappear." He stuck his face around the door. "I had them on when I came in here."

"Maybe you just think you did." I was being a smart-ass.

"Are you being a smart-ass?"

"Yes."

"Get out of the tub and help me look, okay?"

"All right, I'm coming." I wrapped the towel around my body, and when I stepped into the room, I couldn't help but laugh. He was standing in the middle of the room stark naked, blind as a bat, giving instructions to the standing lamp. "Now, you check the East Wing and I'll check the West, and if we come up empty, we'll check the grounds outside."

"Very funny," I said.

"I'm trying—but I'm not in the mood. Can I please have my glasses?"

I walked up behind him and put my arms around him.

"I'll give you back your glasses if you stop worrying about Daddy. I know you're going to charm him."

"Okay." Jimmy turned to finally look at me, his face traced with that endearingly bewildered expression he had when he wasn't wearing his glasses. "Oh, there you are." He smiled and kissed me. I removed the glasses from my head and put them on his nose.

"Oh, there *you* are!" I kissed him back, and he pulled my towel off. It fell to the floor.

"You don't have any clothes on," he said.

"Neither do you," I replied. "You want to make something of it?"

"Let's wait till tonight. Do you mind?" he said as I caressed his body.

"Ohhh, well, okay. If you're sure."

He led me to the bed. At least his depression was forgotten for a while.

On the morning of our dinner date with my father, Jimmy was getting ready to go out for his usual round of auditions. I was busy trying to draw an egg. "The egg is the most difficult object to draw," Jimmy said as he was leaving.

"Why?"

"I'm going to tell you why," he said.

He put the egg on the desk, where the light from the window fell on it.

"Now," he said, "if your gaze moves a fraction of an inch, the light falling on the egg will change. The shadows will change. It will look different every time you look up at it. It's almost like trying to draw a moving object. The egg won't move, of course, but the sunlight does. The changes are imperceptible unless a cloud drifts by. It's an exercise in frustration."

"What?"

"Do one like that, then put away the egg and do one from memory. Have them both finished when I get home."

"Yes, sir." I saluted, and out the door he went, leaving me with my egg.

I sketched until the afternoon light faded, then turned on the lamps and splashed the room with a glow. Suddenly, Jimmy came flying through the door. He was positively cheerful, playful as a puppy, and bearing gifts: a single rose and a bottle of screw-top champagne.

"I found an agent!" he yelled.

"Fantastic!" I yelled back. "Who?"

"Her name is Jane D'eacy. I'm on my way, Diz. Somebody else is out there working for me now. Isn't that great? I'm on my way!"

"I just knew it would happen! How did it happen? Tell me!"

He got a couple of glasses and poured the champagne. "Well, she's building a stable of a few select actors. I ran into a director friend of a friend of a friend and he introduced me to her. She works for the Louis Schurr office. I think she likes me. Hell, I *know* she loves me! Christ! Christ!" he screamed.

I held up my glass.

"Here's to beginnings, Mr. Dean."

"And to happy endings, Mrs. Dean." He threw his head back and made a joyful noise.

"Jimmy, it's getting late. We only have an hour before we have to go meet Daddy."

"Oh, Christ—I almost forgot!"

"No, you didn't."

"Well, I tried to."

"Hey, this was your idea, remember?" I reminded him.

He downed his drink, stripped off his clothes, and as he stepped into the tub he sent me his most dazzling smile. His anxiety about meeting my father seemed to be vanishing. When he was getting dressed, I noticed that he'd borrowed the same blue-and-green-striped tie he had worn to Larchmont.

"Who did you borrow that tie from?" I asked.

"Oh, just a guy I know."

"Well, he has excellent taste." I was curious, but I left it alone. I'm sure he met many guys on his daily rounds and cattle call auditions. I was sure he had borrowed money too, for the champagne.

We didn't have far to walk. The evening was surprisingly mild. As it often is in Manhattan after a snowfall, the streets were covered with piles of dirty slush, making for sloppy trudging.

The little French restaurant, one of my father's favorites, was candlelit and charming. I had dined there before with him; the food was wonderful, presented with quiet style. Everything was a muted apple green: the tablecloths, the napkins—even the walls, where a few pastoral oil paintings hung, all adding to the provincial atmosphere.

Daddy was there at a far corner table browsing the menu, smoking a cigarette and sipping on a Manhattan. When he saw us he got up from the table and, with surprising warmth, extended his strong, pudgy hand to shake Jimmy's. I kissed him on the cheek. We all smiled and settled in.

"Elizabeth tells me you are an actor."

"Yes," said Jimmy, and he mumbled something incoherent.

"What?" my father said, leaning forward.

"A little-known actor, I'm afraid—but I have an agent!" Jimmy blurted out. "And she says she thinks I'll go far."

"Oh, good." Daddy nodded.

"She just signed me today."

"Then let's make this a celebration. Congratulations!" Daddy smiled.

"Thank you," Jimmy went on. "Elizabeth has told me so much about you. I've heard some of your records. You must feel very fulfilled making such beautiful music."

*Thataboy. There's the old charm at work.*

My father chuckled. "Well, I suppose I am, but then not unlike you, I imagine."

"Yes, well, all of us in the arts—how can we not feel superior?"

*Oh my God. In front of my father.*

I jumped in. "Daddy, Jimmy's learning to play the recorder. Isn't that nice?"

"Oh, do you read music?" he asked Jimmy.

"Very slowly," Jimmy said.

"Slowly is the best way when you're learning." My father smiled again.

"Not if you're in a hurry," said Jimmy.

"Well, I'm afraid I can't help you there." Daddy laughed and picked up the menu just as the waiter arrived.

I wasn't ready to give my order, so the waiter turned to Jimmy. "*Monsieur?*"

"*Filet mignon au poivre, s'il vous plaît,*" Jimmy responded.

*So you want to play? Okay, then, we'll play.*

"*Garçon?*" The waiter gave me a half smile, and I continued. "*Je désire un coq au vin et une salade verte.*"

The waiter played along. "*Certainement, mademoiselle.*"

"*Et Monsieur Sheridan?*"

"I'll have the fish." He paused. "For a moment there I thought I was at the Court of Versailles."

Well, that broke the ice. Daddy was in top form, where he liked to be. He seemed to be having a wonderful time being charming and witty and in complete control.

"I think you're probably a very fine actor. You have a quality about you," Daddy said.

"Thank you, sir. That means a lot coming from you."

"Discipline is the key to success. Discipline and determination. Don't let anything stop you. I tell all my pupils the same thing."

"I assure you, sir, nothing will stop me."

"That's the spirit!" Daddy said as he polished off his Manhattan and caught the waiter's eye for a refill.

Everything went well after that. We chatted easily. After dessert, my father offered us a cigarette. His Camels were too strong for me—I preferred Old Golds—but Jimmy took one as two waiters rushed over to fire up their lighters. Daddy asked, "Jimmy, would you like a brandy? Or perhaps you would prefer cognac?"

But Jimmy didn't miss his subtle dig. "I don't drink hard liquor very often, sir," he said, "and I don't speak French. I was just kidding around. Diz and I do that all the time. Most people think we're from another planet, but you caught on right away. It was a great pleasure to meet you, sir."

"Well, I enjoyed meeting you too. I had a good time tonight. You seem to make my daughter happy."

"I try—I guess we make each other happy." We looked at each other, and I felt strangely uncomfortable. Jimmy noticed and kept going. "Thanks for dinner, this was the best meal I've had since Mrs. Sheridan's pot roast."

"Oh, then you've met Elizabeth's mother? Yes, she's an excellent cook." He turned to me and said, "Is she still singing in that prison?"

"Oh, sure," I said. "It's a rough trip for her, but she says she finds it very fulfilling."

"Yes, well, that's your mother. Self-sacrifice always was her métier."

*What the hell does that mean? Enough with the French.*

Jimmy went on. "And I met your daughter Fran. You have a wonderful family."

"Oh, Daddy," I interrupted, "Fran and I both appreciated your Christmas present. Thank you so much." The fact that his hundred dollars helped Jimmy and me move in together I left unmentioned.

"Good," he said. "I invited your sister to join us tonight, but she didn't feel up to the trip. I spoke to her a few days ago and she seemed fine."

"She's big and uncomfortable, but that's to be expected. Other than that, she's okay. Daddy, you're going to be a grandfather. Isn't that exciting?"

"Hell, no! It makes me feel ancient. I'm glad she's there with your mother. They keep each other company. So, Elizabeth, how's your little dance trio?"

"We've played up in Harlem again since I've seen you, and at a couple of small clubs in Brooklyn and New Jersey. We rehearse once or twice a week, but no jobs at the moment. You should come and see us."

"If you ever perform in a civilized part of the city, I might. I wouldn't go to Harlem to see Fred and Ginger dance in the nude!"

That was our cue to say good night. Everything had been so pleasant, I had no intention of telling Daddy that I'd left the Rehearsal Club, or that Jimmy and I were living together. There was a tense moment when we were saying good night. Daddy thanked us for coming uptown for dinner instead of meeting somewhere in the middle. I told him that Jimmy was staying in the neighborhood at the YMCA. I didn't want to ruin what had been such a surprisingly grand evening. When it came to Daddy, I was a coward.

We thanked him again for dinner. Daddy shook Jimmy's hand, and as he hugged me he discreetly slipped me a folded twenty-dollar bill. Jimmy and I were elated. A successful evening with my father was rarely so easily accomplished.

♦♦

Sue had arranged for us to see *South Pacific* a few days later. We were excited. It would be the first time Jimmy and I had seen a Broadway show together. Sue had managed house seats right in the middle of the orchestra, about halfway down. I loved seeing Sue-girl up there on the stage. She was great to watch; her radiant smile made it clear just how much she was enjoying herself. Sue and I never suffered from the same competitive virus that afflicts so many actors; she was my best cheering section, and I hers.

Jimmy was strangely subdued throughout the performance. Every time I peeked a look during the show, he had a defensive look on his face. I knew that watching someone else perform—especially a friend—when you're out of work yourself can be pretty tough. Jimmy was excited about his new agent, but what he really needed was work. He kept browsing through his playbill during the show, and when the curtain fell he told me he'd rather linger at the stage door while I ran backstage to greet Sue and give her a big hug.

Sue threw a postmatinee party the following Sunday, and by then Jimmy seemed to have warmed up a little bit. The place was crawling with cast members from the show. We didn't know anyone, but it didn't take long to feel comfortable. Jimmy mingled well when he wanted to. I spent a lot of time talking to Brock about the trio and possible jobs coming up for him. He hinted that he might need an assistant for the summer if he got the job he was applying for, though I could tell he didn't want to get my hopes up too soon.

A little while later I found Jimmy holding court with a small group.

"But you have to really concentrate and keep your mind wide open," Jimmy was saying.

"Open to what?" I asked.

Someone said, "Jimmy wants to hypnotize someone, but no one wants to volunteer. What about you, Dizzy? He's your boyfriend—you must trust him."

*Oh, swell.* I looked at Jimmy. He winked at me. *What does that mean?* He held out his hand for me to take. *What the hell.* I took it and he led me to a straight-back chair.

He started talking to me quietly. "I won't hurt you. Just relax, take deep breaths, and think of a quiet place—a place that means peace to you. Listen to my voice and put yourself into this place . . . " After a bit, I began to relax, to lean into his soothing voice. As he droned on, I fell into a hole of darkness.

The next thing I knew, I was standing in the kitchen doorway, drinking a glass of water. Sue and Brock were applauding me, and everyone was telling Jimmy how terrific he was.

I looked from face to face. "What happened?"

"Jimmy hypnotized you, kiddo," Brock said, and Sue nodded.

"Really? I don't remember. How did I get here in the kitchen?"

"You were a good subject." Jimmy came and hugged me. "I had a hard time breaking the spell after I gave you instructions."

"Instructions?"

"Yeah, posthypnotic instructions."

Later that night, when we were in bed, Jimmy told me what had happened. After he had put me under, he commanded me to stiffen my arm and told me that I wouldn't be able to bend it—and he was right, I couldn't. That was just an exercise to show everybody I was under. Then, before he woke me up, he said that at some point I would get very thirsty and go to the kitchen and drink a glass of water. That's the first time I became aware of anything.

"I didn't know you could do that."

"Someone showed me how when I was in California. I've only done it a couple of times, but you were the hardest to bring back of anyone I've ever tried it with."

"Listening to your voice, I felt like I just wanted to float away. Just turn the corner and never come back."

"Well, I'll never do that again. I want you here."

Someone must have been watching over us, because Fabio called the next day. A new booking had just come along—a two-night weekend gig in the Bronx. I don't remember the name of the place, but it was a friendly neighborhood nightclub with a big dance floor that gave us room to move around.

It felt fabulous, as always, to be performing again. Jimmy was there on Saturday night, and some of the girls from the Club even showed up. But Jimmy was acting downright sullen and rude—even to me—so I left him alone. I didn't need that kind of attitude on my big night. He just sat at the bar alone, drinking. I suppose he expected me to join him there, but I was all jazzed up after the performance, so I flitted from table to table, saying hi to my friends and dishing the dirt.

Finally, when it was time to go and most everyone had left, I found him at the bar.

"You were a barrel of laughs tonight." I smiled.

He took a sip of his drink but didn't say anything, so I ordered a fast beer for the road.

"I'm sorry." He looked down. "I'm in a bad mood tonight, and I just didn't feel like talking to anyone."

"Does that include me?"

"No, of course not. Besides, I'm feeling better now. It always cheers me up to watch you dance. Were your friends offended?"

"Nobody said anything. Anyway, they know you're kinda weird."

"Just kinda?" He finally laughed and leaned over and kissed me sweetly. "I borrowed money today from a friend, so I got twenty for the rent."

"Me too, plus a little left over—so we're okay for a while. Let's go home, Dudley."

Sooner or later I knew I'd have to tell my parents about my living situation. Mom took it in stride. I guess she just chalked it up as an unfortunate choice her daughter had made.

"You're not ready for that—neither of you. How are you going to live? You know I love Jimmy, but your father is going to hit the ceiling."

Well, she was right about that.

Daddy ranted and raved. I was throwing my life away, not concentrating on my talents. He was wasting his money sending me to summer stock, piano lessons, private schools, and for what? To shack up with some child with the breeding of a cow chip?!

"I just wanted to be honest with you, Daddy. Don't you even care how happy we are together?"

"No. And don't expect any help from me, Elizabeth. I'm afraid you're hopeless. And I do not give you my blessings."

So much for honesty.

Around this time, Jimmy finally got a job. He was to appear on a dramatic television show called *Ten Thousand Horses Singing*. He was happy, but it wasn't much, and he knew he was better than the part.

I don't know which was more difficult to live with, the Jimmy who worked a little, or the Jimmy who didn't work at all. Each of them took his share of opportunities to vent and carry on. It never occurred to me when we began living together that I was getting not only Jimmy but also the full bag of neuroses that came with him. Vile moods, interminable silences, anger, guilt, and tantrums. His mercurial mood shifts were integral to his personality, woven into the texture of his being. I found the best way to combat these negative forces was with humor, but that didn't always work.

One day he came home in a particularly bad mood. He took off his jacket and threw it on the floor. His T-shirt was on inside out.

"What am I doing wrong, Diz?"

"Getting out of bed in the morning?"

"Goddammit! I'm serious."

"Well, then, you're doing exactly what you should be doing. You're looking for work. You're studying. You're pursuing your dream. Right?"

"Sometimes I wonder," he shot back. "How long am I supposed to wait for something good to happen?"

"You're loving me and I'm loving you. That's good."

"Loving you is easy. I'm talking about OUT THERE! An idiot could have done that part I just did."

"Not as well."

He wasn't listening. "It wasn't even a part. Just a few lines. NOTHING'S HAPPENING."

"It will, Jimmy. I know it will."

"If I *live* long enough. I want it now. Jesus, I'm ready. I can feel it. Dammit, I come home to you every night empty-handed. I got no job! I got no money! I'm going through all this bullshit so I can prance around a stage. It's insane! Sometimes I feel like killing myself. Sometimes I feel like just getting a gun and blowing my fucking brains out! Death is the only real mystery anyway."

I hadn't been worried until then. When he said those last few words, very quietly, it scared me. I ran to the window, scaring myself with my own fury.

"Why bother?!" I screamed, "Do it. Go ahead, *do it*. Jump." I opened both windows wide. "You don't need a gun! Go ahead. Do it!"

"We're only on the second floor," he mumbled. I don't think he'd ever seen me this out of control. "I'm sorry—"

"Sorry, my ass. What about me, you son of a bitch?" I shouted. "I couldn't bear it without you. What about me? Either do it now, or I never want to hear you say that again. Ever!"

"Okay," he muttered.

"Promise!"

"I promise."

"Make me believe you."

"You're right. I'm selfish. I couldn't do that to you. I was just shooting my mouth off. I just get so down, Diz, you know?"

"Promise me again."

"I promise," he said solemnly. "I promise on my mother's grave that I will never, ever, speak of killing myself again." He added, "To you." And he never did, in my presence.

As spring approached and the weather warmed, we found the time to get up to Larchmont now and then for some of Mom's good cooking. We borrowed the car and went driving in the country. Jimmy drove sometimes a little too fast, but then, so did I.

On one visit, we went looking for our enchanted cottage in the Westchester Sanctuary for Birds, but when we got there we found someone had secured the front door with a big padlock. It seemed we weren't welcome anymore. *And after I'd gone to all that trouble to clean up the place for them.* But we'd come such a long way we couldn't turn back. Instead we spread our blanket near the stream, had a little picnic of bread, cheese, and fruit, and lay down beneath the low afternoon sun, holding each other and talking. As chilly as it was, we took off our clothes from the waist down and made love in childlike defiance.

April roared into town, and it was getting harder and harder to make ends meet. We managed to give Sophie two weeks' rent, but we'd been late before, and this time she gave us a final warning. I thought about going back to Larchmont, but I needed to be in the city if I was ever going to drum up more work. And Jimmy said he could bunk with a friend if push came to shove. Naturally I wondered who.

One night a few weeks later we were propped up in bed, our favorite place to communicate. It was late at night, but early for us. I was patching a hole in the seat of my blue jeans, and Jimmy was reading an article in a magazine about car racing. I was in one of Jimmy's two white T-shirts, and he was in the other. Out of the blue he asked, "How did you learn to drive so well?"

"I've been driving since I was sixteen. Mom taught me. And then, believe it or not, I drove stock cars on a dirt track in Texas. I've always loved to drive."

"I believe it. You're good."

"Thanks. So are you." And I gave him a nudge with my elbow. "A friend of mine had a souped-up Ford, and he let me race it sometimes."

"Driving is such a natural thing to do. I mean, that's how I feel when I'm doing it," he said. "It's almost like the car is another part of me, but I'm in total control. I love the feeling of being in control of something."

"I know. So do I."

"I know it's not me putting out all that energy, but it feels like a part of me. People talk about the thrill of speed, you know? It's true. There *is* a thrill. Maybe some of it has to do with the danger. Like bullfighting."

"I know. I feel like that too. But I try not to think about the danger. It's such a—such a *clean* feeling, cutting through the atmosphere like that."

"Yeah, *clean*. Yeah!" he broke in. "I never thought about it that way. *Clean*. That's good." He was quiet for a while. "What were you doing in Texas?" he asked.

"It's so dumb. After high school, I wanted to see the world without going too far. So a friend and I went to California on a Greyhound bus. It took us about five or six days. We played gin rummy all the way. When we got there I stayed with a friend of Mom's, and Nancy stayed with her aunt. We saw an awful lot, but I wanted to leave after two weeks. After New York, Los Angeles was so boring. Nancy wanted to stay, so I left by myself.

"On my way back home, I got off the bus in Dallas, where another friend of mine lived. He raced stock cars there. That's when I learned to drive really fast. Every Sunday was family day, so these crazy Texans would hold this meet and drive around this dirt track with their wives or mothers-in-law. Anybody who knew how could drive. There were no trophies or anything. It was just a big outdoor barbecue, Texas style, with a few fender benders thrown in."

"Where did you stay, with this guy?" He seemed more than curious. I didn't answer. "I hate that when you act so mysterious," he grunted.

"Well, you have your secrets too, you know."

"Not from you."

I laughed. "Oh, please. You're always running around out there, seeing this person and that and borrowing ties from guys. Always busy doing your 'important things' out there. I never ask you about any of it."

"Nothing out there is as important as what we are in here. That's the truth." I didn't say anything, so he went on. "But I will tell you something that's been bothering me for a long time."

*I don't think I want to hear this.*

"There is this friend, a producer who helped me find work in California. His name is Rogers Brackett. I lived in his house out there for a while. He taught me a lot. He's very intelligent and sensitive, and he was really kind to me. He's well connected. He was the one that got me those two little movie jobs. He took me out to dinner a lot, and he introduced me to his rich friends, who he thought could help my career. To tell you the truth, I liked all the attention. I guess I needed it.

"Well, anyway, he was coming to New York and asked me if I wanted to go. I jumped at the chance, because I knew this was where the theater action was. You remember, Jimmy Whitmore said this was where I ought to be. So I took the train from L.A. with Rogers. He booked a private compartment for just the two of us."

There was a long pause. My heart jumped as I lay there waiting. He looked so sad.

"He came on to me, the first night, on the train." Ah. *The other train story.*

"What do you mean, 'came on'?"

"I'm trying to tell you. I knew what he was, but I guess I was stupid enough to think it wouldn't happen. He didn't threaten me or anything, but he gave me the impression that our relationship depended on this moment. I decided to go along with it. I succumbed to him. I felt bad afterward. Really strange, like a whore. I felt really uncomfortable selling myself like that, so I left him in Chicago, where he had business to take care of, and came to New York on my own."

"You succumbed?"

"Yes," he said, ignoring my sarcasm. "I didn't enjoy it. Christ, he's old enough to be my father. He was very lonely, and I know how that is. I'm not lonely now, because I have you, but I was then, and confused and probably a little scared. So I just sort of let it happen. I figured, what the hell. I never thought I'd find a love like ours. If I had known I was going to meet you, I would never have—uh, well—shit, you know."

As I listened to him, I watched his eyes fill with tears. I believed him. Of course I believed him. But now I couldn't help but wonder if there were other things he hadn't told me. I felt hurt and betrayed, but part of me was desperately trying to understand.

"Why are you telling me this?"

"Because we agreed, no secrets. Remember? Anyway, that was a long time ago."

"Why didn't you tell me sooner?"

"'Cause I was ashamed."

I knew Jimmy had an experimenter's heart. He'd told me he wanted to try everything. As an actor, he wanted to experience all human emotions. But this confession hit me hard. I wasn't shocked, exactly, but suddenly our magical world together, the one we had spun with such good care, was no longer pure. And my mind flew. I began remembering times when he came home in the middle of the night or at dawn, all smiles, but with little one-line explanations: "I fell asleep on the subway." "I met these actors and we stayed up talking till the bars closed." I knew he was an insomniac, so it never entered my mind to doubt him. Now all kinds of inarticulate questions and doubts were flooding my mind. I was silent.

Jimmy went on. "Rogers is in New York again. He wants to help nurture my career." *His career, my ass.* "He has important connections in the theater. He said he can open doors for me. This is an amazing opportunity—but I don't want to lose you. For the first time, I'm starting to like my life in New York. I finally have an agent, and I'm going up for bigger parts. So I want to spend some time with Rogers to try—"

I finally found my voice. "Some time. What do you mean, 'some time'?"

"—and explain how I feel about you. How we feel about each other. I love you. You are the most positive, the realest thing that has ever happened to me. Please believe me."

I wanted to stop listening. I didn't want to hear this. "What do you mean, 'some time'?"

"As long as it takes for me to explain to him how I feel about you. Then I want you to go with me to his apartment. Okay? Just let me talk to him first," he added.

"Let me get this straight. You want me to go with you, hand in hand like Hansel and Gretel, to this man's apartment so that he can see we're a couple?"

"Well, yeah. Will you?"

I felt a chill run down my spine. "You knocked me for a loop there, Dudley. Can I think about it?" I didn't know what else to say.

"That was not an easy thing for me to tell you, Diz."

"Do you think it was easy for me to hear?"

He reached for me, but I pulled away and buried my face in my pillow. I heard him get out of bed and go into the bathroom, heard the toilet flush, heard him brush his teeth, heard him come back. I turned and watched him as he hurried into his clothes. I felt nausea twisting its way down my throat. I wanted to leap out of bed and tear his clothes off so he couldn't leave. But I couldn't move. He grabbed his jacket, looked at me, and said, "Please believe me. Everything is going to be all right. I love you with all my heart. I want to be with you. Only you. Don't worry." And he was out the door.

I sat on the bed and tried to pull myself together. What bothered me as much as the train episode was the dawning realization that Rogers must have been in town for a while. Maybe quite a while. Long enough to lend him a tie, and lend him the rent, and who knows what else?

I hated the deceit. I felt physically ill. My stomach was churning. I had to find a place inside myself to put my pain and disillusionment, and then seal it off if I possibly could. Intellectually I knew I might be able to sort it out; emotionally, there was no way. I was a wreck.

I knew I didn't want to be here when he returned. I needed to think, and I didn't want to seem so available to him. But I didn't want to wake up Sue, either, and I couldn't go to Larchmont and bear up under the questions Mom would toss my way. I really had no place to go. I turned out the lamp and lay there in the dark, feeling sick and angry and confused, but hanging on to Jimmy's last words to me: "Don't worry." I started to cry. It felt good to be doing *something.*

I finally fell asleep, and I was interrupted only much later, when I must have heard a key in the lock. I distinctly heard the door creaking open, and I bolted upright and turned on the lamp. Jimmy was standing over the bed. He looked like hell, and my heart went out to him. He was drunk, and I didn't want to ask him where he had been.

"Where have you been?"

"It doesn't matter," he said. "I couldn't stay away from you any longer. I'm so tired. I just want to sleep. Please, just for now, can we just sleep?"

"*Suuure.*"

I opened my arms and he fell into them. He was crying and I was crying and we curled around each other, kissing tears away. I shut out everything but what the moment held. I tried to think of something else, anything else, but I couldn't.

*Everything will be all right. I know it will.*

When I was too exhausted to worry anymore, I fell asleep.

I awoke to the sound of someone else at the door. I looked at the clock on the desk, and it was ten in the morning. Sunlight was slicing through the room and Jimmy was still asleep.

*Oh, go away. Please go away.*

I stood behind the door and opened it a crack. Sticking my head around the corner, I whispered, "Who is it?"

"It's me, and I've got bad news for you, Dizzy." It was Sophie. She looked grim.

I opened the door wider so she could see Jimmy sleeping.

"I'm sorry, I've done everything I can. There's nothing more I can do. I don't own this dump, you know. The owner wants you out by noon, day after tomorrow. He wanted you out tomorrow, but I talked him into an extra day."

"What?" I said loudly. Jimmy stirred. "Is that legal, Sophie? Can he really do that?"

"Yeah. You know this is a hotel. It's not like regular apartments. You didn't sign a lease. You're supposed to pay in advance here, by the month. You know that. You kids were a week late last month, and this month is almost over and you've only paid for two weeks. I'm sorry. You'll have to forfeit your key money. I can't protect you anymore. I'm really sorry. I like you kids. My husband would have liked you. But those are the breaks, you know? Life stinks." She patted my hand and was gone.

I turned to Jimmy, who was wide awake. "Did you hear that?"

He nodded, rubbing his eyes, sliding his fingers through his hair.

"What are we gonna do?" I sat on the bed. "What in the hell are we going to do?"

"We knew this might happen, Diz, just not so soon. Can you go back to the Rehearsal Club, just temporarily, until we get some money?" He tried to pull me toward him, but I yanked away.

"And then what?" I was unraveling. "And where are *you* going to stay? No, don't tell me. I know where you're going." I started shouting, "No, I can't go back to the Club. I gave up my place there, remember? There's a waiting list a mile long. And I can't go to Mom's because I have to be here in the city to rehearse. Oh, shit. Goddammit to hell."

I went into the bathroom and slammed the door, sat on the toilet sobbing. After a while I got up and washed my face so I wouldn't look pathetic; the cold water felt good, and I stayed there, leaning over the sink, splashing my face, until I heard Jimmy knock.

"Are you okay?" he called through the door. "Please come out and talk to me. Everything is going to be all right."

"Nothing is all right. After last night? I'm still trying to get over *that*. You and that man. Oh, God! That's where you're going, isn't it?"

"I don't know. I don't want to. I don't think so. I have to talk to him." He was mumbling so quietly, I could barely hear him.

"What?" I yelled.

"That man is not what you think he is to me."

"I think he's a queer . . . *and so are you*," I screamed at the top of my lungs. I was sorry the minute it came out.

I desperately wanted to take back my words. I opened the door.

Jimmy was standing there, fully dressed. "I'm sorry I ever told you. I thought you were different. I thought you would understand. But you're just another stupid cunt."

"How *dare* you call me a cunt, you little prick!"

Then it really got nasty. I don't remember all we said, but our words were like long-dormant poisons spewing out of us:

"Queer!" "Cunt!" "Bastard!" "Whore!" And he jumped on the bed, reached for his cape and horns, and yanked them from the wall. Then he was out the door, slamming it behind him. I ran to the door, yanked it open, stood in the hall, and screamed after him: "Olé! You bastard!"

The room never felt so small and ugly. I was humiliated for both of us. All I could think of was to run. I was out the door and down the stairs before I could think twice.

As I passed the desk, Sophie looked up. "I'm sorry."

"It's not your fault, Sophie. I'll turn in my keys tomorrow. I gotta find a place first. I'll be back."

I remember walking to the park, but that didn't make me any happier. I know I wandered the streets. Finally I bought a newspaper and decided to look for a room. How could I pay for a room? What the hell was I going to do?

I automatically headed for the Rehearsal Club and Sue. I didn't want to tell her about Brackett or the fight. I just wanted to borrow enough to get a place to stay and think.

She was there, thank God. The sight of me in her doorway must have scared her; she pulled me into the room, hugged me, and sat me down.

"My God, you look like hell. What are you doing here?"

She looked so concerned, I started to laugh. "I'm sorry. I have a little problem and I didn't know where else to go."

"Of course you didn't. I want you to come to me. How can I help?"

"It's so complicated. Jimmy and I had a big fight. They asked us to leave the Hargrave because we were always late with the rent. Jimmy has friends to stay with. I can't come back here. I don't want to go to Larchmont. I just want to get a little room somewhere. I'm always asking you for help, I know. I'm an idiot. You have an idiot for a friend."

Sue smiled. "Yes, I guess I do."

"Well, I suppose that's better than 'I told you so.'" I smiled back. "O Lord, Sue, I keep making messes that I can't seem to get out of without your help."

"You act with your heart instead of your head, Dizzy. It's not a bad thing, but sometimes it leads to trouble. Asking you to be wise would be a waste of time. I can give you about twenty dollars. That should get you a room with a little left over. That's all I can manage at the moment. Surprise me—do something sensible with it, okay?"

"Sensible. Right. How do you spell that?" I put my arms around her. "Thanks, Sue-girl."

"Anytime, Diz-girl. But do me a favor and just stay here for tonight. We'll plump some pillows on the floor, give you a chance to calm down, make some decisions in the morning. Miss Carleton will never find out—and if she does, so what?"

I didn't even have to think about it.

# 7

Once again Tony came to the rescue. He had family, friends of family, and friends of friends all over the city, so I called him from Baden's on the chance that he might know of a room somewhere. He told me to call him back in about ten minutes.

"Okay, Diz," he said when I did. "I found you a place. It's a little room on the West Side." He gave me an address—some friend of an uncle, cousin of a friend, someone of a someone. "Ask for Big Tony," he said. Then, "Are you and Jimmy split?"

"I don't know, Tony. It's complicated."

"When do you want to rehearse?"

"Soon. I'll call you. Thanks, Tony."

"Hey, anytime. Forget about it. Good luck, Diz. See ya soon, right?"

"Right."

The address was on the West Side, all right—*waay* out west, in the low Forties, off Ninth Avenue on the upper fringes of Hell's Kitchen. It wasn't as bad as it sounds; a few blocks west was the Hudson River and the piers where the luxury liners docked.

I went up the steps of a neglected brownstone, pressed the little black button that read SUPER, and was buzzed in. I pushed the door open and found myself greeted by a bizarre vision—an enormous, oversize man in a dark double-breasted suit with a flashy tie, coming down the hallway in my direction.

"You Dizzy?"

"Yes. Tony said to ask for Big Tony?"

"Surprise! Ha-ha-ha-ha. Wanna see the room?"

"Sure."

Big Tony opened a door leading down to the basement.

"Downstairs—end of the hall next to the boiler. Number four. It's open. I'll wait here—that is, if you don't mind? Ha-ha-ha-ha."

A basement apartment in an old brownstone in New York City can be chic indeed—quaint and adorable, with a private entrance and a little garden in the back. This one wasn't. It was one little room at the end of a narrow, dimly lit hallway. The room was so small that I couldn't open the door more than halfway, because the bed was in the way. Amenities included a well-worn dresser; a tiny basin with a mirror above it, smaller than an eight-by-ten glossy, hanging from a nail by a string; and a closet almost as big as the room itself. It might have been more accurate to call the whole thing a closet with half a room attached. There were no windows, of course. But it was clean and right next to the common bathroom. *Perfect*, I thought. *This is for me.*

I scurried up to ground level. "I'll take it. How much?"

"Ten a week. But hey, you're a friend of Tony's. So make it eight bucks, okay?"

"Okay."

"That's eight bucks up front—always up front, *capisce*? No sad stories—I heard 'em all. My mother died, my bookie left town, my pimp dropped me, ha-ha-ha-ha—I'm just kiddin' ya, kid. Tony told me to look after ya. Any guests, just keep it down, *capisce*?"

*Guests?* "Yes, I kapeesh, and thank you. I really appreciate it. Are there any rules?" I asked as I handed him the money.

"Yeah, one—don't burn the joint down! Ya wanna receipt? Ha-ha-ha-ha!"

Big Tony turned out to be a pussycat. I always felt safe in his care. With his loud, piercing, stuttering, ascending laugh, he seemed to always be cracking himself up. I didn't run into him every day, but whenever I did he was dressed in a suit and ready with that machine-gun laugh.

As beat as I was, I walked uptown to the Hargrave to collect my things. Suddenly the Hargrave looked shabby to me; the smell in the lobby was unpleasant, and Sophie was nowhere in sight.

When I opened the door to our room, a pain shot through me. Jimmy had been there. The closet door was wide open, hangers spilled across the floor. His books and stuff were gone, and red thumbtacks sprinkled the walls where Jimmy's drawings had hung. So I removed mine too, pulling them from the wall one by one. *Books on Table, Egg with Afternoon Shadows*, trees in various stages of foliage—I crumpled them all and threw them in the wastebasket save for the barest of my trees, which I left behind. As I left it, the room looked threadbare and seedy, which I'd never noticed while

Jimmy and I were together—in truth, as it was. There was a long rip in the faux lace curtains. There were brown rust stains in the bathtub; faint spatterings clouded the washbasin mirror. Useless red thumbtacks pocked the walls like measles. How funny, I thought, and started to cry again.

Sophie was downstairs now. "Jesus! Are you all right?"

"No," I sniffed. "I just came to give you my key and say good-bye. Was Jimmy here?"

"Yeah," she said. "About half an hour ago. You just missed him. He rushed through the lobby with his stuff, slammed the key down on the desk, and said, 'She knows where to find me!' No good-bye, no nothin'. What does that mean? I heard you two fighting yesterday."

"Yeah, I bet they heard us in Jersey too. I'm sorry. I wish I could tell you, but it's so complicated. I'm sorry." More tears. "We had to split up for a while. I don't know what's going to happen." I put my key on the desk. "Thanks for everything, Sophie. You've been a real pal."

"I'm so sorry, dearie. The owner's a *putz*. I wish I could have done something more. Could you use a couple of bucks, Dizzy?"

"No, I'm all right. But thanks." I picked up my stuff. "Oh, by the way, I left you a little memento on the wall. If you don't want it, just toss it."

I *still have a few bucks,* I thought. *What the hell, I might as well go in style.* I hailed a cab and hopped in. I was miserable. I began to realize that I had started the whole thing. *Why did I have to call him a queer?* I'd never felt so alone.

It was dark when I got back to my new home. I dumped my clothes on the bed, spread them out, and lay down on top of them, covering myself with my coat, sobbing myself to sleep.

It must have been in the middle of the night that I found myself standing over the little washbasin, a razor blade in my hand. I had no idea how I got there. Water was running over my wrist, which I had begun to slice open. *What? I don't want to die.* I looked into the mirror. My face was all scrunched and wet from crying. The moment was so melodramatic, I burst out laughing. And it was over. There wasn't much blood, just a little trickle—not enough to do any harm, but enough to leave a little scar to carry around with me as a reminder of how foolish I might have been. I wrapped a sock around my wrist and lay back down, too exhausted even to think.

When I opened my eyes again, the light was still on in the room, and I took it as a good sign that I was ravenously hungry. I looked down and saw my wrapped wrist. Only a little blood had seeped through. *What the hell was I thinking! What happened to my beautiful life? Where was Jimmy? I miss him. Goddammit, what happened? It was all my fault. I've got to find him—and apologize, at least.*

I got dressed and left my little hovel, heading crosstown to Jerry's Bar. If Jimmy still cared, he would look for me there.

It was around noon when I entered the bar. A few of the regulars were there, but it was a little too early to be crowded. Without stopping to chat, I rushed to the back phones; maybe Sue or somebody had heard from Jimmy.

There he was, in a phone booth, looking miserable. He hadn't seen me yet, so I let him suffer for a little while before

I gently tapped on the glass. He finally saw me and dropped the phone, and we were in each other's arms.

"I was going crazy. Are you still mad at me?"

"Jimmy. I'm so sorry for the things I said—"

"No, Jesus, I am. I didn't mean any of it—"

"Neither did I. It was my fault. I started it."

"Dizzy, maybe you're right. Maybe I *am* . . . what you said."

No. I knew he couldn't be. "You made a mistake, that's all."

"I know that now. I can't tell you how sleazy it made me feel."

"You're wrong. You're not a queer and I'm not a cunt. I don't even know what a cunt is."

"Neither do I."

"It's down there somewhere, isn't it?"

"Somewhere."

We smiled and kissed and talked, all at the same time. Finally I caught my breath. "Our first fight. . . . Well, our first big fight."

"And we survived. How about that?" Jimmy smiled.

"How about that," I said, suddenly feeling very shy.

"I looked for you at the Rehearsal Club when you weren't at the Hargrave. Jesus! Where have you been?"

He must have asked everybody in Jerry's if they'd seen me, because once they saw we were together all the patrons started cheering and applauding. Instead of answering I turned toward the bar, took Jimmy's hand, and curtsied. Catching on immediately, Jimmy gave a low, solemn bow; then I twirled under his arm to his other side, and curtsied again, giving them what they wanted. Finally we fell into our booth in the back, and I ordered a burger and a Coke.

"I did go to the Club," I told him. "I stayed with Sue, that first night."

"I shouldn't have told you what I did," Jimmy said.

"Yes, you should have," I interrupted. "You thought I'd understand. I should have. But I do now. I really do."

"Jesus, I just let it happen."

"Don't—you don't have to explain. I don't want to hear any more."

I wolfed down my burger as we talked and talked. When we were finished, Jimmy took my hand. "Let's get out of here. Can we go somewhere? Do you have a place?"

"Yeah." I laughed. "Wait till you see it!"

I wanted to ask him where he was staying, but I didn't. This time I kept my mouth shut.

I took Jimmy back to my little room. The minute we sidled our way into my new home, Jimmy laughed out loud. "This is smaller than a bird's nest," he roared. "I love it!" I started laughing with him. And I fell in love with my little nest from that day on.

We lay on the little single bed undressing slowly, melting into each other like rain into a pond. We were more passionate than I think we'd ever been; my feelings reached beyond joy and exhilaration to something deeper, more primal. When I began to feel myself building toward a climax I let it hang and hover, waiting for Jimmy to join me, and when I heard him moan I knew we would make it happen together. I couldn't stand it, but I did. It went on and on, until at last Jimmy heaved a long sigh and stopped.

"No, no, please don't stop! There's more."

"More?"

"Yes!"

He joined my rhythm again, and I climaxed once more. Even my toes were trembling. I was in a place beyond any I'd known before, the greatest sex of my young life.

We lay there side by side together, drenched in perspiration, just touching hands. Neither of us spoke for the longest time. Then finally Jimmy turned to me and smiled. "Now that was—," he said, and in unison we finished, "—really something!"

"That wasn't bad, Dudley."

"Aw shucks, ma'am."

"Do you think you can ever do that again?"

Jimmy looked at me incredulously. "Maybe, but it would probably kill me."

"Yeah, me too, but"—it came to us both at once—"*what a way to go!*"

With the tip of his finger he gently touched the fading little cut on my wrist, but he didn't say a word about it. "Did you bring your sketchbook?" he asked.

"Top drawer of the dresser."

He got the book and a charcoal pencil. "I want to make you a present." He started to draw.

I tried to peek, but no dice. When he finished, he presented it to me proudly: he had filled the page with a drawing of a big window, with a tiny bull way off in the distance. I thanked him with a kiss.

"You need a window in here with a little bull, to remind you of me."

"What did you do with the sketches you tore off the wall?" I asked.

"Threw them in the street. You?"

"The wastebasket. I tidied up and I made the bed. I don't know why."

"Without us in it, the place looked really sad."

"I know. I've been crying for days. I must look like hell—I'm sorry."

"You're beautiful. You need sleep, some food, maybe someone to love you."

"Not anymore."

"Are you sure it's okay for me to be here? We must have disturbed everybody in the place."

"Were we noisy?"

"Oh, yeah!"

We talked for a long time, totally open. I told him how I'd felt after our fight, what it had been like to leave the apartment, even about Big Tony. And I told him my fears for him, for myself, for us. He tried, again, to explain his relationship with Brackett. I listened. I wanted so badly to be grown-up about something I didn't understand. I knew in my heart that he loved and cared for me deeply. And I decided I had to understand, even if I didn't. I needed him and he needed me. He wanted nothing from me but total loyalty, support, and love. In short, everything. Which was just what I needed from him.

He asked me, again, if I would go with him to Brackett's apartment.

"I know you're probably confused about this," he said, "but I think it's important for Rogers to realize how much I love you. I want him to see just how important we are to each other. You and me, I mean. Maybe it will help, maybe it won't, but I want him to know how much I love you."

Well, that helped me make up my mind. I could feel Jimmy's nerves, could feel the hold this man had on him, and my jitters had now been replaced by an overwhelming resentment. I needed to meet Rogers Brackett and get this whole thing out in the open and over with, as soon as possible.

"Let's go," I said.

"Now? You want to go now?"

I nodded. "Yeah, let's do it."

He smiled at me and caressed my cheek with his hand. "I saw a phone upstairs in the hall. I'm going to call and tell him to expect us. I'll be right back."

"Okay. If you run into Big Tony, just tell him you're my pimp." And I mimicked Big Tony's laugh. "Ha-ha-ha-ha!"

I went to the bathroom and took a shower. I thought of leaving my body smelling of our love but decided I didn't want to share that with anyone—Rogers Brackett least of all. Jimmy showered too, using my one towel. We dressed hurriedly and set off for the shoot-out.

Rogers's place was downtown on the West Side, about a dozen blocks or so. It was a beautiful day—it would have been a beautiful day whatever the weather—so we walked. We needed time to plan.

"What do you want me to do, Jimmy?" We were holding hands, taking our time.

"Just be yourself."

"Is Brackett a nice man?"

"He's nice enough."

"What I mean is, should I be nervous about meeting him? I'm not."

"I'm nervous enough for both of us," Jimmy said.

I stopped and looked at him. "I don't understand. Does he mean that much to you?"

"No! No, not emotionally. It's hard to explain. He used to intimidate the hell out of me. He knows that I know he's smarter than me—well, not smarter, but he has more knowledge. And he's, I don't know, sort of *wise*."

"Well, he's a lot older than we are, but being wise doesn't mean anything if you're twisted or nasty." *That didn't come out right.*

"He's done a lot for me. I'd like him to do more, you know? Broadway, his connections and all. We could have a good friendship, if he'd just stop hitting on me. I keep telling him that I'm not that way. He says he isn't so sure."

"Well, I'm sure. My God! Jimmy, after the way we made love today, how could you possibly think you're anything but a stud? A bull?"

"El Toro de Studdo—that's me."

"*My* El Toro de Studdo, savvy?"

"Sí, I savvy."

I thought of Brackett as a predator. A well-connected old queen, paternal and maternal at the same time, taking advantage of a starstruck, impressionable kid who grew up without a father or a mother. But I knew if I told him how I felt, it would only make things worse. The whole time we spent walking to Brackett's, I did my best to shake off my lingering discomfort. I couldn't stand thinking that Jimmy was pre-

senting me as a trophy, using me to make a stand with
Brackett: *See, Rogers, this is my girl, my woman, we're in love. She
is the one I want to have sex with. See, I'm not a queer. I'm a normal
man.* But of course that's exactly what I thought.

"Don't get mad at me for saying this, but are you ashamed
of me?"

"Oh, God, Dizzy, no. You're worth a hundred Bracketts."

"A hundred Bracketts, huh?" I started to laugh. "I'll see
your hundred brackets and raise you two."

And off we went, skipping down the street:

> *One hundred Bracketts of beer on the wall.*
> *One hundred Bracketts of beer.*
> *If one of those Bracketts should happen to fall*
> *There'd still be . . .*
> *Too many Bracketts of beer on the wall.*

And on and on.

We arrived high on silliness—our most powerful defense.
No one could break through it.

Rogers Brackett lived in a building famous for its notable
occupants over the years, including the literary types of the
1920s and 1930s. The building was tasteful and charming,
just like Brackett himself. We were announced from the
lobby. Stepping out of the elevator into an attractive hallway,
I noticed that everything was beige: the walls, the carpet,
even the sconces with their little beige candleholders.

A door immediately opened down the hall, and there was
the man himself, right on cue. I had to refrain from laughing

out loud. Rogers Brackett was color-coordinated with his own hallway: casual but elegant in beige shirt, beige trousers, beige loafers. And his hair? You guessed it.

He waved to us gracefully. "Hello, James. [*James?*] You're a little late, as usual. This must be your lovely lady friend." And he presented me his hand, palm down. *What am I supposed to do, kiss it?* "Welcome to my humble little pied-à-terre." *Oh, not the French thing again.*

I took his hand with an air of confidence and gave it a good shake. I felt calm and in control. "Thank you," I said, and Jimmy and I entered hand in hand.

"Jimmy has told me so much about you." He smiled warmly.

"Oh, dear, I hope it's nothing I have to live up to. That's not fair, I hardly know a thing about you."

Jimmy giggled. I could tell he was getting a kick out of this.

The living room was tasteful and neat, color scheme a creamy beige. Flowers were beautifully arranged in crystal vases, lamps glowed, and a cheerful little fire popped away in a lovely old-fashioned marble fireplace.

"Please," said Rogers, "make yourself at home."

Jimmy held my hand tightly and led me to a pretty velvet couch facing the fireplace. "This is real comfortable," he said, and I wished he hadn't. Still, he never let go of my hand.

"May I get you something to drink? Jim, would you like your usual?" *His usual.* He was moving toward what I'd guessed to be the kitchen when Jimmy leapt up. "I know what she wants. I'll get it." And he was gone.

A warm fire was crackling, and Brackett placed himself in front of the hearth. He picked up a brandy snifter and rolled it around expertly in his palm, taking a big whiff, then a little sip. Then he casually draped his other arm on the small mantelpiece above the fireplace, an actor carefully poised on his mark. He turned to me and the play began.

"Jim tells me they call you Dizzy. How cute. How did that happen?"

*Cute?* I had a feeling he already knew. But I went ahead and told him about my sister.

"And which do you prefer, Dizzy or Elizabeth?"

"I'm used to Dizzy."

"Well, then it's definite." He smiled. "Dizzy it is."

I couldn't resist. "And what should I call you? Roger with an *s*? I've never heard of that."

A slight hesitation, and then a forced smile: "Neither have I."

Just then Jimmy entered, carrying two opened bottles of Champale. "Dizzy's mom is a singer—and she makes a wild pot roast." He ducked back to the kitchen, and came right back with two glasses.

"Really? Where does she sing?" Rogers asked.

Together we chimed, "She sings 'Sing, Sing, Sing' at Sing Sing!"

"What? Sing Sing, the prison, you mean?"

We both nodded. Jimmy poured my drink and we clinked.

"To Casey."

"To Casey."

"Well, isn't that interesting," Brackett said. He didn't bother to ask who Casey was, and we didn't bother to explain Mom's vaudeville days.

"Mom was a concert singer," I explained. "She had quite an interesting career performing with my father, mostly in Europe, but she doesn't give concerts anymore. She goes up to the prison on Sundays, once a month, to sing for the prisoners. They appreciate it, and she finds it very rewarding."

"Well, good for her," Rogers said with a patronizing air. "I understand your father is also a rather well-known pianist."

"No 'rather' about it. Surely you've heard of him."

"Yes, yes I have."

Jimmy squeezed my hand, obviously enjoying himself. There was an awkward moment of silence.

"You have a very lovely apartment," I said.

"Yes, thank you. I quite like it myself," Rogers chuckled. "Especially the fireplace. Many of the old buildings have fireplaces. They really make a room cozy. Do you have a fireplace?"

Jimmy giggled.

"I'm afraid not," I said, laughing. "My apartment is pretty . . . cozy as it is."

Jimmy changed the subject. "I told Rogers about your father's recordings."

Rogers was solicitous as we chatted about Daddy. How many records had my father made? What was his background, training? Blah, blah, blah.

"You're very fortunate, having such an impressive musical background. Jimmy tells me you dance."

"It's my joy in life."

Jimmy jumped in: "You should see her move. I've never seen anyone move so gracefully."

"So you've said." Rogers was curt.

"Yes, he does go on a bit about my dancing. I'd stop him, but frankly I love it."

I was listening to myself speak, not quite sure I knew where this sophisticated badinage was coming from. I must have been tapping into my boarding school upbringing, my Upper East Side society training. I'd tried so hard not to be the lady my father wanted me to be, I was surprised to find it came so naturally.

Rogers dropped some names, most of whom I'd known since I was little: Robert Benchley (my sister's godfather); the famous tenor Frederick Jagel (a schoolmate's father); Alec Wilder (an acquaintance of my father's). But finally he stopped. He could see I wasn't impressed.

I heard myself continue: "My training has been mostly Modern—Hanya Holm, Martha Graham—so I probably need a stronger ballet background. I'm just not happy holding on to a wooden bar, bending my knees while some over-the-hill lady slams her stick on the floor to keep time. It's so strict and rigid. I know I need the strength, but the hell with it." Rogers laughed. "The first dance teacher I ever had was Anita Zahn, a pupil of Isadora Duncan. Miss Zahn was a good friend of Daddy's, a very good friend."

"Aaah . . . ," Rogers said, and got busy revolving his brandy snifter.

Jimmy was surprised. "I didn't know that!"

"Well, you don't think I tell you everything, do you?" I said coyly.

Rogers seemed uncomfortable, trying to get a word in edgewise between us two lovers. "I'm not too familiar with the world of modern dance, but more with ballet and, of course, literature and theater. Tell me, are you planning on following a career as a dancer?"

"She sings too!" Jimmy burst out.

"My, is there anything you can't do?"

"There must be," I answered.

Jimmy laughed. "She rides a mean horse. Won a medal in a horse show in Madison Square Garden."

"Ah, so you're a championship horsewoman too?"

"Horsegirl, actually. When I was eleven or twelve years old, I began studying at a riding academy."

"My, my. That's very impressive."

"Not really—there were many great riders there. But what was impressive, I suppose, was the name of the school: the New Canaan Mounted Troop of America. Uniforms and all. After a couple of years I became an instructor on scholarship, and I rode all the time—after school, weekends, and summers."

"I always found horses terribly intimidating," Brackett added. "I understand they're not too bright."

"Yes, just like people—some not too bright and some quite intelligent. Oh, they're so wonderful! All they need is for you to show them who's boss. A lot depends on how they're treated. Just like people," I repeated knowingly.

"Would you care for another Champale?"

"No, thank you. I'm afraid I must go. I have a rehearsal. This has been so pleasant, I hate to tear myself away, but I really must go. Jimmy wanted us to meet and I'm glad we did." I took Rogers's hand. "You've been very gracious."

"You're a charming girl, Dizzy. Glad you stopped by. I hope we meet again sometime."

"You never know," I said, smiling.

Jimmy stood up. "I'll walk you out." He turned to Rogers. "I'll be right back."

Once we were out in the hallway, Jimmy wheeled me around and hugged me.

"You were so great in there. You didn't let him get to you. I think you got to him. I'm so proud of you."

"Yeah, I was kinda good, wasn't I?"

He kissed me tenderly, and we made plans to meet later. He said he had to clear up some things with Rogers, and he went back inside as I headed for the elevator.

I was sure now that what Jimmy wanted was both of us: me to fill his heart, and Rogers to fill his head with knowledge and guidance. I think Rogers wanted too much from Jimmy in return—more than Jimmy was willing to give. At least that's the way I saw it that day.

From that afternoon on, Rogers Brackett seemed to fade out of the picture. He had been instrumental in steering Jimmy toward a career that was about to open up. I don't believe that Jimmy was gay in his heart, at least not at that time. I'm sure of that. But I knew how driven he was to become an actor. *You can drink a glass of wine with dinner, I* thought, *but that makes you a drinker, not a drunk*—a simplistic thought, I knew even then, but that's the way I chose to see it.

In this respect, as in so many others, I felt I understood Jimmy because we were so very similar. Neither of us had grown up very comfortably. We were both shy, and I think each of us lacked perspective on the real world. We were not well anchored; we both needed constant assurance of love. And we found in each other a source of strength and balance. We had no plans, just faith—blind though it may have been— that everything would work out for the best.

That night, when Jimmy showed up at my room, it was as if we had been through a trial together and had survived and triumphed. We were consumed with glee.

"Hey, let's celebrate," he said. "Let's have a party."

"Here?"

"Why not?"

"That should be cozy, even without a fireplace."

"I'll light a match."

"Perfect. Let's make it a cocktail party. I'll serve champagne and caviar—you know, keep it simple."

"Oh, yeah, and some of those little cocktail weenies."

"Perfect. Champagne, caviar, and weenies."

We spent the rest of the night giggling, making love, and composing our guest list: Albert Schweitzer, Noël Coward, Tracy and Hepburn, Queen Elizabeth, Big Tony—and, of course, Moondog.

## 8

The middle of May saw a flurry of activity. Brock was hired as resident choreographer for the summer at a resort area called Sommers Point in Ocean City, just outside of Atlantic City—down by the old New Jersey shore! He asked me to be his assistant for the summer, to work on the musicals and also appear in them. We would be doing one show at night and rehearsing another during the day. Sometimes the theater would devote a week to another troupe's play, which would give us a breather, but most of the time Brock and I would be working away. A crank-'em-out kind of theatrical experience for sure, but a job doing what I love.

I was thrilled. Jimmy was ambivalent. He said he was glad for me—but he wanted me to commute.

"I don't think so," I told him. "I have no car, Jimmy. And I can't take the bus. It'd cost too much, take up too much time."

"I don't want to stay here alone," he interrupted. "Oh, Christ, I'll miss you. Who will I pick on? Who will make me smile?"

"Tell me not to go and I won't go," I said.

"It's your chance to dance every day, Diz."

"I know, but I don't want to be away from you all summer."

"It's not China, for Christ's sake, it's just New Jersey. I'll come visit and you can come to the city on your day off."

"I guess so. I'd love to do it," I said.

"I gotta be honest, Dizzy, if it was me, I'd go. You know I would." I appreciated his being straight with me.

"Well, maybe Brock can get you a job down there."

"Doing what?"

"Oh, I don't know. Doing a monologue between acts. An entr'acte with flair. Maybe you can wander through the audience, sell hot dogs."

"You're just too funny for me."

I didn't have to leave until the end of June, I told him. There would be plenty of time to figure out what to do.

Brock wanted to get a jump on the summer, so he rented a studio in Midtown where we could get started on all three musicals: *Best Foot Forward*, *Finian's Rainbow*, and *Brigadoon*.

I was in heaven. I was guaranteed at least two good parts: I would have a chance to be funny as the Blind Date in *Best Foot Forward* and, better yet, a solo dance number as Maggie in *Brigadoon*—the funeral dance in the last act. We started working a few evenings during the week, and afternoons every weekend.

One evening Jimmy came to pick us all up for a night out after rehearsal. He'd planned the whole evening but wouldn't tell us anything about what he had in store. When he arrived, Brock was showing me a new lift we were going to use in *Brigadoon*—the bird lift, it was called—and it was tough. I would run at him and he would bend as I jumped, catch his hands on my pelvic bones, and lift me high into the air to carry me across the floor. We had to time it just right to make it look smooth, so we were drilling it over and over again.

Jimmy was pacing in the corner, anxious to go. Sue was our audience and she was directing us like a traffic cop. "Too fast . . . Look out . . . you're listing to the left . . . That last one was awful! . . . It's supposed to look *effortless* . . . why don't you try it again?"

Brock interrupted, "Why don't you give us a break? It's just gonna take practice and time."

Jimmy grunted. "That's time we don't have. I don't want to miss the movie. We have to see it from the beginning." No one was paying any attention to him.

I must have come running at Brock a hundred times, over and over, being lifted when we got lucky, falling on top of him when we didn't. Then, out of nowhere, we heard a shrill whistle. Everyone stopped to look around—and there was Jimmy, standing in the doorway, his fingers between his teeth, his pants dropped around his ankles. That boy knew how to draw an audience.

"Good Lord!" Sue shrieked. Brock snorted. I was used to Jimmy by now; I just chuckled. "Well, you have our full attention. I'll go change. Let's go to the movies." I ran off to change.

I could tell Brock was upset by Jimmy's behavior. Any other time Jimmy would have been interested in watching us work out choreography, but something had obviously happened to sour his mood. One of his favorite roles was the child who had to get his way, and if he didn't he could be despicable. If his feelings were hurt or if he felt betrayed, he could be unforgiving for days. On the other hand, once he managed to get his way, he could be sweet, gentle, and endearing—on his own terms, naturally. More than anything, though, he needed attention, to touch and be touched. From me he demanded constant demonstrations of my love. It was so evident that he was turning to me to make up for some emptiness inside of him, to fill him up and heal his wounds. It was a lot to expect from someone so young, someone with her own needs, but I tried.

We arrived at the movie house on Forty-second Street. *Has Anybody Seen My Gal?*, the marquee read. We couldn't believe it. "You dragged us out to see *this* stupid movie?" Brock asked.

"I have my reasons," said Jimmy, a mischievous smile creeping over his face. Sue was silent. I guess we had all decided to placate him. He was being mysterious, and we were getting curious.

We settled in, popcorn and Cokes all around. Suddenly, it was clear why we were there. There was Jimmy up on the screen, walking into a soda fountain, ordering something from Charles Coburn, that wonderful actor, who'd somehow been roped into playing a soda jerk in this B programmer.

"Hey, gramps," said Jimmy's character. "I'll have a choc malt, heavy on the choc, plenty of milk, four spoons of malt, two scoops of vanilla ice cream, one mixed with the rest and one floating."

We heard scattered titters around us, and Jimmy slid down in his seat. If this was Hollywood's idea of snappy teenage dialogue, no wonder the youth of the time felt alienated. But Brock, Sue, and I clapped and whistled. When the scene was over, I whispered to Jimmy, "Is that the only scene?"

"Yeah, this movie stinks. Let's go." He seemed embarrassed by the crowd's reaction, and I felt sorry for him. Sue and Brock had had enough of his moods and they decided to stay, so the two of us slipped out together.

Walking home, Jimmy asked, "Why am I such an asshole, Diz? I spoiled your rehearsal and for what? I didn't realize it would be that bad. It was bad, wasn't it?"

"Yes," I said, "but you looked terrific. The camera loves you, and you did great with what you had to work with—dumb dialogue." Jimmy grunted and I kept going. "Let's face it, Brando couldn't have done any better."

"Brando wouldn't have done it in the first place."

"Well, not now, he wouldn't. When you're as famous as he is, then you can do whatever you want. I bet he did some small parts when *he* was starting out."

"Yeah, *Streetcar*. Now *there's* a fuckin' small part to launch a career."

"I guess you got me there. But he started on the stage. He must have said 'Dinner is served' somewhere, sometime."

He knew I would tell him the truth; I knew it wouldn't make him feel much better.

The unexpected arrival of an old Los Angeles friend of Jimmy's gave us a welcome diversion that spring. Bill Bast was an aspiring writer; the two had been roommates in L.A., and now Bill had come to New York to look for work. I liked Bill. He was bright, witty, and far more sensible than Jimmy and I ever were.

Our first meeting occurred in Central Park. It was a gorgeous day, so I'd decided to rehearse beneath the sun, the grass between my bare toes.

I could see Jimmy loping across the lawn, waving. Trailing behind him was a boy who looked about the same age, nice-looking, pale-skinned with dark hair—a boy who seemed as comfortable as Jimmy was high-strung. Jimmy danced up to me; I leapt into his arms, he swung me high into the air, and as I was coming down our feet tangled and we crashed to the ground together like a pair of rag dolls. As we were rolling around, laughing and sparring, I looked up at Bill.

"Hi," I panted.

"Dizzy, meet Bill." Jimmy smiled.

"Are you really Dizzy?" Bill asked.

"I try to be," I answered.

"I guess you'd have to be, hanging around with this guy."

I nodded. "You've got a point there."

Jimmy giggled. "Bill just got in from California, so I'm showing him around. I helped him get a room with two beds at the Iroquois, so now I have a place to flop when you go to New Jersey. Wanna go get something to eat?"

"Sure," I said, but nobody moved. The sun was strong, and a breeze had wafted up to cool us. It was much too pleasant to move on. We lay on our backs on the grass and looked up at the sky. Three fast friends relaxing in Central Park, full of joy, full of ourselves, full of New York City.

Count on me to break it up. "I'm *huungry*."

Jimmy yanked at my pigtail. "You're *always* hungry."

"That means she's alive and well," Bill said, throwing in a word for my side.

"Thank you," I said. He nodded and smiled. Still, no one moved.

"I think I'm going to like it here," Bill said quietly.

"I hope so," I asked. "Why'd you leave California?"

"New opportunities, more to write about—maybe a new perspective, you know? A change of scene. I'm not sure. Why not? Why the hell not, when I'm still young and ready?"

"You won't always be young, but you'll always be ready." Jimmy snickered.

"Ready for what?" I asked.

The two of them just looked at each other—a private joke, a wink. I let it be.

"Guess what?" I sat up.

Chorus for two: "You're *hungry!*"

"Lucky guess."

Jimmy offered me his hand and pulled me to my feet. The three of us left the park, heading toward Jerry's for lunch. I was still barefoot, my shoes in one hand, the other in Jimmy's rear pocket. It was nice to see Jimmy so relaxed; we'd never spent too much time around other people, but Bill seemed to fit right in with our silliness, and from the start I felt as comfortable with him as Jimmy obviously did.

We headed for the exit at Fifty-ninth and Fifth, down that long, curving bench-lined walk, dotted with people sitting and reading, old habitués feeding their pigeons, and children playing on the grass. We emerged at just the spot where the hansom cabs stood waiting for tourists, their poor old horses standing and nodding in the summer sun. We crossed the street to visit the Plaza Hotel, to show Bill the Oak Room and the lovely Palm Court filled with beautiful people having their tea and whatever. Then it was out onto Fifth Avenue and over to F. A. O. Schwarz, where the three of us had a little playtime before heading to Jerry's and *food*.

Jimmy and I would have great fun showing Bill the city in the days to come. The museums; the planetarium; even Battery Park, where the Staten Island ferry docked; seeing the city through Bill's eyes was like meeting an old friend for the first time.

It wasn't long before Bill found himself a job at CBS—it wasn't much, just enough to pay for room and board and a trifle to spare, while he spent his quality time as a writer/observer. At the same time, Jimmy's agent finally began getting some work for him. Small parts on live TV dramas with names like *Sleeping Dogs* and *Prologue to Glory*. Then a part on a radio show for the U.S. *Steel Hour* called "Abraham Lincoln" caused a little flurry of interest in Jimmy, and other small jobs started coming along. I was happy for him. He, of course, wanted more. He craved the center ring and the respect he believed would come with it. And while he was waiting I held him, and whispered to him to hold on.

# 9

By the time I was with Jimmy, I was an old hand at summer
stock. My first experience occurred during my teens, when
my father arranged for me to serve an apprenticeship at the
Lenox Playhouse in Lenox, Massachusetts. The Playhouse
was right across the road from the Tanglewood Summer
Music Festival. All the events at Tanglewood were held outside—music alfresco, the way it was done on the concert
stages in Central Park and the Hollywood Bowl. When I had
time off I would cross the street and lie on the rolling lawns
with my friends, listening to the musicians rehearsing for
their evening concerts. It was glorious lying there on a perfect summer's day, a rich blend of music and nature, sounds
gliding on the air, their harmonies shimmering through the
trees.

My roommate for that summer was Rosie Thurber, James
Thurber's daughter. Like her father, Rosie had a great sense of
humor. We were both apprentices, working backstage and
painting scenery; before the summer was out Rosie and I had
almost single-handedly dug a long ditch along the driveway
leading up to the theater, for reasons long forgotten. But in
return for our hard work we got to participate in the theater's

acting, singing, and dancing classes, and along the way we learned some handy stagecraft lessons about designing sets and lighting stages. Best of all, we got to appear in that summer's productions. Rosie and I each played medicine bottles in Molière's *The Imaginary Invalid*. Then we performed as lepers in *St. Francis of Assisi*. Not exactly starring roles, but no matter: we were in show business. I'm not sure just what I was ready for when that summer was over . . . with the possible exception of Ocean City, New Jersey, which is after all where I landed in the summer of 1952.

John Dwight, the producer of the Gateway Playhouse at Somers Point in Ocean City, had bought a 1920s-vintage nightclub and casino and given it a jiffy conversion into a summer theater. All he seemed to have done, in any event, was build a stage and line up some folding chairs—as many as possible. Then he lined up some eager actors and apprentices to sweep it, paint it, knock together a few sets, and they were ready to put on a show.

There was a narrow rectangular building in the back of the theater that passed for housing—a set of long halls with cell-like rooms on either side. We were all two to a room, boys upstairs and girls down, and one bathroom on each floor. I wouldn't have been a bit surprised if these little cubicles had been rented out, at one bygone time or another, by the hour. I shared a room with another girl; it was fine for sleeping, but that was about it.

John Dwight lived up the street with his mother in a nice big house. He wore white tennis shorts and sneakers with no socks. Always. He knew how to count his pennies, and he had an attitude about it. The most helpful instruction he ever gave us was also the simplest: "Make it happen." John Dwight was not beloved, and neither was his mother's cooking. We ate every meal at her house: cornflakes for breakfast, apple butter and peanut butter sandwiches for lunch, and dinners that have since been blocked from my memory. As Brock put it himself, "This was a hip-pocket operation."

The actors were for the most part apprentices, working without pay in return for half a room, Mrs. Dwight's "nourishing" meals, and the experience. Brock and I were on salary, but our checks were usually late. We helped keep the place clean, mopping floors and taking care of whatever other unpleasant things needed to be done. With our double-duty schedule of performance and rehearsal we knew we were underpaid, but we gave it our all. And it wasn't easy: two apprentices left after a few days, and another in the middle of the season. No guts, no glory.

The first eight days were spent settling in, getting to know one another. Pecking order was established quickly. Those who knew what needed to be done and how to do it were easily distinguished from those who didn't have a clue. But we all dove in, and day by day our crazy crew grew into a real community.

In the mornings, Brock and I organized exercise classes and dance classes; then Ed Sellick, our musical conductor, led us through vocal gymnastics; that gave him a chance to learn our voices so he could organize the chorus and choose the soloists. The afternoon was given over to rehearsals, reading through a new script, and putting it on its feet.

Bert Griscom was the director of all musical productions. He'd had a long association with the Playhouse, dating back to the start of his parents' summer residency in Ocean City some thirty years before. He had worked in all phases of show business, serving as entertainment director in the United States Air Force, staging shows on riverboats, vaudeville, and burlesque, even mounting spectacles in Hollywood. He had worked with Gloria Swanson, Abbott and Costello, and Dorothy Lamour, and he'd have been glad to tell us a million stories if we'd ever had time to hear them. But we worked twelve- to fourteen-hour days, so any leisure time that came our way was taken up, by and large, with passing out.

It's a challenge, trying to describe the elation that flows through a theatrical troupe after a successful opening night. There is satisfaction over a job well done, of course, but also a family closeness that comes from doing it together, and under a crushing (and rock-solid) deadline. We opened *Finian's Rainbow* on the ninth day in, and the audience . . . well, they didn't *love* it, but they didn't hate it, either. For our part, we were overjoyed. It was becoming clear that we had a cast of some promise. We all hugged and congratulated one another—and the next morning we started work on *Best Foot Forward*.

I made some long-lasting friendships that summer. Alex Burke, Art Ostrin, and Guy Little were my closest friends, along with Brock, of course. Alex we lost to the AIDS virus in the early days of that disease, but Art and I have kept in touch ever since that Ocean City summer; he still lives in New York and is still a very busy working actor. Guy owns and runs a regional theater. Brock, too, would go on to thrive: after some adventures far afield of the stage, he would return to earn a Ph.D. in theater and playwriting. And he became a Presbyterian minister, preaching and teaching in his hometown of Tulsa.

The days I spent with those guys were busy ones, but if we made time, we sometimes got the chance to walk the few blocks to the ocean to unwind a bit on the beach or have a drink at one of the bars. The extended boardwalk of Atlantic City was only a little farther up, and it led right up the coast to that funhouse world of big bars, restaurants, and amusement park rides.

Jimmy and I tried to talk every day.

"I miss you."

"I miss you too. I'm working my ass off here."

"Well, don't work it all off—save some for me. When are you coming to the city?"

"When are you coming to the shore?"

"Soon, I think. I got a bus schedule and I'm working on it."

"Are you staying with Bill?"

"Yeah, but I'm not sleeping too well. I still got those insomnia blues. I'm still wandering around town most nights. I go to some of our places, where you and I used to play, but it's not the same. Life's so empty without you."

"Well, you always have Bill for a playmate."

"It's not the same."

"I hope not. Come see me and I'll make it up to you."

Soon afterward Jimmy showed up for a weekend to surprise me, pleasing me no end. He couldn't stay longer—he had an audition—but he planned to come back with Sue for the final week, so that we could go home together. Perfect: the last show was *Brigadoon,* so Jimmy would get to see me enact Maggie's funeral dance.

That first trip down was nothing but pleasure. Jimmy brought a toothbrush and a few books. "Traveling light," he called it. He wanted to go swimming, so I loaned him back a pair of cutoff jeans he had given me. My roommate wasn't about to give up her bed, but there was an extra cot in Guy Little's room on the boys' floor, and he was kind enough to let Jimmy stay with him. Jimmy slept, read, watched rehearsals, helped me with my lines, and used the time to relax as much as he could. We had to keep him hidden, and we had a fine time making it into a game, which he loved.

Being together, away from the city, was very good for both of us. We swam together and sunbathed together and our love for each other seemed as strong as ever.

"You are my constant thought," he said as we were wading along the shore. "You are my steady light."

"I am your Betty Beacon," I yelled as he pulled me into the ocean.

After the parade of traumas we'd suffered together, it was so wonderful to see Jimmy unwinding like this. Waist high in the surf, I started singing "The Tennessee Waltz." He joined me at once, just as he had when we sat face-to-face in the bathtub, playing with each other's toes, in our little room at the Bevan.

"Tell me," he asked, "do you always have to be in the water when you sing that song?"

"Yes, being buoyant is the only way I can hit the high notes."

"You are my high note, my little diva-doo, my colorful coloratura!" he yelled in my ear. His skin was brown and glistening in the sun. We kissed and clung. We looked up and down the beach, but no one seemed interested in us, so we began rubbing our bodies together, moaning in delight. Letting my hand trace his body beneath the waves, I playfully ran my hand up his inner thigh.

"My God, Jimmy, where's your thing? What happened to your thing?"

"It's still there, it's just shrunk. It's the cold water. Don't you know anything?"

"I know that's the littlest pecker I've ever felt."

"Well?"

"Well *what*, El Toro de Studdo?"

I was rubbing my body against him in burlesque ecstasy, gasping and screaming like a good little actress. Jimmy clapped his hand over my mouth, but I pulled his hand away. "*Ohhh*, that was *wonderful*! *Sooo* satisfying."

"You owe me one."

"Okay."

Jimmy caught the last bus back to the city that night. I know he felt better, but he looked so sad. I felt the same way. At least I had a lot of hard work ahead of me to keep me out of trouble.

I had a small comic role in *Best Foot Forward*, and I found out, for the first time, that I could be funny onstage. It came so naturally I was thrilled. I played the Blind Date, opposite Art, and the whole affair gave Brock a chance to create some inspired choreography, mixing up all the classic moves of the time with a sampling of Brock originals. He made it a treat, and the audiences ate it up.

After *Best Foot Forward* we finally got a Sunday off, a little breather while the theater mounted the play for the coming week. Guy had posted a notice that he was driving to New York right after the Saturday night show to catch a Sunday matinee of *Pal Joey,* and driving back right after the show. As soon as I spotted it, I put my name on the list. I was the only one who signed up. Everybody else was wiped out, or too busy rehearsing next week's play. I made a quick call to Jimmy.

"I've got a nice surprise for you."

"You're pregnant?"

"Yes, twins. Isn't that wonderful?"

"Really?"

"No, not really, Dudley, I got a ride into New York. Should I come?"

"Yeah, and hurry. I'm bored stiff."

"Well, save some for me."

"Okay. I'll meet you at the hotel." And we hung up laughing.

Now, Guy's pride and joy was a chartreuse 1946 Ford convertible, which he loved dearly. When he dropped me off at the Iroquois, Jimmy was out front, waiting. After we kissed, he took one look at the car and gave out with a wolf whistle.

"You like my little speedster?"

"Oh, yeah, she's beautiful! What'll she do?"

"You mean, how fast will she go. I don't know. I've had her up to seventy."

"That's all?"

"Well, that's pretty fast. I gotta go. You guys have fun. Don't do anything I wouldn't do. See you tomorrow—bye."

Guy drove away, and Jimmy and I turned to go. "I know it's late, but do you want to go to Jerry's? Are you hungry?"

"Silly question."

He put his arm around me and we headed off. "Are you sure Bill doesn't mind if I stay with you tonight?" I asked.

"No, Bill likes you. He thinks you're funny."

"How are you two boys getting along?"

"I'm driving Bill crazy, as usual. Our hours are so different. When he's tired, I'm ready to play. Can you believe he doesn't like my recorder playing?"

"Well, maybe he's not a music lover."

"You do, don't you?"

"Do what?"

"You know what."

"Honey, your playing is truly *unbelieeevable*. By the way, have you seen Moondog lately?"

"A couple of times. He seems to move around a lot. I worry about him, all covered in leather in this heat, but he says it doesn't bother him. Mind over matter. He's always pretty serene. He always asks me, 'How's Dizzy? I miss her,' and says, 'She always made me laugh.'"

"Maybe we'll try and find him tomorrow."

We were walking up Sixth Avenue. It was hot, there was no breeze, and the streets were nearly empty, but for an occasional cab gliding by.

"I wish I was in the ocean with you right now," I said.

"Or on our beach, under the stars. Yeah, I've been thinking about that since I got back to the city."

"Why don't you come back with us? I'm sure Guy will let you stay with him again. You did thank him for his hospitality, didn't you?"

"I don't know. I guess so." Jimmy stopped and took my hands. "I miss you so much."

"I know. I miss you too. Come back with me. We'll ride the roller coaster. You can unwind, and we'll walk on the beach along the water and race the tides."

"Yeah, I'm not doing shit here. I wanna go get seashells by the seashore with my Betty Beacon!"

I was beaming, but I was flagging too, so we turned on a dime and headed back to the Iroquois hand in hand. We tiptoed into their room, past a dozing Bill. He opened one eye, grunted "Hello, Dizzy," and rolled over.

Jimmy and I snuggled into bed, and I fell asleep during our last kiss.

W e slept in, until around one. When we stirred, we saw Bill wasn't there; he had left a note saying he wouldn't be back until dark.

"What do you want to do, Mr. Dean?"

"I dunno. What do you wanna do, Mrs. Dean?"

We laughed and made love until hunger set in. Then we showered and dressed, and Jimmy left Bill a note with a silly picture of us standing on the beach, with the caption "Off to the shore with Diz for a week." We left to get something to eat before meeting Guy outside the theater.

The matinee was letting out just as we got there. Guy was exuberant, wide-eyed with thrill over *Pal Joey*, but he was exhausted.

"If you're tired, I can drive," Jimmy jumped in.

"Are you a good driver?"

"Tell him, Diz."

"He's a terrific driver," I said, and that was it. Guy was grateful to Jimmy, but that wouldn't last long.

We wound slowly through the Sunday-in-New-York Midtown traffic. All the theaters were emptying, and the streets were full. I rode shotgun; Guy gave Jimmy directions back to Ocean City, then dozed off almost immediately in the backseat.

Jimmy was in heaven. He loved to drive, and as usual, he was relaxed and happy behind the wheel. The minute we crossed the Hudson River, he became Hot Rod Harry. We went into another gear and over the treetops. There was so much cackling going on behind the wheel, Guy woke up and screamed.

"My God, slow down! Who are you chasing?"

"Hey, man, we're not going fast. I usually drive much faster than this."

I'd been daydreaming out the window, not paying too much attention. I was used to the way Jimmy drove, and besides I liked it.

"Jimmy, maybe you better slow down," I said. "It's Guy's car."

"Maybe we better stop for coffee," Guy offered. "I can take it from there."

"Hey, I'll stop if you want, but why don't I just slow down? I guess everybody's different about speed."

"I guess." Guy was not amused.

"He promises," I added, putting my hand on Jimmy's thigh. We needed to stay in Guy's good graces; I was hoping Jimmy could stay with him again.

Jimmy eased up, and even after we made a pit stop Guy allowed Jimmy to drive the rest of the way—as long as he could sit in front and keep his eye on the speedometer.

Jimmy ended up spending the entire week with us. We were always together—at least when I wasn't in rehearsals. Before long everybody was used to having him around, and he became one of the group—just another crazy actor.

Jimmy was the most unobtrusive of roommates; Guy always claimed he was unaware he was sharing his room. When we were in rehearsals, Jimmy was sleeping. When the cast was digging into one of Mrs. Dwight's dubious lunches, Jimmy and I were sharing sandwiches on the beach or on (or under) the boardwalk, and when we went back to rehearsals in the afternoon, Jimmy headed back to Guy's room to read or have a nap. After I snuck him some dinner, the evening was ours. We had drinks in the neighborhood, at the inn up the hill or at the D'Orios Cafe, where there was a great piano player. And every night we walked the beach hand in hand, scraping our toes in the sand. Like little children, we played games throwing sticks and stones or seashells, and we whispered promises we knew, in our hearts, we wanted to keep.

One day we got the idea to spend the whole night on the beach. No matter how uncomfortable everyone said we would be, it was just too romantic a notion for us to resist, and we chalked up all the naysaying to envy. After all, all that lovey-dovey cooing was bound to be getting on everyone's nerves. But what did we care?

We took a couple of blankets, a thermos of hot coffee, some bundled-up clothes for pillows, and we were in heaven—or under it. We talked and smoked and loved and filled our hearts.

"You know, Diz, when we die, we'll live on clouds and we will find the Little Prince and make him laugh. He'll like us, Diz. Don't you think?"

I found it so dear that he was really wondering if the Little Prince would like us. "Of course he will. He'll *love* us!"

"We'll bring him roses. Maybe a whole basket. Red ones."

"And some yellow ones too. Okay?"

"Maybe he has his princess by now. His rose. You think?"

"I'm sure of it." I thought for a moment. "Do you think there's really a Little Prince sitting up there on his planet looking down at us?"

"I hope there's something up there looking down on us." Jimmy's voice had taken on such a sadness that I looked over at him.

"Don't be sad," I said, "there's a lot to be happy about right now. It might not always be that way, but right now, this is our time."

He turned to me. "I'm not really sad; I was just thinking how awful life would have been if we'd never met."

"I know. I've thought about it too. I think it was fate, Jimmy. I think we were destined to be with each other."

"And you'll always be part of me," he whispered in my ear. "Intertwined for eternity."

"Intertwined?" I giggled. "I like that. Did you read that somewhere?"

"Yeah, on the wall in the men's room at Jerry's."

"Very funny."

We kissed good night for a while, then looked up to the stars and blew a kiss to the Little Prince. When we awoke, at dawn, we were stuck together like two Popsicles.

At the end of the week Jimmy took the bus back to the city, promising to return for the final show. I told him I'd call Sue; she'd said she might be coming, and maybe they could share a ride. As he was leaving he told me he was taking a trip on "the high seas" for ten days, so he wouldn't be reachable for a while, but he promised he'd be back in plenty of time for our closing show. It seemed that Lemuel Ayers and his wife, Shirley, whom Jimmy had met through Rogers Brackett when they weekended earlier in the summer at Ayers's country home in Nyack, New York, had invited a small group of people on a trip to Martha's Vineyard on their chartered yacht. Jimmy had been asked along as part of the crew, along with Rogers and Alec Wilder, who was writing the incidental music for a new play Ayers was preparing for Broadway, *See the Jaguar*. Brackett had recommended Jimmy for a role; Ayers thought he was too inexperienced, but Jimmy saw the trip as his chance to change Ayers's mind.

I'd long since given up any further discussion of Jimmy's relationship with Brackett; I'd made up my mind to trust him, and that was that. As I waved good-bye to him at the bus station, I hugged him and gave him a long look. "Be careful, Dudley, don't fall overboard."

B*rigadoon* was my favorite musical, and Jimmy's too; its fairy-tale Scottish setting and magical storyline, concerning a bewitched village whose denizens come to life for only one day each century, charmed us both—and gave the cast of our little production plenty of laughs. Two days into the rehearsals we were all *rrrrrolling* our *r*s as if we were anticipating the dramatic debut of Sean Connery himself. Only Brock, who was playing the villain, Harry Beaton, strayed from the fold; instead of getting in the way, his Oklahoma drawl made him seem all the more menacing: "I must leave this *currrrsed taaown*," I can hear him bray, and I still smile to think of it.

I played Maggie Anderson, a mute young villager who has fallen passionately in love with the doomed Harry. Toward the end of the show comes a sequence when she dances over the pyre of her lost lover, against a background of mournful pipes, and it was a moment I relished. At one moment there comes a dramatic sweep in the music, when Maggie is carried across stage to lower herself and cover her lover's corpse with her body, and the bird lift Brock and I had worked so hard to perfect brought down the curtain with a grace that thrilled us as much as the audience.

Closing night, the show was sold out. Sue and Jimmy appeared together as promised, and Brock and I made sure they had good seats up front. I was thrilled to have the chance to share that moment with Jimmy, to dance that dance for *him*, and the more I thought about it the more nervous I became. I was in makeup and ready early, so I spent half an hour before the show running around, checking props, chatting with anybody I could find, and generally being a pain in the ass until Brock quietly but firmly told me to get ahold of myself.

Finally, the house lights were lowered and the show began. The first act went beautifully, and I had enough to do that I hardly had a moment to daydream about my big scene in act 2.

At the intermission I had asked everybody to not come backstage until the end of the show, so I stayed in the dressing room with the other girls, listening to the beat of my heart, thinking of Jimmy, all the while pretending to listen to the chatter.

Again, the house lights went down and we were into the second act. The corpse of my lover was carried onstage and placed on a pyre of sticks. The pipes began to moan their lovely, sad melody. I entered barefoot in a black dress and shawl, my hair loose around me. I moved quickly to the body of my love, knelt and pressed my body against his for a long moment, and then began to dance. My arms swept around me as if they had their own life. There was not a sound from the audience. I felt understood and beautiful. With the echo of the pipes' final sounds hovering in the air, I lowered myself once again over my lover, weeping.

The audience responded as if they knew how moving this was for us. When we took our bows for the last time, I saw tears in the eyes of my friends as we lined up across the stage.

Backstage, Sue got to me first. "Dizzy, darling, you were breathtaking! My Gawd, when you did the bird lift, and you didn't fall, and my Jimmy"—Brock—"caught you, I was holding my breath. All those rehearsals paid off. It was perfect!" Susan was very dramatic, and I adored her for it.

Just then Jimmy walked through the curtain. He looked at me and shook his head from side to side. "I can't talk." He just looked at me, and then took me in his arms.

To everyone's shock and delight, John Dwight and his mother threw the cast and friends a party at Vaughn Comfort's Café—"just a stone's throw from John Dwight's Gateway Musical Playhouse," their *Playbill* ad read, "and when we get enough stones we'll build a new Vaughn Comfort's." Jack Newlon, the house pianist, entertained us with his "incomparable rhythms," and some of our musicians sat in. When my Jimmy asked Sue to dance, her mouth fell open— and mine too, for that matter. I couldn't remember the last time I'd seen Jimmy so sociable.

"My Gawd, Jimmy, I didn't know you cared."

"Maybe you'll feel different when I start stepping on your feet. I'm not much of a dancer."

"Well, if you're going to dance with my girl," Brock said, taking my hand, "I'm going to dance with yours." As we were dancing, I realized there was something on his mind. "I'm going to miss you," he said. "I hope we can do this again sometime."

"Thanks for asking me. I learned a lot. When can we start working with my trio again? I can't wait."

"Well, you'll have to muddle through without me. I've joined the army."

I couldn't believe it. "Why?"

"'Cause they asked me." He laughed. "They're drafting everybody my age, but if you join you get to choose your own branch of the service, so that's what I did. I was lucky enough to get into the USO. I'll be leaving in a week. I want to spend it with Sue, but I'll probably see you before I go."

"I don't know what to say. I guess you won't be shooting at anybody, but still—"

"I'll be back, kiddo—we will dance again, I promise. I mean, this whole place has been so unprofessional I oughta report Dwight and this damn theater to the Equity union people. But all things considered, I had a great time."

"Yeah, me too. I never worked so hard in my life, but I did have fun. If you need me to sign an affidavit, let me know."

We all drove back in Guy's car: Art, Guy, Brock, Sue, Jimmy, and me. Somehow Jimmy managed to talk Guy into letting him drive again, but like the smart boy he was, this time he kept the speed under seventy.

The New York skyline loomed before us, so dazzling from a distance at night. I was returning to my home—and yet I was once again without a place to live, not to mention a place to work. Jimmy told me not to worry. He told me he'd take care of me. And yet he could hardly take care of himself.

# 10

It soon became obvious that we were going to have to find another living arrangement.

When Jimmy and I returned to his room that night, the first sound we heard was Bill snoring quietly in the darkness. We sneaked into Jimmy's bed and curled up to sleep in a spoon position, but that was doomed to failure; his favorite side was not mine.

"This might be easier if we slept in shifts," Jimmy said. "I'll watch you sleep and then you can watch me." He was kidding, but it was worth thinking about.

"That won't work," I said. "Watching you sleep will just put me to sleep, unless you can keep me entertained while you're sleeping."

"Well, let's think about that. Maybe I can hypnotize you to do something entertaining while you sleep, so you can rest at the same time. But you'll have to do the same to me."

"I don't know how to hypnotize anyone." I pouted.

"It's easy. I'll show you."

"Now?"

Bill exploded, "Will the two of you please shut up, for God's sake? I have to work tomorrow. Jesus, you're like two silly children, squabbling over nothing."

"We're not squabbling," Jimmy said. "This is the way we are."

"Not on my time it isn't. Now say good night and go to sleep." And he turned his back to us; he never saw us with our hands over each other's mouth, stifling our laughter.

For reasons of finance, space, and sanity, we three decided to find a larger place to share. Bill was seeing a college friend named Toni who was doing double duty as an open-ended tenant and house sitter in a lovely brownstone on the Upper West Side, just off Central Park; she was agreeable to sharing the space, so we all took up housekeeping together and split the expenses.

I just loved the neighborhood. Row after row of charming old brownstones and tree-lined streets, and just around the corner was a stable for some of the horses that pulled the hacks in the park. They would clip-clop under our window, at all hours of the day and night on their way to and from work.

Jimmy and I got permission to goof around in the stables, petting the poor old nags, sneaking them an apple or a cube of sugar when we could. We named some of them: Lightning, Swifty, Demon, names that would give them a sense of pride.

Toni's apartment was wonderful, though not very large: a moderate living room in front, with a long hall leading back to Toni and Bill's bedroom, and a kitchen and bathroom along the way. Jimmy and I shared a pullout couch in the living room. Thankfully, Toni's bedroom had a door one could close, so each couple had a certain amount of privacy.

As often as we could, Jimmy and I strolled over to the park, where we spent hours in a bullring of our own devising:

I stomped and snorted and Jimmy whirled his stained cape. By now our little game had evolved into a highly sophisticated ritual, a game that no one else could play; I wonder whether anyone would have been crazy enough to care.

One warm day we decided to rent a rowboat and venture out into the lake. I handed Jimmy the oars, but he didn't want to row. He wanted to lie back, letting his hands float in the water while I did all the work. I stood my ground.

"This is not women's work."

"What?"

"Rowing you around Central Park."

"We don't have boats in Indiana. We have cows."

"Did you ever row a cow?"

"No. Did you ever row a boat?"

I was silent.

"You told me you were a good rower and canoer in camp. Remember?"

I was silent.

"I guess we could just rent the damn boat, push off, and sit in the middle of the damn whatever it is . . ."

"Lake," I said.

"Lake," he said, "and wait until someone misses us."

I was silent.

"Okay, for chrissake, I'll row you out there, but you have to row me back." Well, I didn't and he did. But I finally got even with him: I explained to him that either he did all the rowing, or else he'd have to give up his exclusive rights to the bullfighter's cape and trade places in the bullring from time to time. That did it: he rowed us all over that damn lake and

back to the dock, and not another word about it. He hated to
be outfoxed, but he knew when he was licked.

Bill was working at CBS, and Toni had a nine-to-five job, but
Jimmy hadn't worked since early June. As usual, money was a
constant problem. I had to get a job. Having been away bask-
ing in greasepaint and applause all summer long, I wasn't
looking forward to sitting in the dark at the American
Photograph Co., retouching my fool head off, even if Mr.
Frog would rehire me.

So I found a job ushering at a little art house cinema, the
Paris, tucked in behind the Plaza Hotel on Fifty-eighth Street
between Fifth and Sixth. Downstairs at the Paris there was a
little greenroom/waiting area with couches and chairs,
where they served coffee, doughnuts, and sometimes even
freshly baked cookies. The coffee cups were bone china, and
there was a never-ending supply of embossed, paper napkins.
Often, when he'd gone too long between meals, I'd sneak
Jimmy downstairs so he could eat something.

The movies were usually foreign with subtitles, but every
so often a film from Hollywood would come our way and cause
a flutter. Such a film was the MGM musical *Hans Christian
Andersen*, starring Danny Kaye and the French dancer Zizi
Jeanmaire. The film was held over so long, and I adored it so,
that before its run concluded I knew the songs and even the
dialogue by heart. I began torturing everyone with my rendi-
tion of the film; I even went to the trouble of sneaking Art and
Alex in a few times so we could all sing the songs together. I
was driving them all crazy, but they were too kind to tell me.

"Inchworm" was one of the songs from the movie, and I insisted that Jimmy learn it so that he could sing it with me. It was a duet of sorts: two different melodies sung simultaneously, blending in miraculous—and I stress the word *miraculous*—counterpoint. At night we lay under the covers while I tried patiently to teach him the song. "I want to learn," he would protest, "I really do. But every time I sing my part I hear you singing yours. I can't help it."

"Don't listen to me. Just listen to you. Here, I'll show you—try it again." At which point I buried my face in my pillow and started to sing along with him. Jimmy couldn't sing, he was laughing so hard. Little by little, though, he learned my sweet song.

We talked and sang, lying together in the middle of the night, the stained bullfighter's cape around us keeping us warm. We tried to keep it down, but we missed our privacy.

One night a worry crept into my head. "Do you think we should look for our own place soon?"

"I would love that, but we can hardly afford being here."

"Hey, Dudley, what if something happens to keep us apart?"

"Whaddya mean?"

"Well, what if one of us gets offered a real fabulous tour, or . . . I don't know. You know, they say success can ruin people."

"Who says that? I went through school successfully, I successfully tie my shoes every morning, I successfully met you, I go to the bathroom success—"

I exploded. "Oh, stop it! You're not funny!"

"Then tell me what the hell you're talking about."

"We've kept ourselves so private from the outside world. We've become so much a part of each other. I guess I'm just afraid that will change. Nothing has ever lasted very long for me."

"Yeah, you're right—for me, either. I don't want to lose what we have."

"I know. When anything goes wrong, as long as I know I can tell you about it and we can figure it out together, I guess . . . "

Jimmy interrupted softly. "I need some air. I'm gonna get some smokes."

"Okay."

He got up abruptly, threw on his clothes, and left without another word. *But that's what I was trying to tell you—I don't want to be alone.* I lay there feeling abandoned, wondering if I had upset him, wondering what the hell was going on. About fifteen minutes later, the phone rang. I answered immediately—we always did late at night, to keep from awakening our roommates—and it was Jimmy.

"Hi."

"Hi. Was it something I said?"

I heard a smile in his voice. "No, my little Maggie, no. It's just . . . I've been feeling the same way you have . . . um . . . afraid we might lose our relationship . . . er . . . that it'll get swallowed up somehow . . . that we'll be torn apart again."

"I didn't mean to be so silly. I feel stupid, being afraid of something that hasn't happened yet. We don't know where our lives are going—"

Jimmy interrupted me. "Why don't we get married? Marry me."

Without stopping to think, I answered, "*Suuurre.*"

"I'm not kidding. I love you."

"I love you too," I said. "Are you coming home?"

"Yes, do you want anything?"

"Yes, you."

"I'm there," he said quickly, and hung up.

I held the phone in my hand for a minute, thinking about what I'd just said yes to. Whatever I was hoping for, I wasn't expecting him to ask me to marry him. Marriage had never entered my mind. I only wanted him to tell me that we would be together, no matter what.

I heard the key turn in the door and he was back. I lit the little lamp by my head and there he was, smiling at me, cigarette hanging out of his mouth.

"Hi, Mrs. Dean."

"Hi, Mr. Dean."

He stripped faster than ever, and all at once he was in bed next to me, pressing his nose against my cheek.

"How do you feel?" he asked.

"What do you mean?" I said, then stopped myself. "No, I know what you mean. And I feel strange. You know?"

"I'm not sure," he said. Neither of us wanted to be the first to try to decipher what had just gone on between us. But I had to plunge ahead.

"Were you serious? You know what I mean?"

"Never more. We could do it. We sorta feel that way now."

"It's pretty crazy, you know? We can't seriously think about getting married. We have no money, no careers; we just have each other, and that won't change if we don't let it."

"You don't want to get married?" He looked a little surprised, a little hurt.

"I didn't say that. It could be fun. We could do it in Central Park. Serve your favorite little cocktail weenies."

"Again?"

"They're good! Moondog could sing the wedding march."

"I know you're being cute, but why not?"

"Well, there's no one else I'd want to live with—ever."

"*Sooo?*"

"Okay, let's get married. When? Do we have enough money for a license?"

I was sitting up now, smoking. Jimmy was lying on his back, one arm behind his head. He was squinting at the ceiling, a thin stream of smoke trailing out of his mouth. He suddenly sat up. "Let's go home!"

"Home where? We are home."

"No, I mean my home in Indiana. I want to show you the farm where I grew up. I want my folks to meet you. Let's go to the farm! It'll be fun to relax and get some home cooking. I want you to see the farm."

"Okay, let's go." I smiled.

He pulled me down to him. "That's one of the reasons I love you so much. Anything is possible to you, isn't it? You're serious, aren't you?"

"Yes . . . if you are," I said. I was touched that he wanted to share his past with me, wanted me to be with him in the place where he spent his boyhood. Maybe he simply needed to reexamine his roots, needed to be on firm familiar ground for a while.

"You know, I'm talking about Indiana. Fairmount, Indiana."

"I know." I nodded. "But how are we going to get there? Hitchhike?"

We stared at each other, our eyes wide open. "Yes!!"

A decision was made. We leapt out of bed, trying to decide what to wear. I packed a few things in my dance bag, which didn't take long.

"Do you want to take Bill along?" Jimmy asked.

"Sure, let's go ask him."

"No, we're not going to *ask* him, he'll only analyze everything. We'll just get him out of bed, into his clothes, grab his toothbrush, and get him out on the road with us before he knows what's hit him."

"You're going *where*?" Bill yelled. "Now? Are you crazy?"

"We, Bill—we are going to Indiana." Jimmy giggled.

We talked him out of bed. Toni sat up, rubbing her eyes, but before she had a chance to say anything, we asked her if she would call CBS for Bill and tell them he was sick.

"Huh? Are you guys crazy?" She yawned.

"That seems to be the opinion here." I sat on the bed. "Toni, please, please call CBS for Bill and the Paris for me. Tell them I had a family emergency or something. Please? Okay? We'll be back soon. It's an adventure."

"Okay, okay. But my God, I*ndiana*?!" She rolled over and went back to sleep.

It's amazing what you can do if you don't waste time thinking about it first.

# 11

I don't remember how much money we had, but I know it was less than ten dollars among the three of us. We caught a bus downtown. The subway would have been faster, but then Bill wouldn't have had a chance to think about what the hell he was doing. I wouldn't have had time to think about how hungry I was, for that matter, and Jimmy certainly wouldn't have been able to figure out the entire first verse of "(Back Home Again in) Indiana" if I hadn't helped him.

Arriving at the West Side Terminal, we switched to a bus that would take us through the tunnel to New Jersey. Finally, we found ourselves standing on the Jersey Turnpike, headed out of town. It was still dark. The air was fresh, but oh so cold! Jimmy was exuberant; he had one arm around each of us, like we were on the yellow brick road.

"I'm gonna show you guys how to do farm stuff. Bill? You can slop the hogs."

"Wonderful," Bill replied.

"And Dizzy? You can milk the cows. You'll like that!"

"Swell, Jimmy. And what are you gonna do while we're working away?"

"I'm gonna supervise, of course. Somebody's gotta ramrod this outfit. We're gonna eat real food and sleep in real beds and we'll get up at dawn . . . "

"I just got up at dawn, and I don't like it," Bill mumbled.

Jimmy started trying different versions of the hitchhiking scene from It *Happened One Night.* He opened his shirt to show his chest, pulled up his trousers to show his leg, then he struck a ridiculous pose and stuck out his thumb. If I'd been driving by I would have stepped on the gas and left us far behind. Bill and I were sitting on some large rocks, leaning against a pole.

"Do you really think someone is going to stop just to see your chest hairs?" Bill yelled as he got up to join Jimmy.

"I don't have chest hairs."

"All the more reason not to stop."

"Go to hell!" Jimmy shouted. I started to laugh at the two of them. Bill was pacing in front of me, crossing his arms, slapping his sides to keep warm, trying as hard as he could not to be taken in by all the fun, but he couldn't contain himself from throwing in an opinion here and there. All I could do was laugh.

"Why don't we all try it," I suggested.

"Try what?" they echoed in unison. "You want to show off your naked chest hairs?" Jimmy laughed.

I picked up a pebble and tossed it at him.

"Do you pluck yours, or just singe them off?" Bill added.

I picked up another stone and threw it at him.

Jimmy piped up, "What did you mean, 'Why don't we all try it'?"

"Well, maybe if we all lined up—you know, like a chorus line—and stuck out our thumbs together . . . strength in numbers and all that, you know?"

"Great," said Jimmy. "Let's try it."

And we did. What a sight we were. Three bums on the road, jeans, cigarettes and all. Bill ripped into a grandstanding finale:

> *Oh the moon is fair tonight along the Wabash*
> *As I long for my Indiana home*

Crescendo, and crashingly bad harmony.

Suddenly, a dirty old Nash Rambler started slowing down. It had to: we were practically in the middle of the road. The driver rolled down the window as he slowed to a stop. "You need a lift?"

"*Yes!*" we yelled together. *Was he out of his mind?! He must be awfully lonely.*

"Hop in." The driver was a big man, hearty-looking, with a nice face and a friendly smile. He got out of the car to help us. "I'll move that stuff on the backseat into the trunk." "That stuff" was a couple of rifles, a shotgun, and two canvas bags.

Jimmy and I hopped into the backseat; Bill helped him get things squared away, then got in the front with our Good Samaritan. We rolled out onto the highway again, driving on in silence. I don't think it was until that moment that any of us gave a thought as to what kind of trouble we could get ourselves into, out on the road alone in the middle of the night.

What if we'd just accepted a ride from an escaped mental patient? Or a prisoner on the run?

Our suspicious benefactor broke the silence. "Where ya goin'?"

Jimmy told him about the highway junction near his home in Fairmount; the driver said he was going right through Indiana, and knew just about where it was. What luck—if we lived, that is.

"That's great!" Jimmy said. "My name is Jimmy Dean, and this is Elizabeth Sheridan." Bill chimed in to introduce himself, and thanked the man again for stopping.

"You're welcome. You look like nice kids. My name is Clyde McCullough. How ya doin'?"

"Not Clyde McCullough the baseball player?" said Jimmy, disbelief on his face.

"Yup, that's me."

"I can't believe this! I can't believe it!" He turned to me and laughed. "This is Clyde McCullough!"

"I know, I heard. That's what he said."

"Yeah, but this is *Clyde McCullough*. He's catcher for the Pittsburgh Pirates!"

"Hi, Mr. McCullough. Just call me Dizzy—everybody does."

Clyde laughed. "That's easy to remember. Just like Dizzy Dean. You all call me Clyde, okay?"

Only then did it occur to me that if Jimmy and I got married, my name would be Dizzy Dean.

I relaxed immediately. A celebrity in our midst—a celebrity guardian angel. The boys started chatting about baseball, and I settled back, safe and drowsy, in Jimmy's arms. As I was falling asleep, I heard Clyde say he was on his way to Iowa; he was going to meet some friends for an exhibition game, and then go off with them for a week of hunting. I was never a fan of hunting, but somehow that night Clyde McCullough's plans sounded innocent indeed.

A hand on my arm, jostling me gently awake. Jimmy's voice, whispering in my ear: "Smell the fresh aroma of the corn muffins, the smoky bacon spattering in the air, the heavenly scent of freshly brewed coffee perking . . ." I opened my eyes, and almost fell out of the car. Howard Johnson's!

We were shown to a table, and I went to the ladies' room to wash the crinkles from my face. I looked like I'd slept on a washboard. When I got back to the table, everyone was laughing.

"What happened?" I asked.

"I just got acquainted with your boyfriend's front teeth," said Clyde.

"I guess you should feel honored," I said. "He only pulls that trick on people he likes."

"Really?" said Clyde.

"No," Bill and I chimed together, which called for another round of guffaws.

Jimmy got up. "I'm going to call my uncle Marcus. Order for me, okay, Diz? You know what I like. Steak and eggs and all the stuff that goes with it."

"Now, don't hold back," said Clyde. "Order whatever you want. Don't be shy. It's on me." And that was that. I ordered everything Jimmy wanted, and anything I could think of putting in my mouth.

I decided to press Clyde a little about his hunting. "What are you going after, Clyde? Tell me you're not going to kill a deer."

"I'd be surprised if we kill anything. Hell, we just get drunk and try not to shoot each other."

Jimmy came back with a report from Indiana. "They're expecting us. I told them about you, Clyde; maybe you could stop over and have a good home-cooked meal with us."

"I wish I could, but I don't think I'll have time. Thanks anyway."

We had another day and night of driving ahead of us, so we were back on the road after breakfast. We all offered to drive in shifts, but Clyde wouldn't hear of it. He drove all that day and into the night again, with no more than two pit stops. Sooner or later, we ran flat out of conversation; words just hung in the air, disappearing into grunts and uh-huhs. I wondered how Clyde managed to stay awake all this time. We were trying to keep awake ourselves, in order to keep him from dozing off. Jimmy and I were still in the backseat snuggling, softly singing, "Two and two are four, four and four are eight . . . "

"You're driving me nuts with that song. You sound like two-year-olds," said Bill.

"We are," Jimmy replied. "We're learning our arithmetic. Pay attention. You might learn something. Eight and eight are sixteen, sixteen and sixteen are thirty-two—"

"Eight and eight *is* sixteen," Bill corrected.

"That's what I said. Its *is* is *are*," Jimmy offered.

"It's not *are*, it's *is*," Bill insisted.

"It's *is* what's it's 'is'?" I asked.

"Oh, shut up. You're going to drive me insane!"

Clyde broke in. "Do you know 'Don't Fence Me In'?" He began to sing: "Oh, give me land, lotsa land under starry skies above . . ."

"Don't fence me in!" we all chimed back, out of tune and loving it.

We stopped for a while to stretch and eat, and Jimmy went to the phones to check back with the farm. He came back to the table with a strange expression on his face.

"Something wrong?" I asked.

"Not exactly," he said. "It's just that my dad's going to be at the farm when we get there. He's coming from California for a visit."

"How'd that happen? Did he know you'd be there?" Bill asked.

"After I called my uncle, he called my dad, and Dad said he could get away. He says it'll be a good time to fix my teeth."

"Is your dad a dentist?" asked Clyde, chewing on a piece of toast.

"Yeah, sort of. He's a technician, actually," Jimmy mumbled.

"You're lucky," said Clyde. "Dental stuff is expensive. I know. I've had a few teeth knocked out. All part of the game, I guess."

Jimmy giggled. "But worth it, right?"

"Sometimes," said Clyde, smiling his pearly whites at us.

It was quiet then. We concentrated on eating. We were all pretty travel weary and into our own thoughts.

All I could think was, *Jimmy and his father.*

On the next leg of the trip the three of us took turns sleeping in the backseat while the front-seat passenger tried to keep Clyde amused (and awake). When I awoke, the sun was just beginning to peek its big orange face above the horizon, and Clyde was just starting to slow down. We were in farm country now, with wooden houses, fences, and barns as far as the eye could see. Grazing cows and horses surveyed their fields while rural mailboxes stood roadside guard; the weather-beaten farmhouses behind them were already lamp-lit, their inhabitants preparing for the day. Some gray barn doors were already open, and wisps of smoke from chimneys curled up into the dawn sky.

Clyde slowed to stop at the junction just outside of Fairmount that Jimmy had described. There was a gas station on one corner, where Jimmy was to call his uncle to pick us up. When the car pulled into the station, Clyde was the first one out of the car. "Are you guys going to be all right? Need some money? Call it a loan, if you want . . . " His voice dropped off to a whisper.

Jimmy and I didn't know what to say. "You've already been more than generous," said Bill.

"We're fine now, Clyde. Thanks for everything," Jimmy chimed in.

A hug for each of us and he was gone, his powerful hand waving a last good-bye. Jimmy made the call to his uncle as we waited, stretching, trying to get our land legs back. I looked around and knew that I was a long way from home. As we were waiting a sudden wave of anxiety about meeting Jimmy's folks washed over me, but it ebbed as soon as Uncle Marcus pulled into the station a few minutes later. Marcus wore overalls, boots, and a checkered shirt with the sleeves rolled up; it was hard to tell his age, he looked so hardy and weather-worn, but his eyes were warm and friendly, and at once I felt more comfortable. Jimmy walked around the car to greet him, and they shook hands and shyly embraced. Jimmy introduced us around, and we all climbed into the car and headed to the farm.

I remember even today how peaceful it seemed as we turned into the driveway and approached the main house, clapboard and tall. We circled around and stopped at the large front porch, where Ortense and their son, Marcus junior, were waiting for us. We were exhausted, but Ortense had made a heavenly breakfast; I had as many bites as I could before my head almost crashed onto the plate. Ortense led me upstairs to a simple little bedroom, where I fell asleep instantly.

When I awoke half the day was gone, but it didn't matter. I went to the bathroom to freshen up, then joined the boys downstairs sitting around the kitchen table. The dishes had been washed and put away and the boys had napped too, and so—hardy, refreshed, and a little antsy—we decided to have a walk around the farm. Summer was long gone, and the good, sweet farm air sent a crisp draft across our faces. It felt fresh and healthful, and I was so happy we had come.

Jimmy took us on a tour of his childhood haunts and pastimes, picking up pebbles with little Markie and tossing them at the trees. In the barn we swung on ropes from the loft, landing in the hay. By the little pond in front of the house we skipped stones, and when we found a BB gun we tried a little target practice. We got in a little time shooting baskets at a hoop overhanging the barn door, satisfying Jimmy's competitive streak along the way.

Marcus had been keeping Jimmy's motorcycle in working order for him, so now Jimmy took his little cousin for a ride. The boy sat behind, wrapping his small arms around Jimmy as they swung up and down the long driveway, a boyish admiration lighting Markie's eyes.

There were cows, chickens, and pigs, and tender greetings from Jimmy. "Hey, Mister Pig, did you miss me?" "Hi there, Miss Bessie. You're a good girl. Yes you are." There were no horses, but Jimmy knew I couldn't wait to go riding, so Marcus arranged for me to go next door to have a ride on one of his neighbor's horses. Jimmy gave me a lift on his motorcycle, and I rode around the neighborhood on a docile mare in foal, cantering across fields as Jimmy twisted and turned on his bike, jumping hedges and yelling at me to look. What a show-off he could be. (But then, what a show-off I could be.)

It was late afternoon when Jimmy's father, Winton Dean, finally arrived. He was a nice-looking man with glasses, sandy hair thinning and graying on his temples, and his features were the same as his son's. *This is what Jimmy will look like when he grows old*, I thought. Father and son hugged awkwardly, and I was struck by how reserved and self-conscious

Winton seemed. His gestures were small and controlled. I don't remember seeing him laugh the entire time we were there. There was no sign that he participated in any of the joys of life; even simple affection seemed beyond his reach. Watching him with his son, I felt a deep sadness. All at once I understood something deeper about Jimmy.

After devouring a wonderful early dinner of meat loaf and gravy with fresh vegetables and homemade pie, Jimmy and his father finally disappeared into another room so that Winton could take some impressions to help provide better replacements for his son's front teeth. Bill and I helped clear and dry dishes, then retired into the living room. When Bill asked to see some of Jimmy's baby pictures, Ortense pulled out the family album, but she seemed skeptical. "Are you sure?"

"Oh, we'd love to see some," said Bill. "Wouldn't we, Dizzy?"

"Not if he was an ugly baby. I don't want to see no ugly babies." They knew I was kidding.

"I know what you mean," Marcus bellowed. "That Winston Churchill thing."

"Excuse me?" Bill was perplexed.

"I know, I know," I said, laughing. "All tiny babies look like Winston Churchill."

"Right!" Marcus pointed at me and winked.

"Well," Ortense said, "I can tell you right now Jimmy was the cutest, prettiest little thing you ever did see." She opened the album and proved her point.

There were only a few baby pictures, but there were others of Winton and of Jimmy's mother—"such a sweet person,"

Ortense said. And yet even as a young man Winton Dean looked preoccupied.

The evening ended early—early for us New Yorkers, anyway. Everyone was ready to sleep, but we hatched a plan that Jimmy would sneak into my room after everyone else was safely in bed.

I waited in my bed, contemplating the wonderful day we'd all had together. It seemed to me it was an *American* day, spent close to the land, full of family and meals and laughter. I was swimming in patriotism when I heard a creaking coming down the hall. The bedroom door squeaked open enough for Jimmy to peek in, then squeaked again as he pushed it open farther, then squeaked one last time as he tried to close it behind him. He scurried across the room to my tiny bed and jumped in beside me, both of us trying to stifle our laughter. He was out of breath.

"I can't stop making noise. The whole house is probably awake by now, waiting to hear what we're going to do next."

"What *are* we going to do next?"

"This is weird, huh?"

"Yeah, and kinda embarrassing. I like your folks a lot. This has been so comfortable and they've put themselves out for us."

"That's the way they are with everybody. That's the way everybody is around here. Just simple folk."

"Strange." I looked at him.

"What?"

"Well, that you grew up in this simple place, with such simple people, and you turned out so complicated."

Jimmy started cackling. I put a pillow over his mouth to keep him quiet and continued: "Maybe that's the problem. Deep down you're just a simple creature, trying to complicate yourself."

"Hey, just because I want to sponge up all there is that's interesting doesn't mean I want to be complicated. I'm just very disturbed when people aren't honest with me or want too much of me, then, I guess I . . . uh . . . *get* complicated."

"Well, if *that* wasn't the most complicated answer I've ever heard—"

He grabbed me, and we started rolling around in the bed, laughing and shushing each other even more loudly. The bed was creaking, and the more it creaked the funnier it was.

"Maybe we better forget this. I'm uncomfortable."

"Yeah, we don't want to shock a house full of simple people with our 'shenanigans,' as my uncle used to say."

But just for fun, before we said good night we bounced up and down on the bed awhile before Jimmy crept and creaked his way back down the hall where he came from. *That'll give them something to talk about at breakfast.*

The next morning, Ortense smiled at me. "Did you sleep comfortably, Dizzy? I know that old bed creaks a lot. I hope it didn't keep you awake." I thought I saw a twinkle in her glance.

"I slept like a baby," I said. "I didn't hear a thing."

"Well," she said, clucking, "gooses and ganders." A *little farm humor, I guess.*

We went to town the next morning. Jimmy wanted to show us around. Fairmount was the very model of a small midwestern town, complete with movie house, barbershop, hardware store, feed store, gas station, drugstore with an ice cream parlor, high school, and, of course, church. Everyone knew everyone and everyone's business. Everyone knew Jimmy, and they all stopped to say hello; we showbiz diehards were a million miles away from the stage, and yet we were having a great time . . . much to our surprise.

Adeline Nall, Jimmy's drama coach, had been alerted that we were in town, and she was expecting us when we got to the high school. Somehow she had arranged for the three of us to talk to her drama class: Jimmy about acting, Bill about writing, and me about dancing. Greeting us in the hallway, Miss Nall was thrilled to see Jimmy; it was obvious how fond and proud of him she was.

The kids were giggling and whispering when we walked into the classroom, as I suppose we would have been if we were behind those desks. Miss Nall stood in front of her desk, held up her hands for quiet, and introduced us.

"Class, we are very lucky today to have a visit from a dear friend of ours, and two friends of his. These three are artists, and they can tell us a bit about what to expect when we leave here if we are interested in pursuing a career in the arts. James, one of my best pupils, is an actor; Bill here is a writer; and Elizabeth is a dancer. They are going to share with us their experiences and maybe a few helpful hints." Then she turned to us with a sweeping gesture. "Your audience awaits."

The three of us looked at one another. The expression on Jimmy's face was loud and clear: "Not me." And I wasn't about to make the first move. So Bill shrugged and stood, bless him;

he walked over to the blackboard, grabbed a piece of chalk, and addressed the class.

"Hi. My name is Bill Bast, and I'm a writer. Of course, that's easy to say—I don't have anything published . . . yet." He smiled. "But I *will*. That's the kind of confidence you need to carry around with you, while you're waiting to be discovered.

"What is writing? Well, it's a way of communicating thoughts and ideas. There are all kinds of writing: poems, novels, journalism, letters, plays. The difference between putting a thought down on paper and making it ready for someone to read is this." He turned to the blackboard and read aloud as he wrote:

I *entered the room and sat down.*

Then he wrote:

The *room was quiet and serene when I walked in. I looked around, chose a straight-backed chair against the wall, sat down and waited.*

The first sentence was an idea, he explained; the second sentence was an extension of the first. "But what's missing to make you feel that you're really walking into the room yourself?"

There was a show of hands. Bill picked a shy-looking girl in the back row.

"Some adjectives to describe the room?"

"Good!" said Bill. "Adjectives convey *feeling*—atmosphere. Let's see now . . . "

*The room was quiet and serene when I walked through the paneled mahogany door. The brass doorknob felt heavy to the touch. I saw I was alone as I made my way over to a small, straight chair against the wall. I sat down on the needlepoint cushion and waited.*

He went on to explain that if this were a play or a movie script, the embellishment would give an actor more clues about how to feel, how the body would accommodate the scene. Then he gave everyone a chance to embroider the scene further. By the time they were through, every last element in the room had been described—even the temperature. The class responded with applause. I was moved; Bill Bast was a natural.

I knew I was next when Bill handed me the chalk, but all I could do was laugh and thank him.

"I don't think I'll put mine in writing. I've never danced and written at the same time." *A few laughs—good start.* "Dancing is a way of communicating too," I ventured. I opened my arms and twirled, and began to move all around the classroom, up and down the rows of desks, showing how the body can express the emotional basics—joy, sadness, indecision. It was a total surprise to the audience, and I heard little gasps.

"Last summer," I continued after a moment, "I appeared in a production of *Brigadoon* as Maggie, a character who is deaf and mute." I gave a brief explanation of the plot. "I had one solo number, all alone onstage. The man I loved had just been killed. He was carried to center stage and I had to show my grief over my loss. The key to choreographing this piece was that Maggie couldn't hear and couldn't speak. So everything she felt had to come from *inside* her. Offstage, bagpipes were playing a sad melody, but I knew Maggie couldn't hear it, so she must have been listening to her own music." And I undertook a version of my funeral dance for them without music. The classroom was still and attentive. When I finished, the class applauded, but more gratifying than the clapping was the look of joyful interest on their young faces. They were *engaged*, and that was how I left them for Jimmy.

Miss Nall's beloved alumnus stood and slowly walked to the head of the class like a bullfighter staring down his prey. Bill and I glanced at each other, our eyebrows lifting in unison.

The first words from Jimmy's mouth were low and breathy: "My name is James Dean and I am an actor." But then he startled us all by roaring back and screaming: "MY NAME IS JAMES DEAN AND I AM AN ACTOR!"

A parade of readings emanated from Jimmy: different entrances, different feelings, different approaches, all wrapped around the same declaration. You could have heard a heartbeat. He entered his scene laughing hysterically, trying to get the words out: "My name is—heh—heh, heh, J—hee hee—*James*—heh, James *Dean*—" He rolled on the floor, trying to catch his breath. Then he leapt up, turned away from the kids, and spun around again, crying, wiping his glasses, and sputtering the same thing through an unholy sob. When it seemed he had torn through the entire repertoire of human emotions, he straightened up all at once, and his normal demeanor returned as if by magic. "My apologies to Miss Nall, the best teacher I ever had."

Afterward we were delighted with ourselves, like professors striding across Harvard Yard.

"I thought your lecture quite good, today, Mr. Bast."

"Why, thank you, James. Yours too was quite excellent."

"Hey! What about me?" I whined.

"Oh, I'm sorry, Professor Sheridan, but I'm afraid I drifted off during yours. I'm sure it was quite adequate." Jimmy looked at Bill. "Did you catch Professor Sheridan's presentation?"

"I'm afraid I was looking out the window at a little bird flying by. But I'm sure she was competent," Bill added.

"Competent, my ass! You can both go straight to hell!"

We returned to the farm and discovered that Jimmy had received a phone call from his agent, Jane D'eacy. He returned her call, then came running into the kitchen, where Bill and I were sitting with Ortense.

"Diz, Ayers wants me to read for *See the Jaguar!*" He was glowing. "I have the strangest feeling. I can't explain it, but I know I'm gonna get it. It's the strangest feeling I ever had about a job."

I'd never seen him like this before. Something in his voice, in his face, was different—was *positive.* And starting from that moment, almost imperceptibly, forces began to pull us apart.

Jimmy could hardly contain himself. Over dinner he recited the entire plot of the show to his folks—from every nuance of his character right down to a few lines he had committed to memory. His excitement was infectious—"What a break!" he exulted; "This could be it! I can feel it, I'm on my way!"—and yet the more he talked the more I felt my stomach tightening.

After dinner was over I went upstairs to pack what little we had in my dance bag. Jimmy stayed downstairs, talking with his family while I stayed in my room and lay on the bed. We'd planned to stay a week, having our wonderful time in Fairmount, but after that phone call Jimmy would want to get back right away. I had a longing to cry, but I didn't. I fell asleep.

It was dark when I heard Ortense tapping on the door, her voice gently calling me down for breakfast. Everyone was up and busy when I got downstairs. Winton Dean was sitting by the window, silently polishing those two front teeth of Jimmy's. I sat down next to Jimmy, and he gave me one of his goofy toothless smiles.

After breakfast Bill, Jimmy, and I took one more walk around the farm. Markie joined us down by the pond. "Hey, Markie," I said, "I really enjoyed meeting you. I hope we can come back sometime and have some more fun."

"Me too."

"Maybe I'll bring you to New York sometime. Wouldn't that be a kick?" Jimmy said.

"Really? Could I really visit you?"

"We'll sure try. I don't have my own place yet, so it would be kinda hard right now. But maybe before too long. We'll see, okay?"

"We better get going soon," Bill said. "One more stone, okay, Markie?"

We all lined up at the water's edge, Jimmy gave a count-down, and everyone skipped one last pebble across the muddy water. Markie's stone went the best; mine plopped right into the pond.

Back on the porch Ortense was waiting with a large bag of food, and I could smell the corn bread as we all hugged her good-bye. We piled into the truck and Marcus carted us down the driveway and back onto the main road, heading toward the junction where he had picked us up only a few days ear-lier. As we hopped off and Marcus's truck pulled away, we set our bags on the road and silently stuck our thumbs in the air.

The first two rides were unmemorable; our third and last, unhappily, was unforgettable. It was almost dark, and we hadn't made it very far at all, when a drunken Texan pulled over in his big Cadillac, opened the door, and said, "Y'all jump on in." He wore a hat as big as his car, and every half an hour or so he took a little snort from a pint of bourbon he had tucked between his legs, which he referred to as his "medicine." He had a severe ulcer, he explained, and after we had stopped to eat he would then pull the car over to the side of the road a few minutes later, throw open his door, and heave out the side every greasy, fried morsel he had consumed. When it was obvious he'd had too much medicine, Jimmy volunteered to drive the last leg home to the city.

What a long ride home—long and solitary. Our drunken friend slept heavily in the front, next to Jimmy; Bill dozed in the backseat next to me, and I sat behind Jimmy, my arms around his shoulders, my head leaning against the back of the driver's seat.

I wanted Jimmy to have his career and I wanted his career to be splendid. But in my heart, unreasonable as it was, I wanted him to want nothing in his life but me. Somewhere along the way Jimmy reached up to hold my hand, and we sped through the night that way, my heart sinking deeper and deeper as we got closer and closer to New York.

# 12

The moment we arrived home, the time and place for Jimmy's audition were set. We all returned to our jobs—Toni had made those phone calls for us, so we hadn't been fired—and when we got home we worked with Jimmy on the script until he knew his audition scene cold.

Off he went the next day. Dirty blue jeans, a T-shirt, and his glasses—which he'd broken when he fell off his motorcycle a few days earlier, trying to show me what a daredevil he was. Bill met me at the Paris after work, and together we waited for Jimmy's return.

I was serving coffee to the next audience waiting to go in when I caught sight of Jimmy coming down the lobby stairs to the lounge. He looked dejected. I quickly pushed aside a pang of pleasure; it was a natural emotion, but I felt immediately guilty. Jimmy sat down next to Bill, but just then the show was over and the next audience had to be seated. I shrugged and motioned to the boys that I'd be right back. When I had ushered the last derriere into the last seat I tore back downstairs, and there they were, laughing together.

"Hi, baby," Jimmy said. "One of my lenses fell out, right in the middle of the audition. Jesus, I started to laugh. What the hell else was I going to do?"

"Are you okay?" I said.

"I'm good, real good." He grinned. "It went all right. Yeah, I feel good about it. They wanna see me again tomorrow."

"Would it be too soon to celebrate?" Bill asked.

"I get off in a little while," I said. "Let's just go to Jerry's and have a beer. You know, a quiet party to celebrate getting through this together. I know you'll get the part—I know it." I *do know it, and what the hell is going to happen next?*

They left, and I finished cleaning up the lounge before wrapping things up and going to meet them.

*See the Jaguar* was a complicated play, full of symbolism and contrivance. Almost everything meant something other than what you might have expected. The part Jimmy read for was that of Wally, a wild mountain boy, naive and childlike, full of curiosity about everything. Wally had been reared by his mother in a locked cage, ostensibly to protect him from the outside world. Just before his mother dies Wally is set free, and knowing nothing of the world he soon gets into trouble again—and ends up in prison, behind bars once again. Ah, the irony. But no matter: they knew Jimmy was perfect for the role—and he got it.

Jimmy worked hard to learn the play. Bill and I helped him run lines as much as we could, and I helped him practice the little song Wally sings. We had fun, but there was a measure of frustration in it as well. Jimmy was more and more reluctant to let himself go, to give himself up to the playful magic that was at the heart of our relationship. He was taking himself more seriously, and in my heart I wondered whether he was maturing while I was merely reverting to my safe and childlike inner world.

Just as it had for me in Ocean City, soon the process of putting up a show was bringing the cast of See the Jaguar close together—though this time it was Jimmy who was part of the family. With him were Broadway veterans Arthur Kennedy and Constance Ford, the leads in the play, along with five or six other cast members. And as he worked on his character Jimmy seemed less and less enchanted with the role he played in real life. Jimmy never spoke very much about the process of getting into character; he himself told me he wasn't sure exactly what happened to him during the transformation. But I knew he wanted no distractions, and I knew that in his position I might have felt the same way. But I couldn't compete with his newfound joy.

One night after a late rehearsal we were in bed, running lines. But Jimmy seemed distracted, and I asked him what was wrong.

"Nothing," he said.

"No, no, there's something," I prodded. "I can feel it."

"Nothing, goddammit. Nothing!" he snarled. "I don't want to dance in the fucking street, or play bullfighter, or make love, or anything right now."

"Who asked you?"

He paused. "Well, I know I've been neglecting you and we haven't had any fun together lately. It's just that my head's so full of this show, it's like living two lives. I don't need that right now. I just don't have any time for you. *I'm working!*" He must have seen the expression on my face, and he backpedaled a bit. "That didn't all come out like I meant it. I'm sorry. I mean, I just have to put all my energy into this role. This play might not run long. It's not all that great. Even I don't get all of it. Do you, Diz?"

I tried to shake off his tirade. "I know what you mean. But *you'll* be wonderful, I promise you."

"I think I will be too, if I can get it down the way I want it—so I can't help you right now. I *can't!*" he yelled. "*Please* let me enjoy this. I've been waiting for this for a long time. Just let me enjoy it—if that's even the right word . . . "

"Yeah, okay." That was it. "Enjoy the hell out of it! Okay? For chrissake, *enjoy* is a *great* word. It's what *we* used to do together, remember? Enjoy?"

"Oh, shit," he murmured.

I jumped out of bed and ran to the bathroom. I leaned over the sink, choking on my own sobs. *Oh, God, why? What the hell's the matter with me?*

I pulled myself up and looked in the mirror. *Who in the hell could love this face?* I patted water on my face and brushed my hair, but it didn't help. My mind was shutting down. But I knew I needed to see Jimmy, needed to be sure I hadn't ruined everything. Again.

The living room was empty; his clothes were gone, and so was he. I ran to the door, hoping to catch him on the street, and almost fell over him, sitting on the step, staring at his script. He caught me before I fell down the stairs.

"Whooa, where you goin'?"

"To put out the fire I started?"

"We started," he said. "Let's just stop this. I need you. Help me. Okay?"

"Okay." I managed to smile. "But inside. It's freezing out here." I took his hand and we headed in. "I'm sorry," I said. "Sorry. Sorry. That seems to be my favorite word these days."

"Yeah, mine too. I'm sorry." He smiled and kissed my hand.

We worked for another hour, warm and cozy under the covers. Then Jimmy fell asleep, his breathing soft in my ear.

A few weeks later, the word came: *See the Jaguar* was going out of town for a few days of previews in New Haven, then on to Philadelphia for two weeks. Jimmy announced that when he came back he was going to move into the Iroquois Hotel. It would be more convenient to the theater, he said, but he also admitted to me and Bill that he no longer wanted to be part of a community-living situation. "I need to be alone from now on. At least for a while."

Before he left town, Jimmy tried to be as honest with me as possible. He told me this was his chance to spread his wings. "This is the most important single event in my life . . . other than us, of course," he added sheepishly. We were still lovers, I believed, but I also knew that our romance no longer burned with the intensity we once felt. Our love had already moved into a comfortable stage, its brilliant colors gently diminishing like a rainbow too long in the sky.

My trip to Ocean City had shown me that we were capable of pursuing our own dreams in each other's absence. But now he was going somewhere, and I was just spinning my wheels, going nowhere. Whenever I tried to rekindle things between us, I only seemed to irritate him. I didn't even feel like dancing. My only strong feelings were for Jimmy.

When the cast finally left town, Bill told me he wanted to move back to the Iroquois. I wanted to leave too, but I had no place to go. Then a serendipitous thing occurred: I ran into Art Ostrin on my way to work, and he told me about a friend of his, Lavonne Slaybaugh, who was looking for someone to share her apartment in a brownstone on Central Park South.

It was too good a location to be believed. I found the building and walked up the narrow, carpeted stairway to the second floor. It was very quiet; I detected a faint odor of furniture polish, and I liked it right away. The apartment was in the front. A *view of the park! It's as if I'd belong to the park*, I thought. *Or will the park belong to me?* I knocked, and a pretty girl with dark hair and gray eyes opened the door.

I introduced myself and walked in. Everywhere I looked I saw comfortable, inviting places to sit or lie down. There were two immense windows, with window seats for viewing, on either side of an old-fashioned fireplace. I suddenly got the feeling I'd returned to the parlor of the Rehearsal Club, and strangely enough I was comforted.

"I'm Lavonne. Make yourself at home." She motioned for me to sit at the dining room table near the door, and I did.

"This is such a fabulous room," I told her. "How many of you live here?"

"Well, there's only one of me living here, but there's another girl, Nancy. Just the two of us now. There were three, but one of us left to get married. That's why we're looking. With three of us, we can afford the rent and living expenses."

She showed me the rest of the apartment. Nancy, who worked in an office, had the one small bedroom off the main room; two pullout couches on either side of the living room, with lots of pillows, were living quarters for the other two girls. There was a tight little kitchen tucked away in the back, and a decent-size bathroom. It might have felt cramped, but the opposite was true: the big room was so spacious, the other rooms around it were almost a relief. Lavonne was an actress, and we hit it off right away. When I told her I worked at the Paris, right down the street, that seemed to put it in place for her. The apartment was mine if I wanted it, and I did.

I moved in immediately—and thank goodness, for the move gave me plenty to occupy my mind. I still missed Jimmy, but getting acclimated to my new surroundings took a lot of my attention. I wrote Jimmy to give him my address and phone number, and he called me several days later; his voice was different somehow, stronger, more confident. He told me about his first night onstage before an audience, and I could feel the energy coming through the phone line from New Haven. How in charge he felt! How powerful! His was a sympathetic role, and the audience loved him from the moment they saw him. It was a discovery for him, a new kind of love.

Two weeks after I had moved in with Lavonne, Nancy moved out and Lavonne took the bedroom. I was next in line. Then a lovely girl named Connie moved in, with a Great

Dane named Lady Pam in tow. Connie, a recent divorcee, was a lot of fun, and we all loved Lady Pam, who became protective of all of us. We all took turns walking her in the park, and Lady Pam was so elegant that not one of us expended a moment's resentment on the millions of dollars it cost to feed her.

We were right in the middle of the city, close to Columbus Circle with its statue and pigeons and hot dog stands and benches. We were right around the corner from Fifty-seventh Street, one of the grandest shopping arcades in the world. And a few blocks to the east was the Plaza Hotel, all acluster with hansom cabs, and my second home, the Paris. I never got tired of sitting in the window of our apartment, looking at the constant parade of passersby. Central Park was a feature film, full of children's noises, old folks on favorite benches feeding favorite pigeons, neighborhood folks brown-bagging their lunches on the grass in the sun. I was used to playing the gypsy, but this was one of the nicest places I'd found to light.

After Brock left town, Sue told me her show was closing soon; worse yet, she was auditioning for a job that threatened to take her on the road too. It was nothing more than a coincidence, but I felt like I was losing all the people closest to me.

I was seeing a lot of Art and Alex. I would sneak them into the Paris, and after I got off we would go to Jerry's for a drink and I'd force them to sing *Hans Christian Andersen* songs, all the way through, just for old times' sake. Fabio and

Tony were jumping from one job to the other, just as they'd always been, but almost always working. We talked of putting the trio back on its feet, and we even met for one rehearsal, but my heart wasn't in it anymore. We never even looked for another job.

Finally *See the Jaguar* returned to New York City. Jimmy called me the Sunday night he got back in town.

"Hi, honey. How's it going? I've missed you." He's *never called me* honey *before*.

"I've missed you too. A lot has happened since I saw you last."

"Yeah, I'll say. Where are you? Is it nice?"

"It's terrific. I'd love to show it to you. When can I do that?"

"That's just it. We have heavy rehearsals for the next two days, before previews. We're going to walk around the stage tonight, just to get the feel of it. My head is so into this, I don't want to stop. I do want to see you, but I just want to wait until we open—then we'll have all kinds of time. I hope you'll understand."

"You don't want to see me at all?"

"Oh, God, yes. I just don't want to be distracted by anything. I'm really digging into this part. Please try and understand."

I paused. "I'm jealous and I'm trying not to be and I really don't understand."

"Jealous of who?"

"Not of who. Of what. All your new friends, sitting around talking about your work—Broadway, for God's sake. All that stuff."

"I know, honey." *There it was again.* "I'm really sorry. But, you know, I haven't done anything to be sorry about."

"Well, if you haven't, then don't be. Okay?"

"Okay, my little mermaid, Maggie. I love you. Thanks for understanding." *There was my Jimmy, finally.* "Look, I will call you after rehearsals every day, and we'll say good night every night."

"Okay. If that's the way you want it. Good night, Jimmy."

I tried to convince myself that I understood, but I was angry. All I knew was that the play had consumed him and taken him away from me. I couldn't have been more upset if it had been another woman, or even another man. I knew that Brackett was hovering about, being ever so supportive, but what bothered me was much more than that.

Jimmy didn't want me to see a preview. He wanted me to wait for the real thing. He had arranged for Bill and me to come to opening night, and to come to the party at Sardi's afterward. He said he was experimenting with subtle nuances in every performance, and he wanted it to be perfect when I saw it. Did I believe him? No, not really. But I couldn't know for sure.

I remember stewing over opening night. I couldn't have been more nervous if I were the one taking the stage. I had nothing to wear! I did have that black number from our tryst at the Bevan Inn, and you can never go wrong with a basic black dress; but all I had to wear over it was an old maroon cloth coat, and I hated it. Lavonne and Connie both offered to lend me one of theirs, but I was longer, taller, and ganglier than anybody else on the earth that night, and nothing fit. I dressed, put on my pearls, did up my hair, and asked Connie to help me with my makeup. I looked exactly as I did the first time Jimmy and I made love, and I couldn't help but wonder if he would make the connection.

I was to meet Bill at the theater. I suppose I could have walked—it wasn't that far—but Lavonne and Connie thought it would be classier if I arrived in a chauffeur-driven car, even if it was a taxi. I was overcome by shyness as I got out of the cab; it seemed as though everybody in front of the theater was looking in my direction to see if I was somebody. Surrounded by such beautiful people, of course, I felt like nobody. I spotted Bill standing over on the side, under the marquee.

"Hi! You look nifty." I could have kissed him. Maybe I did.

"You look pretty good yourself," I told him. "We look like we're ready for the Debutante Ball."

"Well, you do," Bill cracked. "Me, I'm not so sure."

As we stood in line, I asked, "Have you seen Jimmy since he's been back?"

"Once or twice, on the run. We've both been busy. Have you?"

"No. I've talked to him on the phone a few times, but he said he wanted to wait until after the opening."

We were quiet then. Bill picked up the tickets and we were ushered to our seats, which were way down front. We read our programs. My stomach was in knots.

"Are you as nervous as I am?" I prodded. "My stomach won't sit down."

"Well, yeah. I feel a little anxious for him. This is a big deal," Bill whispered.

"I know. God, I hope he gets through his song. He was nervous about that." And then the lights went down.

The play began, and I remember nothing but the rush of emotions I felt as I sat there in the dark, watching not the actor but the boy I knew. I could see everything Jimmy was using to portray Wally, all the parts of his own history he was drawing upon, and it was working for him, just as it worked for him in his real life. He *was* an innocent, misunderstood boy.

I knew he was good, but I was a little surprised at just how good he was. I've never seen anyone as comfortable as he was onstage. As I looked around at the audience, it was obvious that he had totally commanded everyone's attention. Even when the other actors had the stage, and he was just sitting wistfully in his cage, all eyes seemed to gravitate toward him.

There were sound problems that night—most of Alec Wilder's prerecorded music went unheard after the tape broke—and a few other little glitches. But Jimmy was perfect. After the final curtain call, when the lights in the house came up, Bill said we should go backstage to say hello before we left for Sardi's. All I could think of was going backstage to see my father. There would be millions of people there ahead of me, gushing and pushing, making the most of their compliments, until there would be nothing original left for me to say. My stomach was still in flutters, and drifting into nausea, when I spotted the crowd gathered outside Jimmy's dressing room. We were elbowing our way through the door when Jimmy spotted us.

He hugged us both. "Did you like it? Everything that could go wrong did go wrong, but I remembered my lines! Thanks, you guys!" And he was off, whirling around, spreading himself thin so all could fall at his feet. He told us to wait so that he could get his coat and walk with us to Sardi's, but it was only a few blocks, so I told him we'd see him there. I needed the air.

As we walked, I asked Bill if he thought I looked shabby.

"Shabby? Are you kidding? You look great. What's the matter with you?"

"Didn't you see all those rich-looking people with their furs fawning all over Jimmy? Making goo-goo eyes at him, for God's sake?"

Bill laughed out loud. "'Goo-goo eyes?' What the hell's that?"

"I don't know." I couldn't stop whining. "This is his night. I can't help feeling like we don't belong."

"Oh, we belong. We're his friends and we're proud of him. Who belongs here more than us? This kind of a night doesn't happen to many people. He's not supposed to act like himself. He's on a high. If I were you, I wouldn't let him see you like this." He smiled. "Come on, Dizzy, enjoy yourself. We're going to Sardi's to drink champagne!"

When we got to Sardi's, there was a table waiting for us against the back wall, over to one side. I liked that. We could see the whole room, yet we were out of the way. Jimmy arrived to a smattering of applause, and started table-hopping right away. Every once in a while he would wave to us; occasionally he would come over to catch his breath, have a cigarette, and go back to walk the bullring and receive his *olés*.

Finally people started arriving with the early papers, and the reviews we were all waiting for. The play itself fared rather poorly. Lemuel Ayers, who had put so much of himself into it all—from producing the play to creating the costumes and sets—was crushed. But Jimmy's performance was a different story. There were so many New York papers at that time, and most of Jimmy's reviews were filled with enthusiasm. Some reviewers wrote that he showed promise, some loved him outright. But they all agreed that this young man was going places. Jimmy was positively glowing with the acclaim; he was being coaxed from table to table, and every time he approached a new table they applauded.

As he made the rounds, I could see he had already turned a corner. He had begun his odyssey. I couldn't help but wonder what happened to the shy, rumpled, clumsy boy I'd fallen in love with just a year before. The Jimmy being feted that night was a poised young man, self-possessed, gracious, and sociable. And in my heart I suddenly felt like another member of his audience. I was afraid, but I tried not to show it. Watching him, it occurred to me to wonder whether I could summon enough grace to withdraw with class . . . or was it enough class to withdraw with grace? I chuckled.

"What's funny?" Bill said.

"Absolutely nothing." I lit another cigarette.

Sardi's was beginning to clear out; it was late, and the reviews had cast a pall over the room. You can't kick a dead horse too long without feeling ghoulish. Bill finally said good night, and Jimmy turned to me. "Stay with me tonight, okay?"

"Uh . . . are you sure?"

"Don't you want to?" He looked hurt. I was surprised.

"I want to. Yes, I want to. I just thought . . . well, maybe tonight you'd want to be with the cast or something," I mumbled. "I don't know what I thought."

He smiled. "No, I want my Betty Beacon. My steady light. Come with me and let me tread your boards."

I smiled back. "My, my. One Broadway show and we're Mr. Theatrical."

"That's me. And Mr. Theatrical says let's go."

He grabbed my hand and pulled me toward the exit. Dizzy and Jimmy again, going off to play.

The Royalton, where Jimmy was staying, was right across the street from the Iroquois, but worlds apart in class. The lobby was lovely, and once again I felt uncomfortable in my dull cloth coat. But Jimmy was thriving; it was perhaps the first time he'd ever had a nice, steady paycheck, and he was treating himself to a taste of the good life.

The night clerks looked up from the front desk as we walked by. I kept my eyes lowered, but my shame in turn made me furious with myself. Jimmy held my hand all the way through the lobby and up the elevator; not until he closed the door to his room did he let go, and then only to call down and order room service—club sandwiches and a bottle of champagne.

"I've missed you," he said quietly as he took me in his arms. "I know I haven't paid you much attention tonight.

Every time I started toward you, it seemed like somebody else wanted a piece of me. Are you still my little girl?"

I smiled. "Yes, as long as you want me to be."

It had been such a long time since we had kissed, and now we did, and the passion again seemed real. He loosened my hair gently. He was breathing heavily, and I was trembling. We took our coats off, dropping them to the floor; he led me over to the bed and knelt on the edge as I lowered myself onto the pillows. He lay down next to me and we kissed each other hungrily . . . until a knock on the door brought us back to reality. Our food had arrived.

I wanted him to say, "No! Not now! Come back later!" Instead he rolled on his back, and said, "Oh, shit."

Then he rolled off the bed, crashing to the floor with a thud.

"Are you still there?" I asked.

He peered at me over the mattress like Kilroy. "Here I am." Then he hopped up and opened the door for the waiter, who made his way into the room without looking directly at either of us. He put his tray on the desk, then pulled the champagne from the little silver bucket. "Shall I open the wine, sir?"

"Yes, please," Jimmy replied.

The waiter handled the job with a cool professionalism, despite the scene of suggestive disarray before him. I was disheveled, and more than a little embarrassed, but Jimmy was so cool. He seemed to be in his element, signing the check with a flourish. The waiter backed out of the room, as if departing a Buddhist temple, with just the slightest hint of a smile touching his face.

No sooner had he closed the door than we were back on the bed, rolling about and making each other giggle. I knew we were aching for each other, but, as if it were an unspoken pact, we were stalling, prolonging the moment as long as we could stand it.

"I'm so proud of you," I said. "Let's toast to your future."

"I'm so proud of you too."

"For what? My coffee-pouring expertise? The stylish way I wield my flashlight up and down the aisles?"

"Yes," he said, and I whacked him on the head with a pillow.

We each took a sip of champagne, which tasted like it was made yesterday in New Jersey. We put our glasses down and I jumped on top of him, but suddenly he flipped me over and lay on top of me.

He looked at me so tenderly. "What's to become of us?"

I didn't answer. I didn't know.

The question was hanging heavily in the air when the phone rang. Jimmy answered; it was the manager, requesting there be no ladies in the room overnight. It was a house rule, he said. Would Mr. Dean like for the hotel to arrange for a cab to escort his guest home after they had finished their meal?

"That won't be necessary," Jimmy said. "We'll manage on our own." He slammed down the receiver but missed the cradle, and he had to fumble around until he managed to slam it successfully. "I'm so sorry. That son of a bitch told me you have to leave. He said it was okay to finish our meal first, though," he sneered. "Isn't that swell?"

"I'm not hungry." I was near tears, and so was he. The champagne wasn't all that was flat.

"We could go across the street to the Iroquois," I offered. "They know us there."

"I don't know. I'm pretty drained. We had something going here, and now it's ruined. Fuck 'em, I'll put you in a cab myself."

I lowered my head as we made our exit in silence, feeling like a whore. My hands were cold as ice, as if the blood were leaving my body. We walked over to Broadway hand in hand in silence. It must have been about three in the morning. Jimmy looked tired; it must have been exhausting, flying as high as he was all night long without crashing. I let him hail the cab, and as he opened the door I kissed him lightly on the cheek. He held my face in his hands. I smelled the familiar tobacco-soap-alcohol on his fingers. And he kissed me again, lovingly.

"I've missed you."

"It felt so good just to kiss you and feel your arms around me. I missed you too."

"We will continue this night, real soon. I'll call you tomorrow."

I threw myself into the cab as a tear started to trickle down my cheek. I brushed it aside quickly and rolled down the window to say good night.

"Dudley, you were wonderful tonight."

"Hey, if the waiter hadn't arrived when he did, you'd know what 'wonderful' really means."

I managed a smile. "Well, what there was of it wasn't too bad, either."

We were smiling at each other as I cranked up the window. When the cab moved forward, I turned to look out the back. He had already started back to his hotel. I waved, pathetically, to the back of his head.

*See the Jaguar* closed after five performances. Jimmy told me it was pretty grim at the theater the next night. I didn't see him very often, and when we did get together we seemed more like old friends than like lovers. We did make love, a few times, but not as desperately or as passionately as we had. It was all too comfortable, all so uncomfortable.

But *See the Jaguar*, it was already clear, had jump-started Jimmy's career. His stunning reviews led to a flurry of auditions. He moved back to the Iroquois; on occasion I stayed the night with him, and now and then he returned the favor.

One night I asked him, "What happened to us?"

"Nothing," he said. "It's me. I'm all fucked up. There are too many people inside of me."

*Well, you can all go fuck yourselves.* "What if we had actually married when you asked me?"

He hesitated, then shrugged sadly. "I would have stood by you."

I didn't even know what that meant. "Bullshit!" was all I could manage to say.

"I'm sorry you feel that way."

"Yeah, me too."

My father and I had gotten back in touch once again around the same time that Jimmy returned to New York. He had apologized for being so stern with me; it was a first. But he, too, was terribly unhappy. His second marriage was falling apart, and he was drinking too much, though I wasn't yet aware of it at the time.

One evening he called and told me he needed to see me. He was around the corner at the Russian Tea Room; could I meet him? It sounded urgent.

By the time I got there, he was well on his way.

"Hi, Daddy." I gave him a peck on the cheek and slid into the booth. "Are we celebrating something?"

"Quite the opposite, actually. I'm trying to drown my sorrows. Will you join me?"

"I don't feel like drinking. But I'll have a beer with you, I guess."

"What happened?" He smiled. "Your Champale lost its fizz?"

I didn't answer; it was none of his business. Instead I told him about the splash Jimmy had made in *See the Jaguar*. "Did you happen to read any of the reviews?" I asked.

"No," he admitted. "I have no interest in the theater these days, or anything else, for that matter."

"Well, the play got slammed, but Jimmy's reviews were wonderful. I told you he was going somewhere."

"And are you going to this somewhere with him?"

"I don't think so. I haven't decided."

I was sorry I'd mentioned Jimmy at all. I'm sure he didn't give a damn one way or the other. He took a long sip, then suddenly leaned over and took my hand.

"How would you like to go on a trip with me?" he said. "I know you love horses. We could go out west, someplace where you could ride your fool head off."

*What? The last place in the world I would want to be: alone with my father on some dude ranch. Just the thought of it gave me the creeps.* "Uh . . . I don't understand. Do you mean a vacation? It's winter! No! I'm so happy in my new apartment. I have a job. I don't want to leave town right now . . . I don't understand, Daddy." I think it may have been the first time I'd ever said no to my father.

"Well, think about it," he said tersely.

*Oh, God, I've hurt his feelings. What's going on?* He looked hurt—crestfallen. I didn't know what else to say. I felt a nausea rising into my throat. I swallowed it down. "I'm so tired, now. Can I please go home? Let me think about it."

"All right," he said curtly. "I'll walk you to your door."

Standing up to my father was always impossible for me. I don't know, to this day, exactly why. He paid the check and we walked back to the brownstone in silence. I said good night as we were approaching the door, but he said he wanted to come up and talk for a little while before he went home. I was exhausted, but he insisted.

No one was home, except of course for Lady Pam. I sat down on one of the daybeds in the living room. My father came over and sat down next to me. He was quite drunk. His movements were unsteady, his eyes glazed over, and he was breathing heavily. I was becoming alarmed. He began stroking my hair.

"Are you happy?"

"Yes, Daddy, I'm happy. I guess."

Before I knew what was happening, he had pushed me onto my back and was kissing me on the lips.

I was in shock. All I remember was his drunken breath. I was terrified. I cried out, and in that second Lady Pam leapt up and stood over us, as if she were menacing an intruder.

I pushed my father away, mortified and unsteady. He managed to get up, and started mumbling. "What? Sorry . . . I thought . . . I . . . "

I was shattered. At that moment I felt my father's embarrassment, and I was humiliated for him. *What in the hell happened?* Bless Lady Pam for knowing what to do. I put my arms around her and calmed her as my father stumbled about the room. I left him fumbling with the doorknob while I ran to the bathroom to collect myself for a moment. My hands were still trembling, but after a moment I realized I was no longer afraid of him. What I needed was for my father to sober up, and the only thing I could think of was stuffing him full of coffee and food.

We went to a restaurant just a few doors away. Daddy straightened out a little, but the dinner was endless. We small-talked as if nothing had occurred. It's possible that, in his mind, nothing had; even as I found him a cab and sent him home, he never even acknowledged what had happened between us.

Most little girls naturally dote on their fathers. I never did. I idolized my father from afar. He was dashing and famous; being around him was heady stuff for an emotionally sensitive little girl. But he always made me feel like an unwelcome intrusion in his life. Whenever he deigned to allow me to sing a little song for him, or do a dance sequence I was proud of, he always concluded the ritual with a critique of my performance. He was never able to find it in his heart to accept me at face value. And now he had taken whatever little comfort I was still able to find in his company and extinguished it.

My father, my friend Sue, my Jimmy: all were gone now. And I was ready to run. My roommate Connie had just spent two weeks securing a divorce on the island of St. Thomas. She adored being there and talked about it constantly, so when I told her I was thinking about seeking out some new horizons, she knew just what to do: a friend of hers was the district attorney for the island, and she wrote and asked him whether he might have a job available for a young American friend. When he wrote back and told her there might be, that was all the encouragement I needed.

My mom thought I was crazy. "Why so far away? You're leaving your family and friends behind, all because of a letter from some stranger on an island in the Pacific Ocean?"

"The Atlantic Ocean, Mom. Actually, it's the Caribbean Sea—even closer."

"I still don't understand why you're leaving."

"I'm not sure I do either. I know you like Jimmy a lot, Mom, but I was starting to depend on him for my happiness, and he seems to be moving away from me. I want to experience my *own* happiness. Do you understand?"

"I'm not sure I do. But I know how stubborn you are when you fixate on something. Have you told your father?"

"Not yet, and I'm not looking forward to it."

"How soon do you plan to leave?"

"I'm not sure. Maybe a few weeks, maybe sooner. I just wanted you to know. Don't worry about me ... Well, that's stupid; I know you will. But try not to, okay?"

"Why so sudden, dear? It's not every day that people up and move to a different country."

I laughed. "Mom, you're so cute." I hugged her.

"Seriously," she continued, "is something wrong? I mean, besides with you and Jimmy?"

"Oh, Ma." *How could I even say it?* But I had to. I couldn't feel ashamed forever. I had to bring it out in the open. "Daddy ... tried to do something unnatural to me."

"My God—what do you mean, 'unnatural'?"

I told her what happened, as plainly and undramatically as I could. I didn't dwell on my revulsion; I tried to retain whatever sympathy for Daddy I could.

"Oh, Elizabeth, I'm so sorry. People do things when they're drunk that they don't mean. He would never harm you; he loves you." My mother was one of the last innocents on earth. She gave me her blessings, some money, and I left.

I didn't care what my father thought about my plan, but I called to tell him.

"Do you need anything?" he asked.

"No," I said. "Good-bye."

There was one other person I wanted to talk to: Adrienne, soon to be Daddy's ex-wife. Adie wasn't too much older than I, and we were pretty good friends, considering the circumstances. We met for lunch at Sardi's.

I slowly went through everything that had happened that night between Daddy and me, as delicately as I could. She didn't seem to be as shocked as I thought she would. She seemed to understand.

When I finished, she said, "Dizzy, I've always liked you. You haven't had an easy childhood, you and Frances. Your father is not an easy man to live with. In fact, he's not an easy man to know."

"Don't you love him anymore?" I felt oddly defensive.

"There's always a little wash from the boat left behind," she said. "But your father and I have run our course." They hadn't been getting along, she explained, and she felt it was best to end a marriage that should never have taken place. She was much younger than he was; he was good-looking, and famous, and her teacher; no doubt all that was seductive to her. But he was also becoming a serious drinker, and Adrienne knew that was going to be more than she could take.

Adie suggested that I go see a friend of hers, an excellent psychiatrist who might be able to give me a little peace of mind. When I mentioned it to Mom she thought it might be a good idea, which surprised me, given her Christian Scientist background. Moved by curiosity as well as need, I called Adie and asked her to make the appointment.

The doctor's office wasn't far from the Paris, on Fifty-seventh Street on the East Side. I don't remember what the doctor looked like, but I remember the room: plushy and comfortable, with a view of the park. I proceeded to tell him why Adie thought I needed his help. I told him about what had happened with Daddy, and about my opportunity to travel; I never mentioned Jimmy.

"And how can I help you, Elizabeth?"

"I don't think you can."

"What makes you think that?"

"Because I want to help myself."

"And so you are. Just by coming to see me, you're taking the first step toward a cure."

"But I don't have a disease. There's nothing wrong with me. I just want to go away and have some new experiences."

"How do you feel about your father?"

"Not very well."

"Wouldn't you like to feel better about him?"

"No."

"In other words, young lady," he said with a hint of frustration, "you are like a mermaid, sitting on a rock in the middle of the ocean, who has thrown her compass to the winds."

"I guess so." And then, "Yes!" I *loved* that image. I wanted to be that mermaid—*was* that mermaid—and he had just handed me my passport.

I got up and said, "Thank you, Doctor."

"We have a few minutes left."

"I think I've found out everything I needed to know. Thanks again."

He looked at me quizzically. "You're welcome." I turned and left and never went back.

I've never forgotten those words. A foolhardy mermaid, tempting the fates.

♦♦

I couldn't wait to tell Jimmy about my mermaid plans. I called him, and we made a date for him to come over to the apartment when no one was around. Surprisingly, he didn't want me to go. Over a cup of coffee, we talked of the future, his and mine.

"Do you know what you're doing?" he asked me.

"No."

"Why do you have to go so far away?"

"Funny—that's what Mom said."

He took my hand and looked at me over his glasses, forlornly. He knew I couldn't stand that Kilroy look of his.

"Because the opportunity's there, and it really appeals to me. The more I think about it, the more excited I get. If I stay here, I can't see beyond years of chorus work, or ushering and pouring coffee. There's no purpose to my life right now. I'm so proud of you, but I'm jealous too. I don't want to just tag along. You wouldn't want that either. I'm not a coattail hanger. I want you to fly, but I want to fly too. I need a life of my own now. I need to go."

"I understand." It was a whisper. "It's hard to think of us not together."

"We haven't been together for quite a while. I mean really together, like we used to be."

"It might have seemed that way to you, but I knew in my heart that you were here, available when I needed you—"

"That's one of the problems. I don't want to be just 'available' when you need me. I don't know what I want, but I know that seeing you now makes me more sad than happy. There's no place for me in what's happening to you now. Your life is changing so fast, I can almost see your head spinning."

"It stops spinning when I'm with you." He was being so sweet, I couldn't stop the flow of tears. "Oh, please, Diz, don't cry. I'll keep you safe." And he took me in his arms.

"You can't," I said. "You can't, now. When we were together and we were locking out the world, I felt safe. But now everything is different. I want to go away before I get too scared to try."

"I will never, ever forget you."

"I won't let you."

"You'll be coming back. I know it."

"Probably."

"We'll write."

"Yes. We'll become paper mates." We were lying on pillows, in front of the fireplace. Jimmy was on his back, holding me to him. "And when we're famous they'll sell our letters for trillions of dollars to the Museum of Modern Art. The museum will put them on display, and people will pass by in hushed reverence, shaking their heads in wonder."

He picked up the ball. "But someone—a very clever thief—will come along and steal them from the museum. He'll be caught, but before they reach him, he'll throw the letters away. They'll fall in one of the doorways where Moondog sleeps. Not being able to read them, of course, Moondog will stuff them in his bag to use for wrapping his fruit and vegetables . . ."

"However," I jumped in, "Sue, who knows Moondog, will have become a regular since I left New York, stopping by all the time to say hello, bring him some fruit."

Jimmy was excited now. "She'll happen to see our letters, tell Moondog about them. And they'll decide to split the reward."

"Reward!?"

"Of course. By now the whole town—no, the whole world—will know. The reward will be a million dollars." He stopped. "Do you think that's too little?"

"Definitely."

"Okay, then. Two million. And a car."

We were laughing now.

"I love you, Mr. Dean."

"I love you, Mrs. Dean."

And that was that.

## 13

Flying into the town of Charlotte Amalie on the island of St. Thomas early in 1953 was an unforgettable experience. The airstrip is right on the ocean, and when approached from that side it's a piece of cake. But on every other side it's surrounded by steep hills, and planes have to squeeze down through a slim pass before drifting onto the strip. Taking off with any kind of crosswind, in either direction, is just as harrowing. Once on the island, it's easy to choose staying forever rather than facing the plane ride out.

The airport was small, just a few hangars here and there. The only commercial planes that flew there were leftover cargo ships used in World War II—they were DC-3s, I think. The planes held thirty or forty passengers; there were two flights a day, in and out.

The minute I walked off the plane, the sweet tropical air touched my skin. I was excited, tired, impatient. Everywhere I looked, there were fresh flowers for sale. A steel band was playing as I walked inside the airport, and the rhythms were so infectious that I found myself keeping time as I walked. It may sound strange, but I felt right at home.

There were several booths scattered inside the airport, each representing one of the many hotels on the island, enticing whoever would stop a moment and listen to the spiels of greeters extolling the virtues of their hotel. The colorful posters behind each booth beckoned: Bluebeard's Castle, the Virgin Isles Hotel, a host of smaller inns and guest houses, and my new home, the Caribbean Hotel, where Connie's helpful friend had found me a job.

Swaying to the music, I shuffled through the airport and jumped in a cab. We didn't have far to go: the Caribbean was just around the corner and up the hill. Everything in the town of Charlotte Amalie was different from what I was used to, and yet exactly what I was expecting. The hotel was a long, two-story, white wooden building, secluded among palm trees, frangipangi, and tropical greenery. It was built on a cliff, almost completely surrounded by water. A long veranda graced the front of each floor. Each room had a private balcony, with lounge chairs and a dining setup. Here I could mend my broken heart; here I could recover my balance.

My job was to solicit tourists for the hotel when they arrived off the plane from Puerto Rico; in return I received one of the smaller rooms at the hotel, free meals, and fifty dollars a week, and I tried to save every penny. Each day I sat behind a little booth at the airport, greeting each planeload of travelers as they arrived. I caught on quickly, and garnered my share of customers, but it wasn't very difficult work: there were only two flights a day, so I got to spend most of my time on the beach across the street from the airport. In the evenings, I sat at the main bar in the dining room, schmoozing with the guests and enjoying the floor show, which featured a wonderful calypso band called Richard's Orchestra. I made friends with the musicians and learned to sing all the calypsos they taught me.

After a few weeks on the island, I was tan and relaxed. I still had no great ambition, but it didn't seem to matter. I was taking life as it came along.

The caretaker and gardener who worked the property was a sweet man named Noah. I noticed that among his many jobs he took care of a horse, which he kept in a small enclosure near the hotel. One day I asked about the horse. He was a quarter horse, Noah told me, a bay stallion named Generalé with a small white blaze on his forehead. I asked if I could ride him sometime.

"Do you ride well? He can be a handful sometimes. He loves to run. I used to race him. He was *muy rapido*, very fast, but he's gotten lazy. I don't have time to exercise him. I think he is mad at me, and I don't blame him, but what can I do? I'm so busy. So much to do here. *Mucho trabajo*. Savvy?"

"Yes," I said, laughing. "I'll make him happy, I promise. I love to ride and I'm good at it, so please don't worry. We'll get along."

Noah showed me where he kept the tack, and handed me a bridle. "I'm sorry," he said, "all I have is a small racing saddle. Is that all right?"

"Yes, that's fine. But I think I'll ride him bareback the first time."

"Are you certain?"

"Yes. Does he like to swim?"

"He loves to swim."

"Good." I walked over to the makeshift corral. When I started to approach Generalé with the bridle in my hand, he flipped his ears up at me, tossed his head, and whinnied softly.

"Well, aren't you a sad-looking beauty?" I said as I opened the gate. I wished I'd had an apple or sugar cube to give him, but he let me walk right up to him and tickle his nose. "Hello, Generalé. We are going to be great friends, I just know it." He whinnied again, as if in agreement. He accepted the bridle without too much fuss. I led him out of his little corral and walked him around, talking to him softly all the while.

"What a good boy. You're kind of fat for a racehorse, you know that? I'm gonna get on your back now, and then you and I are going for a little ride. Okay?"

I lay myself over his back so he could feel my weight. So far, so good. I slid off, clutched a handful of his mane, and Indian-mounted him. He started to rear, but I let him know who was boss right away and he settled down. We headed for an almost deserted beach I had discovered. As soon as we reached the water's edge, I gently pressed his sides with my knees; he began to trot; then, when I leaned forward, he saw what I was after and took off running. Not too fast, but fast enough. Up and down the beach we went, back and forth, until he was lathered up pretty good. I pulled him up and walked him into the gentle surf, then slipped off and let him swim on his own. Taking care to stay away from his churning hoofs, I swam with Generalé along the coast. Then, when we'd both cooled down, I walked him out of the sea, remounted, and rode slowly back to the hotel.

"Did you like that?" I cooed to him. "It's the most fun I've had in a long time." I removed his bridle and put it away and currycombed him, talking to him all the while. "I've got to go now, but I'll see you tomorrow and we'll do it again. Okay?"

I gave him a long hug, and turned to find Noah standing nearby.

"Thank you so much for letting me ride him," I said.

"No, I thank you. I watched you two, and he likes you. I can tell. You may ride him anytime."

"I like him too," I said. "I'll be by again tomorrow." And I hurried off to meet the last plane of the day.

Generalé and I started going out together every day, and soon he made a miraculous transformation. He lost all his extra weight, his coat began to shine, his neck arched, and his ears were pricked most of the time. Riding this noble animal, so strong and proud and majestic, I couldn't help feeling I'd found another way to be alive, another way to be free. Generalé was intelligent; he knew joy and power, honesty and devotion. He would see me coming and toss his head in anticipation, and once we were on our way I would throw my arms around his neck and whisper in his ear. All he needed was to be loved and cared for, and for me nothing could have been easier.

We rode along the beaches, through the town, up and over hills into landscapes of breathtaking beauty where tourists are almost never seen. Along the stretch of grass alongside the runway we raced the airplanes as they took off, and day after day we beat the smaller aircraft with ease. And nearly every day we swam in the ocean together, side by side.

We were seen everywhere on the island, my hair as long as Generalé's tail; eventually someone even wrote a calypso song about us, a naughty number called "That Girl, She Love Her Horse Too Much." I could only be flattered: at last I had become an island girl.

My job was pleasant; I enjoyed greeting the tourists and luring them to the hotel with tantalizing promises I hoped would be kept. But I can't say the same for my boss, Mr. Feldstein, who took an uncomfortable interest in me from the day I started. He was a round, balding, greasy little man, and a lecherous son of a bitch. I was able to keep him at bay for a long time, until one day when he summoned me to his room. He'd hurt his back, he said. Would I massage it? I was repulsed by the hairy expanse of flesh he exposed to me, but I was naive enough to wonder whether this may have been part of my job. I gave his neck and shoulders a quick rubdown, but I couldn't bring myself to go into the woods; I made an excuse and got the hell out of there as fast as I could.

Now, Mr. Feldstein was a gangster type, and once I left his room all I could do was imagine all the horrible things he could bring down on me if he so desired. I thought about paying a visit to the D.A. who had gotten me the job in the first place, but Mr. Feldstein really hadn't done anything but ask me to massage his back, and I didn't think that was against the law. So all I could do was try to avoid him as much as possible.

The next time he summoned me, it was late at night. The bar was just closing, so I fortified myself with a couple of stiff drinks and went to his room with more than a little trepidation. He opened the door—he was wearing a white terry cloth bathrobe—and asked me in.

"You wanted to see me, Mr. Feldstein?"

"Yes, I thought we could have a pleasant chat, maybe a little massage, like before." He made it sound like a question, but it was a command.

"I'm really not a massage person," I said. "And I don't feel comfortable doing this."

"Doing what?" he barked.

"Well . . . just being here."

"Well, you're with the boss." He laughed. "So relax and forget about it." He started toward me. I screamed, began to sob, and ran for the door, his loutish voice calling after me, "Hey, you!"

The phone was ringing when I got to my room. It was Mr. Feldstein. "Listen, girlie, I don't know what you think is going on here, but I don't like it. And I'll show you how much I don't like it. You're fired! How's that, girlie? I want you out of here tomorrow." And he slammed down the phone.

That was all right with me. I'd managed to save some money, so I rented myself a pretty little room near the center of town. Charlotte Amalie was as picturesque as you can imagine: tiny cobbled streets lined with small, wooden, capriciously painted houses nestled on steep hillsides, each of them enjoying a breathtaking view of Caribbean waters as far as the eye could see.

My new home was halfway up a hilly street known as Commandant Gade; the early settlers of the Virgin Islands were from Denmark, and *gade* is the word for street in Danish. I took a room on the second floor of this tall wooden structure, across the hall from a landlord whose dog would bite if his master didn't like you. I paid my rent, so he liked me. My room had a four-poster bed as its centerpiece, with mosquito netting I lowered at night for sleeping; the floor was covered with the woven matting that is used everywhere in the islands, and I bought myself a small, furry throw rug to put by my bed for my bare feet to fall upon when I got up in the morning. I had a hot plate, a small bureau and armoire, and a balcony with a view of the world around me.

I racked my brain trying to think of ways to make a living. What did I know that people would pay to learn from me? Dance! I sent out feelers to everyone I knew about starting classes for children, and the reception was encouraging. I also started practicing the piano in the afternoons at several of the clubs I frequented at night. My father and sister had managed to teach me a few keyboard basics through the years, so I started accompanying myself, singing the calypsos I'd learned, and managed to get a few jobs here and there entertaining tourists in the afternoons while their cruise ships rested in the harbor.

If this all sounds as though it happened too easily, it did. Never for a moment did I think I would fail to accomplish anything I started out to do. Though my heart was badly cracked, I was finding solace and relaxation in the rhythms of Charlotte Amalie. I was making enough money to pay my rent and live the good life; my classes were growing, and so was my repertoire. Little by little I started singing other songs besides calypsos: show tunes, Irish ballads my mother had taught me, French folk songs I'd learned in school, and of course a few songs from *Hans Christian Andersen*. My accompaniment was simple, almost adolescent, but I got by, and nobody seemed to care. Whenever I ran into a passage I couldn't handle on the piano—and there were many—I would just sing louder and play softer. Between songs I would chat with the customers and have a drag from my cigarette (there was always one smoldering in the ashtray) and a sip of my rum and Coke. I felt like Rita Hayworth in *Gilda* or Marlene Dietrich in that movie she did with John Wayne and a bunch of palm trees. But there was no John Wayne . . . yet.

My neighbor downstairs was William, a ballet dancer from the States. He was in his thirties, very pale, very gay, and a very sweet man. William had put together a dance troupe for Carnival—St. Thomas's answer to Mardi Gras—and some of them, including William himself, took classes from me. One of the features of Carnival was a dance contest that drew entrants from all over the Caribbean, and William asked me to help choreograph a number for the troupe.

I have never in my life experienced anything remotely like the exhilaration of Carnival in St. Thomas. Let me see if I can convey something of its excitement to you: imagine a main street maybe ten blocks long, lined with fancy jewelry shops, colorful stores, guest houses and bars, and a great big liquor store carrying the finest booze for no more than two dollars a bottle. Come the start of Carnival, people begin flowing out of every doorway, rushing to every balcony, window, and door. Coming from the edge of town, a mass of people led by a steel band parades down the street, ringing its calypso call throughout the streets. As they approach the center of town, their faces are filled with pure joy. Thousands of feet shuffle along in a leisurely dance step called the tramp, moving inch by inch in time to the rhythm. The mass moves forward sinuously, like one great organism, moving back and forth, up and down, in time to the mesmerizing beat. You're smashed against your neighbor in front, the tramper behind smashed against you. The beat goes on, and all's right with the world.

That first Carnival in St. Thomas, I felt as if I had an angel on my shoulder. William and I worked hard on our program for the dance contest, because winning was very important to all of us; I choreographed the routines, and William gave me a place as a dancer as well. We couldn't wait to present our show to the judges . . . and when we did, we won, jubilantly.

The other great Carnival event that captured our imagination was the big horse race a few days later. There was a racetrack on the far side of Charlotte Amalie; the track was small, the purses were small, and the jockeys, like me, were oversize and undertrained. During Carnival there was a six-hundred-dollar purse: three hundred for the winner, two hundred to place, and one hundred to show. So of course I couldn't resist entering with Generalé, pitting my darling horse against horses imported from all the neighboring islands. Generalé and I trained every morning; then, the morning of the race, I brought him down to the beach to watch as the crude native sloops of our competition arrived, their single white sails billowing in the wind, each one bearing a horse, tied to the mast, to be raced that day.

Post time, and the grandstand was crowded, almost out of control. After each race the crowd threw whatever they could onto the track: pop bottles, food, personal belongings, each other; those who'd bet on losers booed and shouted until the track was cleaned and the parade for the next race appeared.

There were six horses in our race. We were to go around the track twice, ending where we started. There was no starting gate, so we brought our horses up to a line drawn across the track. When the horses were abreast, which sometimes took a while to arrange, a man standing on the side dropped a red flag hanging from the end of a stick, and we were off.

The word for speed has several meanings in the dictionary, but what I felt at that moment, though I was used to Generalé's power, was something else. The other jockeys clicked and chirped at their horses; the sound of twenty-four hooves filled the air, as dirt and dust flew in the faces of every horse behind the leader. It was incredible. I could feel every beat of my heart.

Five seconds into the race, and we were dead last. But we'd managed to stay with the field. As we started around the track for the last time I let out a holler—"*Now!*"—and Generalé exploded like an engine primed with jet fuel. *Bang! Bang! Bang!* We passed each horse as if it were standing still.

Then it was over; then we had won. Not by a nose, but by at least two lengths.

The crowd began roaring at us, throwing bottles still filled with beer. I guess nobody had bet on the bay.

I split my share of the purse with Noah; he was so happy with us that he gave me the horse to keep, for as long as I stayed on the island. We were a family now—two mouths to feed, and plenty of money to do it. I paid a month's rent in advance, bought a bag of apples for Generalé and a new work outfit for me, and put away a few dollars for a rainy day.

A wonderful place to live and work; daylong workouts with Generalé; that series of ludicrous triumphs at Carnival—it was as if I were a child again, but one whose heart was finally full of the joy and pleasure I had never found within my own family. And it occurred to me that I was beginning to understand what Jimmy must be feeling. I heard from him occasionally, long letters with funny anecdotes and pictures or short, angry notes venting about some passing annoyance. I still missed him. In the letters I wrote him I tried to describe what I was doing, but it was impossible to explain the rhythms and colors of island life—of my life.

Jimmy had moved back to Hollywood and secured a contract with Warner Brothers. I could tell from his letters that he felt he was being swept away, without much time to think about where he was going. Much of his time was devoted to racing cars; he'd won a few races, he said, and it was the only time he felt completely alive. The studio wasn't very happy about him risking his life, but—as I well knew—nobody was going to tell him what to do.

I thought about Jimmy all the time, but I tried to make new friends. One of them was a construction engineer named Justus Villa, whom everyone called Pancho. He was tall and beautiful, the color of caramel, half Caucasian and half something darker. Pancho was from Brooklyn, with the accent to prove it; he was wise beyond belief and had a wicked sense of humor, and he treated me like a lady. And I came to love him.

At this time, I was working at Bluebeard's Castle on the weekends, performing at an open-balcony restaurant that overlooked the harbor. Pancho would come sit at the bar and listen to me sing. He was far more mature than I was, but my little-girl ways, my naïveté, and my bawdy mouth seemed to please him. He had two small children, a boy of eight and a girl of six, whom he'd enrolled in my dance class. Pancho and I became lovers, and the four of us quickly became a family. When I explained about Jimmy, he said he understood; he had been in love before too, he said, but he wanted me to be his wife and mother to his children.

Without thinking it through very clearly, we became engaged. I asked him if we could take it slow, but he was insistent and kept pressing me for a wedding date. I panicked. I became ill. He didn't know why. I started sleeping all the time; I lost my appetite and became feverish. Pancho took me to the hospital, where I stayed for a week. The doctors called it a nervous breakdown. I guess too much had happened too quickly, and my emotions had grown unstable. I loved Pancho, but not the way I loved Jimmy. I just couldn't marry him. He was incredibly understanding, but in the end he told me he had to think of his children and their future. He wanted a wife; I didn't want a husband, or to be a mother to someone else's children.

And so we said good-bye. And soon thereafter, with sadness but no regret, I said good-bye to my lovely little island, my new friends, and my beautiful horse. My plane took off, we made it safely into the air, and I was going home.

# 14

My psyche was in bits and pieces when I withstood the jolt of settling back into life in New York City. I didn't understand what had happened to me. I had come home to heal, but that wasn't happening. I was supersensitive to everything around me. I felt defenseless. All the hurt and humiliation, all the bitter disappointment I had shrugged off throughout my life, were coming back at once. I was morbid one minute, ecstatic the next. I cried and laughed for no reason.

I spent time with my mother, whose instinct told her that the best treatment she could offer was to leave me be. I was grateful to her, and yet I longed for a measure of comfort and understanding I could never open myself up enough to invite. I took greatest solace in the piano, and I practiced and practiced and extended my repertoire all the time. My mother still sang up the river, and once a week took a train into the city to sing with her accompanist for a few hours; both of us seemed able to lean on our artistic outlets for strength and balance.

When I visited the city, I often stayed with Sue—she'd returned from the road to take a cute little apartment on the Upper West Side—or with Lavonne on the East Side, or Art and Alex in Midtown. Friends were important, and I was grateful, but I didn't seem to fit in anywhere. If I was confused before I ran to the Caribbean, I was stunned, almost paralyzed, now. I had been away for about a year and a half, but it seemed like a lifetime. I looked for work, but halfheartedly. I missed the leisurely island life, and I missed Jimmy even more. Our love had made the city a fabulous playground; now it seemed grim and ugly. It was early autumn, and gentle winds were breathing on the doors in the evenings, but even the park was a drag. *Autumn in the city, for Christ's sake. They write songs about how beautiful it is.*

Jimmy's career was well into its steep ascent. From his second Broadway play, *The Immoralist*, to several prestigious television shows, his work was being reviewed with excitement. But the most exciting news was coming out of Hollywood, where he'd been chosen for the lead in the film adaptation of a John Steinbeck novel. Although *East of Eden* hadn't yet been seen by the public, advance word was already out about the performance of this young actor named James Dean.

I'd been staying with Art one weekend, in his old railroad flat on Eighth Avenue in the Forties, and I'd promised to help him throw a Sunday evening get-together for all his actor friends who were working in shows. When I got back from a shopping run, Art told me Jimmy had called. "It's the damnedest thing," he said. "He's in town, and he ran into Fabio on the street. Fabio told him you were back from St. Thomas, and that you were staying here. Sooo . . . I invited him to stop by for the party. Is that okay?"

"Sure. Okay. I'd love to see him. But do you think he'll really come?"

"He told Fabio he would." It took a minute to sink in.

We dug into the preparations: dips, salads, and a bunch of goodies. I was glad to be distracted from my thoughts. But when party time came and all our friends started arriving, I felt as if my nerves were wired directly to the doorbell. I told myself to calm down, but it didn't do any good. I flitted around, pouring wine, passing plates, listening and watching.

Lavonne was there; Fabio arrived, looking great. We schmoozed about old times, old jobs, even old dance steps. We agreed that the Sheridan Trio had deserved better than it got. Theater stories were flying around the room, and everyone was having fun. I was on my way to the kitchen with an armload of dishes when the doorbell rang again. I ran to the kitchen to dump the stuff and ran back to open the door.

There was Jimmy, the movie star. We both reached out at the same time; we hugged so hard and for so long that I lost my breath. I pulled back to get a look at him; he looked almost the same, maybe a little heavier, but it was his clothes that made me exclaim, "My God, you look so Hollywood!"

"Oh, no, don't tell me that!"

Jimmy was wearing a white turtleneck sweater and a raincoat thrown loosely over his shoulders. I was sorry the moment the words left my lips, but it was true: he looked every inch the movie star, wonderfully tan, well fed, and successful. Finally I heard a throat being cleared, and Jimmy stood aside to introduce two guests: his agent, Jane D'eacy, and a young man named Leonard Rosenman.

We joined the party, and I made hasty introductions all around. Art took over serving for a while, and I sneaked into the kitchen to catch my breath. I was standing over the sink, rinsing a glass, when I felt my pigtail being tugged. It was Jimmy, of course. He pulled my hair around to the side and stood next to me, watching the water run over my fingertips. No one spoke for a moment; we just stood there, side by side. I found myself relaxing.

"Are you all right?" he asked.

"Yes," I lied. "You?"

"I don't know," he said. "I'm just glad to see you. Tell me about island life."

I tried. I tried to fit it all together for him. I tried to make him feel the tropics as I did. I blurted out, "Wait till you see my horse! You'll love him."

"Maybe I will, someday. Are you going back?"

"I was happy there. My life kind of opened up for me. I didn't have to struggle as much as I do here." I asked again, "Are you all right, Jimmy?"

"Sometimes," he said. And we were quiet again.

I dried off my hands and we went back inside. Jimmy had a tight hold on my pigtail and wouldn't let go. I fell into chatting with Leonard Rosenman, the composer who'd written the score for East of Eden. He asked me about my father; Jimmy had played Daddy's records for him. We chatted with Lavonne, and Jimmy told her he remembered her fondly, especially one afternoon when the three of us discussed religion and Jimmy asked if she thought Jesus was divine. He remembered showing us how to walk backward, against the wind, like Marcel Marceau.

Lavonne later told me how touched she was that Jimmy was so sweet to her, but then again it was easy to be nice to a girl as lovely as Lavonne. The others at the party weren't so lucky. Jimmy was restless the whole evening, anxious to have some time alone with me. When one friend came over to say good night I started to get up from the couch to say good-bye, but Jimmy held on to my hair and wouldn't let me go to the door. He was rude to almost everyone. I guess I was flattered, but I was embarrassed for him too. The party was clearing out rapidly; Jimmy was emptying the room with his crass behavior.

"I'm going to Grand Central as soon as I help Art clean up," I told him. "You want to ride over in a cab and drop me off?"

"Yeah," he said.

Jimmy said good night to his friends Leonard and Jane, who left while I was clearing dishes and straightening up. Jimmy thanked Art for letting him crash the party, I gave Art a big hug, and Jimmy and I were off into the night to hail a cab.

The minute we settled in the backseat, Jimmy took my hand. I rested my head on the seat and closed my eyes. My thoughts shuffled through the past few years, then stopped when the past and present came together, and here we were: Dizzy and Jimmy, side by side.

I was drifting along when Jimmy let go of my hand. "Do you want a cigarette?"

"Yes," I said.

"Me too," he said, giggling. "Do you have one?"

I smiled. "A great big movie star like you, and you still can't afford to buy your own cigarettes? You haven't changed a bit."

"Was I supposed to?"

"I was hoping you'd be exactly the same. Maybe I was hoping *we'd* be exactly the same."

"Things never are," he said: a note of sadness.

"I know. But being with you like this, even for just this little while, I'm beginning to feel nothing's lost, you know?" I needed to know he understood.

"Nothing's lost," he said, his eyes bright. "Nothing's lost between us. It never will be. You're a part of me and I'm a part of you. I take you with me wherever I go."

"So do I. You were there in every sunset I—" Jimmy leaned over and kissed me before I could continue. The cab stopped suddenly, but it didn't matter.

"Grand Central," the cabdriver said, shutting down his meter. I opened the door and stepped out. Jimmy paid the driver and we walked through the doorway and down the great marble staircase, where we'd danced long ago. Jimmy was humming softly. We walked slowly toward the train; I was sure he wanted to start to play, just as we always had, but neither of us seemed to know how to begin. We just stood there, silently, holding hands.

"I know so many people now who could help you," he said after a while. "Why don't you think about coming to Los Angeles and working out there? I could help."

*Tell me to come live with you, and be your love again, and I'm ready to go with you right now.* "Maybe someday, but right now I'm thinking about going back to the West Indies. I started something down there. I'd like to see where it takes me."

We hugged one last time, and he whispered in my ear, "I'll always love you, Diz."

"I know," I said. "I'll always love you too."

We said good-bye and made plans to see each other in a few days.

"Maybe we can take a walk in the park before I have to go back. I'm not even supposed to be here. I'll call you."

We kissed once more, with tenderness, and I pulled away and ran down the platform toward the train. I looked back just before I boarded and saw him standing there, head cocked to one side, a lost puppy. He looked small, too small for his trench coat.

The next morning he called. The studio had tracked him down; he had to get back to Hollywood right away for some postproduction work. "This is what I hate about this fucking business, they never leave me alone. I wanted to walk in the park with you. I'm so sorry."

"I know, so did I. But I loved seeing you again. I'm so very proud of you."

"We'll write?"

"Yes, we'll write."

"Friends?"

"Friends."

"Good-bye, Dizzy."

"Good-bye."

I hung up the phone, still thinking of that last kiss. I felt at peace, just knowing that he still loved me. That's what he had said: "I'll always love you."

And I believed him.

# 15

I'd been sending off letters, looking for a job in the Caribbean, and a few weeks after Jimmy left, one of them finally paid off. A singer was needed in a club called the Music Hall in Puerto Rico, four weeks guaranteed, with options. I immediately sent a wire accepting the job, packed a bag, called a few friends to say good-bye.

Mom drove me to the airport. We hardly spoke on the way; there was little to say. I knew my restlessness saddened her, if only because she never truly understood it. She walked me to the gate, and I kissed her and told her I'd write.

"Be careful, dear, and let me know how you're doing. I worry about you."

"I know. I'm not sure I know what I'm doing, but I just have to hang on to the thing that's making me feel alive right now. Do you know what I mean?"

She looked curious. "You mean performing?"

"Yes. Mom, you've got to know what I mean. Having an audience? That's like lifeblood for me right now."

She smiled back. "Yes, I do. These days I'm just singing to entertain myself, though; I'm sure my prisoners would be entertained if I just stood on my head." We both laughed. "Still, it makes a difference."

I hugged my mother, and turned again to leave her.

San Juan was a picturesque delight. With its dozens of luxury hotels and casinos lined up on either side of the beachside Condado Strip, it was a tourist mecca. The weather was gorgeous, the currency American, the people more than willing to speak English when I couldn't follow their Spanish. The Music Hall, which sounded so huge and impressive by name, turned out to be a nice-size cocktail lounge, right off the lobby of a first-rate movie theater. There was a long bar and a few tables, with a piano on a small stage at the end of the room. The place was well lit and cozy, and during breaks, if I didn't feel like mingling, I could sit in the back row of the theater and take in a show. Best of all, it was only a short plane ride to St. Thomas, and Generalé.

On my very first day off, I caught the early plane to St. Thomas. I hadn't seen my island for quite some time, and I'd missed it.

The moment I arrived I ran all the way to the Caribbean Hotel to look for Noah and Generalé. The first place I checked was the little corral, and there they were.

"Well, if it isn't our old friend, Elizabeth. Your son has certainly missed you."

"I'm back. I'm working in San Juan now, but I couldn't wait to come and see you. Can I take a ride?"

He patted me on the back. "If you don't, I won't be able to explain it to your horse here."

Generalé just stood there stock still, staring me down. No little dance, no pricked ears, no whinny, no nothing; he was cross with me, and I couldn't blame him. I approached slowly, and started talking to him softly.

"Hello, my beautiful boy. I know you're mad at me. I'm so sorry I had to go away and leave you. I said good-bye, remember? I missed you very much and I thought about you every day. I'm back now, and I'm going to see you often. Look what I've brought for you!"

I'd had the foresight to bring along a peace offering—a nice, big, red apple. I held out my hand with the apple and he gave a little snort, reached for it, and it disappeared. Then he pushed his nose under my armpit, and forgave me.

I put on his bridle and a little riding saddle. Noah gave me a foot up, and we were off. We rode up into the hills, feeling the warmth of remembering, of coming home; then we headed down into the town, taking time to say hello to a few old friends, one of whom told me that Pancho had gotten married and seemed to be happy. I was glad to hear it, and relieved.

I headed for Generalé's favorite beach near the hotel across from the airport, and let him run up and down the water's edge a few times where the beach was deserted. He'd put on a little weight, but he was still fast. I had my bathing suit on under my jeans and T-shirt, so I quickly peeled off my clothes and walked him into the surf. And we swam, side by side, soothed by the blue and green of the Caribbean waters.

San Juan was a very creative place in those days. The Ballet de San Juan was an accomplished troupe with a large repertoire, and the Graphic Arts Department at the Instituto de Cultura was world-class. Many great local painters came out of the area during the 1950s and 1960s, and of course every year the Casals Festival brought noteworthy musicians from around the world.

San Juan was discovered by Columbus in 1493, and the Old City was more than four hundred years old. The original Spanish architecture had been maintained and preserved; the streets were paved with blue bricks that had been used as ballast in the Spanish ships that docked there in the early sixteenth century. Palm trees and small cafés dotted these cobbled streets, which ran straight up little narrow hills branching out from the main plaza in the center of town.

The club where I worked was just across the lagoon, not far from the Old City. I built a following quickly there, and before long I was assured that the job was mine for as long as I wanted it. My hours were nine at night until three or four in the morning, and the manager and a few of the regulars saw to it that no one messed with me. When we closed for the night, more often than not several of us would go around the corner and have breakfast at Al's Little Club, where a few of us would sit until dawn. Then I would call a cab and go home to my little apartment—usually alone, but not always. Those early-morning hours catered to artists, entertainers, musicians, casino dealers, hookers, convivial alcoholics, and anyone else reluctant to put the night away. Night people are my kind of people; they don't ask a lot of questions. Live and let live is their code, and I loved that.

I slowly built a life for myself in Puerto Rico, full of strong friendships and fleeting acquaintances. Statesiders were known as continentals, and I was the only female continental entertainer on the island at the time—a claim I make only because I remember reading it in *The Island Times*, a weekly English-language newspaper.

Along with rice and beans, music was among the most popular Puerto Rican staples. Calypso singers like the Mighty Sparrow and my old friend the Duke of Iron were everywhere, along with many great bands (including my old friend Noro Morales). There were wonderful performers, but no one did what I did—whatever that was—and I was glad of that.

One of the friends I made was Eddie Fernandez, son of a very prominent San Juan family. Eddie helped me find a decent place to live when I first got to the island, but after a while I was invited to move in with some friends, Mike and Stork Pease, a geologist and his wife, and their two small children. They lived in a beautiful, sprawling condominium, with plenty of room and an awning-shaded veranda that stretched the entire length of the building. It was perfect for parties, and the Peases loved to entertain. It was a full life, but I kept striving for more.

For a while, Eddie and I took acting classes from the celebrated Puerto Rican actor Juano Hernandez. He'd had prominent roles in the movie adaptation of the William Faulkner novel *Intruder in the Dust* and *The Trial* with Glenn Ford, and played the old trumpeter who taught Kirk Douglas how to blow the trumpet in *Young Man with a Horn*. In order to be accepted into his class, you had to write an essay on why you wanted to become an actor. I don't remember exactly what I wrote, but instead of listing my summer stock credits, I wrote how I felt when I was dancing. I was accepted, and so was Eddie. I learned a great deal from those classes, and from Juano: patience, timing, and most of all how to be true to a character by being true to yourself.

The Peases' home was across the street from a hotel right on the Condado Lagoon, and for a while I took classes at the water-skiing school there. As a natural athlete and a dancer, I became pretty good at it—at least good enough to stay on my feet and learn a few simple tricks without falling into the water. The trainer, Vic, also owned a Le Mans Allard that he used to race at Ramey Air Force Base, one of the few Strategic Air Command bases in the world. Ramey was located on the northwest tip of the island, sur-rounded by the ocean on three sides. Vic was so busy with his classes that he had very little time to race, and when I told him I'd raced stock cars in Texas he was delighted to let me take his Le Mans out on the straightaway there. I drove it around the island for a while to get the feel of it; then, after much begging, Vic drove me out to Ramey one early Sunday morning to get acquainted with the track. Foolishly enough, I was allowed to enter a race that afternoon; I came in dead last, but I was happy just to finish.

I raced a few more times that season; I ate a lot of smoke, but I loved adding driving to my bag of diversions. One day I remember entering a race in the afternoon, entertaining at the Officers' Club during the cocktail hour, then driving back to San Juan in time to play the first set at the Music Hall. I thought of Jimmy, of course, when I was driving; he'd written to tell me he'd even won some trophies, and I couldn't help wondering whether on some Sunday afternoon we might both have been racing at the very same time, a continent away from each other.

And, on the Sundays I didn't race, I would take the early plane to St. Thomas and ride my horse. I'd wanted to fill up my life, and I had. It was crowded and exhilarating, and I was happy again.

# *16*

It was the autumn of 1955, another beautiful day in the Caribbean. I was in St. Thomas, astride Generalé. I'd gotten into the habit of landing at the airport, mounting the horse, then racing the plane I'd come in on as it took off on its return trip. Generalé wasn't as fast as he'd been during our training for Carnival, and we hadn't won yet, so the pilot had raised stakes on our bet to five dollars. But a few weeks earlier we'd ended in a dead heat, and I knew we had it in us. So that afternoon, when the pilot referred to Generalé as "that old plug," I couldn't resist.

"Care to double our bet? Ten bucks?"

"You got a bet, but you're throwing your money away."

"We'll see," I replied.

When we got to the airport the pilot waved and started revving the engines. We took our places by his side. I peered up at the pilot, took the reins in one hand, and playfully flipped him the bird. He grinned, gave a thumbs-up, opened the throttle, and we were off. My knees tightened around Generalé's belly, I could feel his whole body tremble, and we got a jump on him. This wasn't the Kentucky Derby, but it was a race we wanted to win. We streaked off down the airstrip, neck and neck with the plane, and when we reached the end of the runway, we won easily. When the plane lifted off I waved; the pilot dipped his wings, barely clearing the hills above the harbor.

"He better pay me!" I said to Generalé. "But he'll probably say I cheated, because we got a head start."

We went across the airport road and over to the beach, which was public but so out of the way it attracted few bathers; I'd come to think of it as our own private beach. That day, as usual, we had the beach more or less to ourselves. The only sign of life was the music I could hear drifting from a radio nearby. Farther down the beach a few locals were swimming; just beyond, hanging out in front of a group of palms, a few frogmen from the navy's Underwater Demolition Team recognized us and waved.

Generalé was walking with his head down, pushing his nose toward the sand. Now and then he bobbed all the way down to sniff the salt spray; when a wavelet bumped his nose, he'd do a funny little sideways dance. Once we'd cooled down, we bounced up to the trees near the round bar outside the club. I waved to the bartender, a Jamaican named Twelve, who yelled as I pulled up.

"Nice to see you, Elizabeth girl." A smile lit up his handsome face, its ebony skin set off by blue-green eyes—the legacy, no doubt, of European colonists in his family tree. When we'd first met, I asked him about his name. "Were you the twelfth child of the family?" "Oh, no," he said. "I am the twelfth son. I also have five sisters. Seventeen of us in all." "Wow. That's a big family!" I whistled. "Well, there's not much to do in Jamaica." He laughed.

Twelve had taught me some calypsos, and he was also in the habit of throwing bits of island wisdom my way—odd things that seemed meaningless at first but often helped in a pinch. The first time I met him I was wrestling with a terrible bout of tropical flu. I sneezed, and he flashed his radiant smile. "La Monga?"

"Yes, terrible. The worst."

"Whenever I have La Monga, I attack the sea," he said with considerable gravity. "It works every time, but you must attack fiercely."

I was puzzled. *Attack the sea fiercely?* But later that day I tried it; I was a strong swimmer, and I gave it everything I had. The next day I was better.

I tied Generalé to a tree nearby, humming along with the little plastic radio sitting on the bar. *You smile a song begins; you speak and I hear violins . . . it's magic.* I started to reminisce, moving to the music. I remembered slow-dancing with Jimmy for the first time, our bodies pressed together, my breasts against his chest, his breath warm on my neck. I picked up two palm-frond hats lying discarded on the sand, shook the sand out, and fitted them one inside the other. Then I filled the hats with water from the outdoor tap and ran them over to Generalé before the water leaked out. His furry lips started twitching even before I reached him, and I had to refill the hats before he was satisfied. Then it was my turn, and I headed for the bar.

"How you been, Twelve?"

"Mighty fine, girl, but you look like you've worked up a sizable thirst." The muscles in his arm flexed as he polished a glass with a blue-and-white bar towel. "You want one of them rum Cokes you always askin' for?"

"That sounds too good to say no." I pulled up a stool, scooped up a handful of nuts from a bowl on the bar, and watched while he built my drink.

That dark coolness, so smooth on the way down. A tall skinny glass, lots of ice, a half a shot of dark, smoky Myers's rum, mixed with a half a shot of the lighter Old St. Croix. Coke to the top. A long straw, a squish of lime, and a delicate stir. I removed the straw and raised the glass. Rum and Coke was tough to handle in the morning—something I'd learned the hard way—but tough to beat.

"To you, Twelve. Here's to old friends."

"Old friends . . . to you right back." He raised the half-empty Coke bottle he'd opened for my drink.

I took a taste, holding it on my tongue, then filled my mouth with another, savoring the cool, tingling bittersweetness before letting it slide down my throat. My stomach grumbled when it hit; I hadn't eaten anything since the night before, and the nuts had only made me hungry. I ordered a Cubano sandwich and settled in.

Twelve's little plastic radio was playing the calypso classic "MaryAnn," a favorite I sang all the time at the Music Hall. The music was what I loved most about the Islands: calypsos, danzas, boleros, merengues, cha-chas, sambas, salsa before it was called salsa; even the most progressive hot Afro-Cuban jazz was easy to find. Every little *colmado* and cantina had a jukebox, and everyone had a radio. I was always dancing. Sometimes, after my last set, if I was feeling frisky, I'd ask someone to lift me up onto the bar, and dance the length of it, negotiating the land-scape of bottles and ashtrays with abandon. Everyone got a big kick out of it—especially the guys sitting at the bar.

I had another sip of rum and Coke, and started dancing in the sand. "Oh, yeah," Twelve said, moving with the beat.

> *All day, all night, Miss MaryAnn,*
> *Down by the seaside she sifting sand*

"Oh, yeah." Arms wide to the side, I swayed and sang, cir-cling the bar.

> *Even little children join in the band*
> *All day, all night, Miss MaryAnn*

I tramped over to Generalé, I kissed him lightly on the nose.

"Oh, yeah," Twelve called out, joining me on the sand. We tramped together side by side, laughing and singing.

The song ended and Twelve went back to the bar, but I kept on tramping, eyes closed. Twelve laughed.

"What?" I opened my eyes.

"Look at you dancin', girl, makin' your own music."

I hadn't even heard the song end. I was still out there, shuffling and sifting sand and singing to myself.

And then I heard a voice saying something about a car crash in California. The voice sounded serious. It was some-thing about a young actor.

*Wait a minute.*

"What did he say?" I asked Twelve. "What's he talking about?"

"Some guy, some movie guy out there in Hollywood—he was jus' killed."

"Who was it? Did he say who it was?"

"Dunno." Twelve leaned across the bar and turned up the sound. There was a lot of stuff about lost promise and unique talent and the tragedy of genius, taken from us at only twenty-four.

"The rising young star of *East of Eden* . . . "

I leaned against the bar.

" . . . and *Rebel Without a Cause* . . . "

I opened my mouth and tried to breathe. No. Don't say his name.

"James Dean."

*Jimmy.*

Twelve was talking to me, but it was as though he were underwater. His lips were moving, but I couldn't hear a sound. I stood frozen as Twelve leaned over in slow motion, reaching for me.

*I have to get out of here. I have to get away.*

I couldn't move until I felt Twelve's hands on my shoulders, gently shaking me, breaking the trance.

I wheeled, ran over to Generalé, and shoved my foot into the stirrup, forgetting I'd loosened the girth. As the saddle swung underneath his belly, I hopped back and fell.

Generalé whinnied and steadied himself.

I staggered toward the dangling saddle. Ripping the buckle of the girth open, I threw the saddle and blanket on the sand, untied the reins, and pulled them back over Generalé's head. Then I grabbed a handful of mane and swung myself up onto his back.

"Go, Generalé. Go. *Vaya.*" My throat felt as though it were squeezing closed. The words rasped like sandpaper.

He whinnied again and took off down the beach. *Get me out of here.* I wanted to scream, but I couldn't; my mouth was so dry, no more sounds could come out. It felt as if my entire body were closing down. I could hardly see. I could feel nothing but the urge to get away, to escape the past few minutes.

Generalé tore off, galloping toward the end of the beach. We were flying, my cheeks stinging, my eyes blurred, my legs held against his flanks, my tears dropping on the wind. *Faster, goddammit.* Generalé was so lathered his flanks were foaming. I was slipping off, holding on, hugging his neck now as we spun around toward the water's edge. The heavy musk of his sweat filled my nostrils, then merged with the salt spray that splashed up around me.

*Attack the sea.*

Generalé was breathing heavily as we rode out through the breakers. A torrent of water hit me, smashing me off his back, away from his flailing hooves. I punched my way through the surf, fighting the waves fist over fist, as though I were beating down a hidden enemy. Again and again I punched the water, panting and gasping, until finally we were beyond the waves, swimming side by side. Exhausted.

Finally, too spent to go on, I grabbed for Generalé's mane and let him pull me where he would. If he wanted to swim out to sea, I didn't care. I relaxed in the warm current, my body numb, my mind still on fire. I could hear him now, his voice whispering to me: "I love you, little girl. My little girl."

*Jesus, Jimmy!*

I closed my eyes. We were dancing naked in front of a mirror, laughing and singing and kissing and feeling.

> *When we walk hand-in-hand,*
> *The world becomes a wonderland . . . it's magic . . .*

I was drowning in him. I inhaled the tobacco and soap odor of his face and hands. I could feel his teasing fingers under his bullfighter's cape, his hands running lightly along my body, his eyes, his touch. *Oh, God, Jimmy.*

I don't know how long Generalé and I swam, but finally his hooves struck the sandy bottom, jarring me out of my reverie. I regained my footing, rested my hand on his neck, and we walked back onto the beach.

Generalé rolled on his back in the sand, his legs straight up in the air. I flopped down next to him and lay on my back, gazing up to the sky where his hooves seemed to be pointing at the sun. *Jimmy.*

I wanted to see him and touch him and feel his arms around me; I would have given anything to know what might have been.

I remember nothing about how I got back to San Juan. I had a job that night and I made it there on time. But I was badly wounded. I looked at the tiny scar on my wrist, and I knew I would never try that again. But I wanted to die.

*What am I going to do?*

♦♦

I would go to work, and play, and sing my songs and talk with the customers and smoke and drink, even laugh and dance, just as I had before. The real me observed all that from afar, looking down, as if I were watching a movie of myself.

Those were the easy hours. After breakfast at Al's Little Club with the gang, when I couldn't put it off any longer, I would go home alone and sit on the beach and watch the sun rise, and I would try to convince myself that it was a new day.

I put enough of the pieces of my life back together again to function, to live and make a living, but there was no real joy in my life. I had my friends, and I had my memories. But I couldn't sleep enough, I couldn't drink enough, I couldn't attack the sea fiercely enough, to alleviate the pain of my loss, or fill the empty space where Jimmy used to be in my heart.

> *In the wee small hours of the morning . . .*
> *I lie awake and think about the boy . . .*
> *if only he would call.*
> *In the wee small hours of the morning,*
> *That's the time I miss him most of all.*

I mourned a long time for Jimmy. Then I tried to get back into the rhythm of life, and live my own to its fullest. I just wanted to be happy again . . . and, after a while, I was.

Shortly after Jimmy's death *Rebel Without a Cause* was playing at the Music Hall. It had been there for a while, but I hadn't yet been able to bring myself to cross the threshold into the theater.

Finally, one night after my first set, I walked into the back of the theater. There were no empty seats; it was as crowded as it had been since it had opened. So I stood way over in the corner and watched. There on the screen were Natalie Wood, Sal Mineo, and Jimmy. Wandering around the old mansion Sal Mineo's character had told them about, leaping in and out of the empty swimming pool, playing tag; finally exhausted, sitting down to rest on a stone bench. Jimmy nestled his head on her lap, with Sal on the ground at their feet. Natalie whispersang a lullaby; Sal told them the story of his father. Jimmy reached over to stroke Sal's head, to comfort him . . . and then, suddenly, I heard him say it: "*Suure. Suuuurrre.*" The way he'd said it to me, the way I said it to him. There it was, a gift for me. I stood in the dark and began to cry.

That night, instead of joining the gang, I went straight home. I went to bed and tried to sleep, but I couldn't shut my thoughts off. Instead I got up and poured myself a drink, lit a cigarette, took out all Jimmy's letters, and read them again and again. Crying and drinking and crying. Finally, I gathered up all the letters and staggered to the beach.

The moon was full. I gathered up enough driftwood and twigs for a funeral pyre, and set it afire. I crushed all the letters and drawings into a ball and threw them into the fire—not one at a time, sifting through the memories, but all of them at once. I would never lose their words, of course; I knew them all by heart. Now all I had left was what I could remember.

I watched silently as the pile went up in flames, then flickered and curled into ash. I could almost hear Jimmy reciting his favorite passage from *The Little Prince*:

> *In one of the stars, I shall be living*
> *In one of them I shall be laughing*
> *And so it will be as if all the stars were laughing*
> *When you look at the sky at night*
> *You, only you, will have stars that can laugh*

With the bagpipes playing in my head above the hiss of the surf, I began my own funeral dance. The sparks from the last remaining embers were riding the wind, dying in the air, like brief fireflies. For a few moments I felt lighter, almost at peace. I knew Jimmy would be laughing in the stars, just as he always promised.